Men'sHealth®
TOTAL
FITNESS
GUIDE
2009

Men'sHealth®

TOTAL FITNESS GUIDE
2009

RODALE®

© 2009 by Rodale Inc.

Rodale books may be purchased for business or promotional use or for special sales. For information, please write to: Special Markets Department, Rodale Inc., 733 Third Avenue, New York, NY 10017

Printed in the United States of America

Rodale Inc. makes every effort to use acid-free ∞, recycled paper ♻.

ISBN 13: 978–1–59486–995–2

ISBN 10: 1–59486–995–2

Book design by Susan Eugster

2   4   6   8   10   9   7   5   3   1   hardcover

LIVE YOUR WHOLE LIFE™

We inspire and enable people to improve their lives and the world around them

For more of our products visit **rodalestore.com** or call 800-848-4735

Contents

Introduction

Are you a believer or an achiever? Two-thirds of men *believe* that they are physically fit, but a paltry 13 percent actually are. No matter which category you belong in, it's a safe bet that you'd like to be fitter and stronger. This book is the key to your success.

To create this fitness guide, we talked with the experts, pumped the iron, ran the miles, and played the sports to bring you the very best fitness information that's available anywhere. With this book, you'll sculpt the body that you've always wanted and become a bigger, bolder, better you.

We kick the book off with a kick in the pants—to help you lose some weight if that's what you need. In Part One, Lose Weight, you'll find our best fat-fighting tips. Here's what to eat—and when to eat it—to burn fat, build muscle, and transform your body. Then, on the flip side, we spent months analyzing menus, nutrition labels, and ingredient lists to identify the restaurant industry's top 20 worst meals. These dishes should come with a warning—and now they do. Also, we'll tip you off to the one trend in restaurants that you can actually use to your advantage to enjoy big flavor—and a smaller belly. After all that, if the needle on the scale is still refusing to budge, we'll give you 10 reasons why you might not be losing weight even if you're doing everything right. Then we'll give you 13 ways to maintain your motivation.

Because we know you're busy—who isn't?—Part Two will help you Get Fit—fast. You'll learn how to update the classic pushup for a total body transformation. Use our simple workout to build your best body in just 1 hour. Then take your workout to the next level with our 15-minute workout boosters. If your workout is getting a little stale, you'll see how to beat boredom with four simple steps.

In Part Three, we'll get to the meat of the matter and help you Muscle Up. You'll find out how to start your workout with a 3-minute stretch to build muscle quicker. Discover how the classic deadlift will work wonders on your physique. Then build a firm foundation with the simple squat. You'll also pack on size fast with eight simple exercises we bet you've never done before. Later, America's top strength coach shares his secrets for explosive gains. And you'll gain size quickly by following the lead of two NBA superstars.

Part Four is where you'll really get down to business with some heavy-duty, hard-working workouts. Spot Train to build bulging biceps, bolder shoulders, a transformed torso, and a rock-solid midsection.

Test Yourself

Before you start your fitness transformation, use the following fitness tests to gauge your current levels of strength, flexibility, and endurance. After 5 weeks, repeat the assessments. Snap a digital photo now and another after 35 days, and your new body image will be all the proof you'll need.

Test your strength. Do as many classic pushups as you can without stopping, but use this precise execution: Take 2 seconds to lower your body until your upper arms dip below your elbows; pause for 1 second; then take 1 second to push your body up. This ensures that you'll perform the test identically each time you take it.

Test your flexibility. Place a yardstick on the floor and put a foot-long piece of masking tape across the 15-inch mark. Sit down with your legs out in front of you and your heels at the edge of the tape, one on each side of the yardstick. Put one hand on top of the other and reach forward over the yardstick as far as you can by bending at your hips. The number your fingertips touch is your benchmark.

Test your endurance. On a treadmill or on a flat course outdoors, run or walk 1.5 miles as fast as you can and record your time. (Warm up first by walking or jogging at an easy pace for 5 minutes.)

This section is your ticket to a better body, one part at a time.

Run Fast toward a better, fitter you in Part Five. First, you'll learn the best way to warm up. Then you'll up the tempo with a little speed conditioning. You'll rule your next race with our training techniques. Running a little ragged? Break out of boredom with our build-your-own triathlon plan. Last, harness the power of your mind to get strong and lean.

Part Six, Have Fun, is where you'll find the best advice on improving your game. Here you'll get new game with the training secrets of some of the biggest names in sports. Discover how the University of Florida's men's basketball team trains. Ramp up your playbook with five trick football plays. Find your center of power with an NFL veteran. Pick up the world's fittest quarterback's simple plan for success, and more.

This book is bursting with the best fitness tips and workouts to build your best body ever. Here's to the bigger, bolder, better you!

PART ONE

LOSE WEIGHT

BY JEFF VOLEK, PhD, RD, AND ADAM CAMPBELL, MS, CSCS

Trade Your Belly for Biceps

Here's what to eat—and when to eat it—to burn fat, build muscle, and transform your body

magine, for a moment, that you can control what your body does with the food you eat. You instantly stop storing nutrients as belly flab, and instead transform them into sleeve-busting muscle. And because you're using incoming calories to build more muscular pecs, shoulders, and arms, you automatically burn your stored fat for energy. Consider it the panacea for the modern male body: Your biceps grow as your love handles shrink.

With the Targeted Nutrition Tactics (TNT) Diet, this can be your reality. The TNT Diet is a cutting-edge eating plan based on research at the University of Connecticut. It's designed with a simple purpose: to help you simultaneously lose fat and gain muscle. And whether you're a heavyweight with 30 pounds of pure fat to drop or a lean guy who wants to pack on some serious size, you can customize the TNT Diet to your goals.

Hungry to get started? Read on to discover how TNT can dramatically remodel any body, including yours.

The Science of TNT

To understand how TNT works, you need a primer on glycogen—the carbohydrates stored in your muscles. Unlike your fat stores, which can expand to what seems like an infinite level (read: you can grow fatter and fatter), your glycogen tank has a limited capacity to store carbs. Think of your car: If it's a midsize, it probably has a 14-gallon fuel tank. Try to fill the tank with 20 gallons, and the extra 6 will spill out onto the pavement. It's the same way with carbs and your glycogen tank.

So this is where the problem lies: Once your glycogen tank is full, the excess carbs you eat overflow into your bloodstream and are shuttled off to your liver, where they're converted to fat.

What's more, eating carbohydrates raises your blood levels of the hormone insulin. That's important because when your glycogen tank is full, insulin puts both your muscle cells and your fat cells in growth mode. That's great for your biceps, but it's a horrible scenario for your belly.

Now for the good news: Low glycogen levels, which you can achieve with the right eating strategies and exercise, change your body's response to insulin. While insulin still signals your body to build muscle, it no longer keeps your fat cells in growth mode. Why? Because your body makes refilling your glycogen tank a priority, in case of an energy emergency. So it sucks any carbs you eat into your muscles to be stored as glycogen for later use. As a result, your body must turn to fat as its primary fuel source.

This creates the ideal internal environment for remodeling your body. Think of it as flipping a cellular switch that allows you to burn fat as you build muscle. The next step, then, is to implement the nutrition (and exercise) tactics that give you complete control over that switch.

What to Eat When

It's a trend among nutritionists to talk about "good" and "bad" carbs. And while we certainly agree that some carb sources are

The TNT Time Zones

1. Fat-Burning

The nutrition tactic: A low-carb diet

The benefits: Speeds fat loss, regulates your appetite, and reduces heart disease risk

When you'll use this tactic: Most of the week. A low-carb diet is the foundation of TNT.

Why it works: Limiting your carb intake helps keep your glycogen and insulin levels low—and your body in fat-burning mode. Whats's more, studies show that low-carb diets reduce both hunger and heart disease risk.

What to eat: Eat any combination of foods from the three categories listed next until you feel satisfied, not stuffed. During this Time Zone, steer clear of foods containing more than 10 grams of carbs per serving, particularly those made with flour or sugar (bread, pasta, rice, baked goods).

High-quality proteins: Beef, poultry, fish, pork, eggs, cheese, and protein powder

Low-starch vegetables: Any vegetable except potatoes, corn, and carrots

Natural fats: Avocados, butter, coconuts, cream, nuts and seeds, olives, olive and canola oils, and sour cream

Don't worry: Contrary to popular opinion, research shows that saturated fat doesn't raise your risk of heart disease, especially when eaten as part of a low-carb diet.

Sample Menu

Breakfast: Denver omelet with sausage

Morning snack: Handful of almonds

Lunch: Grilled chicken thighs, steamed broccoli

Afternoon snack: Celery with ranch dressing

Dinner: Rib-eye steak, mozzarella-and-tomato salad, glass of red wine

2. Reloading

The nutrition tactic: A high-carb diet

The benefits: Boosts muscle growth, instantly inflates your biceps, and allows you to eat pizza

When you'll use this tactic: Up to 2 days a week, depending on your goals. For convenience, we recommend weekend days.

Why it works: The carbs you eat will induce a surge of insulin, and this will drive a flood of muscle-building nutrients into your muscle cells. The downside is that you won't burn fat quite as fast as during the Fat-Burning Time Zone.

What to eat: Focus on having protein and carbs at every meal. Again, eat until you're satisfied, but not stuffed. And while you should emphasize the foods listed below, also know that this is the best time to satisfy your cravings for candy, chips, and even takeout pizza. We don't recommend these foods for your health, but we do realize that most guys won't follow the guidelines of this diet—or any other diet—100 percent of the time. So feel free to allow one of your Reloading Time Zone meals to be a cheat. It won't sabotage your progress.

High-quality proteins: Beef, poultry, fish, pork, eggs, cheese, protein powder, milk, and yogurt

Fruits and vegetables: Any type of produce

Nutrient-dense carbs: Beans and 100 percent whole grains—bread, oats, pasta, and cereal

Sample Menu

Breakfast: Cold cereal with fresh blueberries

Morning snack: Apple with sliced cheese

Lunch: Hamburger, sweet-potato fries

Afternoon snack: Fruit yogurt

Dinner: Spaghetti and meatballs, large salad

3. Muscle-Building

The nutrition tactic: Workout nutrition

The benefits: Dramatically accelerates muscle growth and speeds recovery

When you'll use this tactic: In the window of time 60 minutes before you lift weights to 30 minutes afterward

Why it works: Resistance training primes your muscles to grow; all you have to do is feed them. So during this time, you'll always include protein, which provides the raw material for muscle growth without inhibiting your ability to burn fat. And if you're okay with temporarily slowing down your fat loss, you can also down a hefty dose of carbohydrates, which will boost muscle growth to an even greater extent.

What to eat: Depending on your goals (see "Your Body, Your Plan" on page 7 to find the right TNT Diet plan for you), you'll eat either a snack that contains only protein or one that provides both protein and carbohydrates.

Protein-only guidelines (TNT Plans A and C): Drink a protein shake (mixed with water) that provides a blend of at least 40 grams whey and/or casein protein, and little to no carbs and fat. (We like Nitrean, available at atlargenutrition.com.) Or simply have the same amount of protein from a whole food, such as 3 ounces of tuna.

Protein + carbohydrate guidelines (TNT Plans B, D, and E): Drink a protein shake (mixed with water or milk) that provides a blend of at least 40 grams whey and/or casein protein, 40 to 80 grams carbohydrates, and little to no fat. (A good choice: Biotest Surge Recovery, biotest. supplements.net.) Alternatively, opt for a 16-ounce carton of low-fat chocolate milk or a classic turkey sandwich (but hold the mayo, because fat slows protein digestion).

better than others, we've found that the total amount of carbs, and when you eat them, are more important. So we've based the nutrition tactics in TNT around what we call Time Zones. (They're explained here and on page 7.) Think about it: Eat carbohydrates at the wrong time—when your glycogen tank is full—and your body stops burning fat and starts storing it. But eat carbs at the right time—when your glycogen levels are low—and those carbs help you build muscle without increasing the size of your gut.

Using this concept of "well-timed" and "poorly timed" carbs, the TNT Time Zones allow you to customize your diet for any goal. That's because we've used these Time Zones to create specific eating strategies that provide you with a range of body-sculpting options. One end of this spectrum (see "Your Body, Your Plan" opposite) is designed for maximum fat loss; the other, for maximum muscle. And in between, you can vary the degree of each with simple tweaks to your diet.

These options allow you to find the plan that works best not only for your goals but also for your lifestyle. For example, if you have 25 pounds to lose, you'll see the fastest results with Plan A, a low-carb diet. If you want more flexibility, you might choose Plan C, which is still great for losing fat but lets you load up on carbs one day a week. And, of course, if you want to gain muscle as fast as possible, Plan E would be your choice.

One caveat: For best results, we recommend that no matter which goal you choose, start with Plan A for 4 weeks. This trains your body to learn to use fat as its primary source of energy, and that makes each of the other plans more effective. (If you already follow a low-carb diet, go ahead and jump to the plan of your choice.) Once you've followed Plan A for 4 weeks, use the chart to find the plan that best fits your body-composition goals.

Your Body, Your Plan

Use the chart below to determine your TNT eating strategies. For instance, if you choose Plan C, you'll follow the Fat-Burning Time Zone guidelines Sunday through Friday, except for the period around your workout (Muscle-Building Time Zone) (The Time Zones are explained on pages 4–5.) On Saturday you'll adhere to the Reloading Time Zone. In addition to any drinks listed in each Time Zone, have as much water, unsweetened tea and coffee, and no-calorie drinks (such as diet soda) as you desire. You can also have up to two alcoholic drinks a day, such as wine or light beer.

These plans range from the maximum fat loss of plan A to the maximum muscle building of plan E.

	PLAN A	PLAN B	PLAN C	PLAN D	PLAN E
The Fat-Burning Time Zone (low-carbohydrate)	7 days	7 days	6 days	6 days	5 days
The Reloading Time Zone (high-carbohydrate)	0 days	0 days	1 day	1 day	2 days
The Muscle-Building Time Zone (workout nutrition)	Protein only	Protein + carbs	Protein only	Protein + carbs	Protein + carbs

The Final Tactic

You can't build a beach body without exercise. That's why a key ingredient of the TNT Diet is weight training. It's not just the top strategy for building muscle, but it's also the most effective form of exercise for torching fat. In fact, research shows that lifting weights not only burns as many calories as, say, a moderate-intensity run, but it's also ideal for stoking your metabolism and reducing your glycogen levels. So to achieve all the benefits of the TNT Diet, combine the nutrition tactics in this section with a 3- or 4-day-a-week total-body weight-training program, such as any of the total-body workouts in Part Four.

For the complete TNT eating and exercise plan—which includes 24 weeks of workouts—pick up a copy of *TNT Diet: Targeted Nutrition Tactics: The Explosive New Plan to Blast Fat, Build Muscle, and Get Healthy.*

To see hundreds of guys who've lost thousands of pounds on the TNT Diet, go to MensHealth.com/transform.

BY BILL HARTMAN, PT, CSCS

Fuel the Burn

Lose the last 10 and reveal your abs just in time for summer

Any man can tell you: Dropping a few pounds is one thing; becoming Brad Pitt-in-*Fight-Club* lean is quite another. Which is why you'll never mistake Jared Fogle for Tyler Durden. After all, if torching that last bit of belly flab were as easy as eating 6-inch sandwiches, the Subway guy would surely be sporting a six-pack by now.

The fact is, the closer you are to achieving legendary leanness, the more stubborn your fat stores become. It's really self-preservation: Your body is designed to protect your fuel reserves from running too low, just in case food becomes scarce. And while that might have been a handy biological feature in the Paleolithic age, it's hardly necessary in 21st-century America. The secret to disabling this? Igniting your metabolism.

By learning how to fire up your body's internal furnace with exercise, you can accelerate fat loss and finish off your gut for good, revealing the chiseled muscles hidden beneath. All it takes is a little knowledge, coupled with a steady dose of physical effort. We provide the first half of that formula here; your charge is to handle the second.

How to Lose That Last 10

No matter which exercise you choose, there's only so much fat you can burn during, say, a 30-minute workout. And research shows that the better trained you become, the more your body's "exercise efficiency" improves, meaning the same amount of activity burns fewer calories as time goes by. For instance,

University of California at Berkeley scientists determined that to avoid age-related weight gain, avid runners need to boost their weekly mileage by 1.7 miles every year.

So to lose the last 10 pounds, you have to think beyond how much fat you burn during your workout. Instead, focus on the amount you burn during the other 23 hours and 30 minutes of your day—while you're sitting at your desk, lounging in front of the television, and lying in bed sleeping. And to achieve this benefit, you need to hit the weights and do interval sprints. By knowing the right combination of sets, repetitions, rest periods, and exercises and the best method of cardio, you can create a workout that not only burns as many calories as a 4-mile jog, but, unlike that jog, also unleashes a flood of fat-burning hormones that stoke your metabolism for hours after you exercise. The result: Your body's fat-burning furnace runs on high all day long, even when you're sitting on the couch. Here's how to build the perfect metabolism-boosting workout plan, step by step.

Do 8 to 15 repetitions of each set. Doing your 1-repetition max may make you feel like a big man, but if your goal is not looking like one, then you're better off pumping out more reps. Research shows that performing sets of 8 to 15 repetitions stimulates the greatest increase in fat-burning hormones, compared with doing a greater or fewer number of repetitions. The one caveat is that you have to use a weight that provides an adequate challenge. For instance, doing 8 repetitions with a weight you can lift 15 times won't be very effective. After all, it's only about 50 percent of the work your muscles are actually capable of performing. Instead, you want to give between 90 and 100 percent of your full effort for any given repetition range. A good way to gauge how you're doing: If you start to struggle by your last repetition, you'll know that you're in the ballpark.

Perform two to four sets of each exercise. Turns out, it doesn't take much weight work to rev up your metabolism. Ball State University researchers discovered that fat-burning hormones increase when you complete just one set of an exercise. And while doing more sets boosts your hormone levels to an even greater extent, there is a cutoff: In a recent study, Greek scientists determined that there is no difference between doing four sets and six sets of each exercise. So consider two to four to be the optimal number of sets for speeding fat loss, depending on your current level of fitness. For example, you'll want to use the low side of this recommendation when you're just starting out, and increase your number of sets as you become better conditioned. After all, losing weight by losing your lunch is never the goal. (For a complete workout that combines all the metabolism-boosting principles we're outlining in this section, see "Your Six-Pack Plan" opposite.)

Rest no longer than 75 seconds between sets. Look around any gym, and you'll find that rest periods are usually dictated by how chatty a man's workout partner is. But by closely adhering to specific rest periods of no

longer than 75 seconds, you can speed fat loss. Here's how it works: Doing sets of 8 to 15 repetitions results in the accumulation of a chemical called lactate in your blood-stream. And high lactate levels are associated with an increase in the release of fat-burning hormones. However, resting too long between sets allows the oxygen you breathe to help clear the lactate from your bloodstream. Keep your recovery time short, though, and you'll keep your blood levels of lactate—and fat-burning hormones—high. That means more fat is burned while you rest.

Your Six-Pack Plan

Build muscle and lose fat with this 4-week training program

The Weight Workout

Alternate between weight workout A and weight workout B, 3 days a week, resting at least a day between sessions.

Perform each pair of exercises as alternating sets. That is, do one set of the first exercise, rest for the prescribed amount of time, then do one set of the second exercise, and rest again. Repeat until you've performed all the recommended sets.

Note that the sets, repetitions, and amount you rest between sets change from week to week.

WORKOUT A

1. Split squat + barbell lunge
2. Romanian deadlift + standing dumbbell press
3. Dumbbell bench press + chinup

WORKOUT B

1. Front squat + close-grip chinup
2. Dumbbell stepup + barbell bench press
3. Standing barbell shoulder press + dumbbell face pull

WEEK	SETS	REPS	REST
1	2	15	75
2	2	15	60
3	3	12	75
4	3	12	60

The Interval Workout

Alternate between interval workout A and interval workout B, 2 days a week, on the days between your weight workouts.

To perform the intervals, run or cycle at the fastest pace you can maintain for the duration of the sprint time. Then slow down to a pace that's about 30 percent of your full effort for the recovery time.

Repeat until you've completed all the prescribed intervals for each workout.

WORKOUT A

WEEK	INTERVALS	SPRINT TIME	RECOVERY TIME
1–2	4	30 seconds	90 seconds
3–4	6	30 seconds	90 seconds

WORKOUT B

WEEK	INTERVALS	SPRINT TIME	RECOVERY TIME
1–2	3	60 seconds	180 seconds
3–4	5	60 seconds	180 seconds

MUSCLE CHOW

Fast and Healthy

Mussels are the original fast food. They cook in about 3 minutes. Even better, they pack lots of protein. Rinse them well and discard any that have already opened. Once they've cooked, toss those that haven't opened.

GARLIC AND TOMATO MUSSELS

- 1 teaspoon extra virgin olive oil
- 1 small yellow onion, diced
- 2 cloves garlic, minced
- 2 pounds mussels
- ½ cup water
- 1 cup dry white wine
- 1 large tomato, chopped
- 2 tablespoons fresh parsley, chopped

In a large pot, heat the oil over medium heat. Add the onion and garlic, and sauté until lightly browned. Then add the mussels, water, and white wine. Reduce the heat to low and cover with a lid. After 3 to 4 minutes, the mussels will begin to open. Remove the lid, add the tomato and parsley, and cover again for a minute. Transfer the mussels to two large bowls and spoon on some of the sauce from the pot.

Makes 2 servings

Per serving: 545 calories, 56 g protein, 27 g carbohydrates, 13 g total fat, 2 g saturated fat, 2 g fiber, 1308 mg sodium

Work your entire body. How much you elevate your metabolism after your workout is directly related to the amount of muscle you activate at any one time. So you'll want to focus on movements that work multiple muscles, as opposed to those that attempt to isolate muscle groups. For instance, you'll experience a much greater boost in metabolism by performing 10 repetitions of the squat, compared with 10 repetitions of an isolation exercise, such as the biceps curl.

In addition, by training your whole body each session, you'll work the most muscle possible. A University of Wisconsin study found that when men performed a full-body workout involving just three big-muscle exercises—the bench press, power clean, and squat—their metabolisms were elevated for 39 hours afterward. What's more, they also burned a greater percentage of their calories from fat during this time, compared with men who didn't do a total-body workout. The take-home message is clear: Complete an intense full-body weight workout 3 days a week, resting a day between sessions, and you'll keep your metabolism humming along in a much higher gear at all times.

Alternate between two exercises. Why spend more time in the gym than you need to? Each time you do a set of an exercise, rest, then follow with a set that works muscles that weren't involved in the previous movement, and rest again. For example, you might pair an upper-body exercise with a lower-body move, or an exercise that works your chest muscles with one that hits your back. Once you've done one set of each exercise, repeat the process until you've completed all the planned sets of both movements.

This method is called "alternating sets" and allows one group of muscles to rest while another group works, and vice versa. The benefit? You can limit your rest periods, which will keep your lactate levels high while giving specific muscles more time to recover between sets. It's a strategy that helps offset fatigue and ensures that you give your best effort to each set.

Monitor your lifting tempo. Remember, your goal is to work your muscles as hard as possible on each repetition of each set. And that means you need to control the speed at which you raise and lower the weight. By performing an exercise too fast—for instance, lowering your body quickly and "bouncing" up from a squat—you take some of the stress off your muscles and place it on your tendons. The trouble is, stressing your tendons doesn't boost your metabolism the same way that challenging your muscles does. (At least not that scientists know of yet.)

As a general rule, try to take 3 seconds to lower the weight, and then pause for a second before lifting it. This helps eliminate the elastic energy that allows you to bounce, forcing your muscles to work their hardest on every repetition.

Skip the long runs. Sure, aerobic exercise burns calories. However, if you're already dieting—and you'd better be if you want to see your abs—studies show that distance running does little to further enhance fat loss. Most likely this is because aerobic exercise doesn't boost your metabolism after your workout.

But that doesn't mean cardio can't help: High-intensity intervals—such as short sprints of 30 seconds or more, interspersed with a slow jog—are great for accelerating fat loss. Why? Because they're similar to weight training. After all, a 200-meter sprint challenges your lower-body muscles hard for 30 seconds or more, just like a set of 8 repetitions of the squat. So by doing a few intervals on the days you don't lift weights, you can spike your metabolism even higher.

Boost Strength and Melt Fat with One Workout

Running hard, backing off, and repeating is great for your ticker, fat loss, and muscle, which is why this isn't the first time we've suggested intervals. But here's a new spin: Instead of resting or slowing down between sprints, fill the gaps with basic weight exercises.

"This is a great way to do strength training for guys who hate it," says Jim Liston, CSCS, of catzsports.com. And vice versa: Can't make time for a cardio day? Now you don't have to. Do each circuit without resting between exercises, unless specified below.

Circuit 1

Do 5 rounds, then rest for 2 minutes.

EXERCISE	TIME/REPS
Sprint on a treadmill at 10% gradient or use a stairclimber	40 sec
Dumbbell squat (in rounds 1, 3, and 5 only)	10 reps
Body-weight squat (in rounds 2 and 4 only)	20 reps
In round 1: do a front bridge	40 sec
In round 2: side bridge on left arm	40 sec
In round 3: side bridge on right arm	40 sec
In round 4: front bridge	40 sec
In round 5: hold bottom of a pushup	40 sec

Circuit 2

Do 3 rounds, then rest for 2 minutes.

EXERCISE	TIME/REPS
Run or climb at top speed	80 sec
Rest	20 sec
Pushup	30 sec
Dumbbell bent-over row	10 reps

Circuit 3

Do 4 rounds, then rest for 2 minutes.

EXERCISE	TIME/REPS
Run or climb at top speed	60 sec
Single-leg rotation squat	5 reps/leg
Ab exercise of choice	60 sec

Circuit 4

Do 3 rounds, then stop.

EXERCISE	TIME/REPS
Run or climb at top speed	40 sec
Rest	40 sec
Hold bottom of a pushup	40 sec

Exercise Descriptions

Dumbbell Squat

Stand with a dumbbell in each hand, arms at your sides, feet shoulder-width apart. Bend at the hips and knees to lower your body until your thighs are parallel to the floor, then press back up. Take 2 seconds to lower yourself and 2 seconds to press up.

Single-Leg Rotation Squat

Holding a dumbell in your left hand, balance on your right leg. Slowly bend your knees to lower your body toward the floor while reaching toward the outside of your right foot with the dumbbell hand. Push through your heel to return to the starting position.

Dumbbell Bent-Over Row

Stand holding a pair of dumbbells in front of your thighs with an overhand grip. Bend forward at the hips until your upper body is almost parallel to the floor. Pull the weights up toward your rib cage until your elbows pass your torso, then slowly lower them.

Front Bridge

Lie facedown in a modified pushup position, with your forearms resting on the floor. Your elbows should be under your shoulders and bent 90 degrees. Tuck your chin so your body forms a straight line from your heels to your ears. Forcefully contract your abs and glutes.

Side Bridge

Lie on your side with your forearm on the floor under your shoulder, and your feet stacked together. Contract your glutes and abs, and push your hips off the floor, creating a straight line from ankle to shoulder and keeping your head in line with your spine. Hold the position.

BY MATT GOULDING

Avoid Death on a Plate

The U.S. food industry has declared war on your waistline. Here's how to disarm its weapons of mass inflation

NET WT. 1.5 OZ (42.5 g)

Sure, a turkey burger sounds healthy. But is it, really? Not if you order the Bella from Ruby Tuesday, which packs a whopping 1,145 calories. (And yes, that's before a side of fries.)

To further enlighten you on the prevalence of preposterous portions, we spent months analyzing menus, nutrition labels, and ingredient lists to identify the food industry's worst offenders. Our primary criterion? Sheer caloric impact. After all, it's the top cause of weight gain and the health problems that accompany it. (As you read, keep in mind that 2,500 calories a day is a reasonable intake for the average guy.) We also factored in other key nutritional data, such as excessive carbohydrates and fat, added sugars, trans fats, and sodium. The result is our list of the 20 worst foods in America. Eat at your own risk.

20. Chicken Selects Premium Breast Strips from McDonald's (5 pieces) with creamy ranch sauce

830 calories
55 grams total fat
4.5 grams trans fat
48 grams carbohydrates

The only thing "premium" about these strips is the caloric price you pay. Add a large fries and a regular soda and this seemingly innocuous chicken meal tops out at 1,710 calories.

Change your chicken: Twenty McNuggets have the same impact. Instead, choose Mickey D's six-piece offering with barbecue sauce and save yourself 530 calories.

Calorie Conundrums

We took to the streets with six of the worst dishes in America and asked 60 people to estimate the total calories in each. Here's how they did.

Outback Steakhouse Aussie Cheese Fries

Actual calories: 2,900
Estimated calories: 1,884

Bob Evans Caramel Banana Pecan Cream Stacked and Stuffed Hotcakes

Actual calories: 1,540
Estimated calories: 1,070

Taco Bell Fiesta Taco Salad

Actual calories: 840
Estimated calories: 659

Chili's Awesome Blossom

Actual calories: 2,710
Estimated calories: 1,028

Burger King Triple Whopper Meal, King-Size

Actual calories: 2,220
Estimated calories: 1,616

Ruby Tuesday Bella Turkey Burger

Actual calories: 1,145
Estimated calories: 619

19. Jamba Juice Chocolate Moo'd Power Smoothie (30 fluid ounces)

900 calories
10 grams fat
183 grams carbohydrates
166 grams sugar

Jamba Juice calls it a smoothie; we call it a milkshake. In fact, this beverage contains as much sugar as 2 pints of Ben & Jerry's butter pecan ice cream.

Turn down the power: Seventy-five percent of this chain's "power smoothies" contain in excess of 100 grams of sugar. Stick to Jamba's lower-calorie All Fruit Smoothies, which are the only menu items that contain no added sugar. And always opt for the 16-ounce "small."

18. Pepperidge Farm Roasted Chicken Pot Pie (whole pie)

1,020 calories
64 grams fat
86 grams carbohydrates

The label may say this pie serves two, but who ever divided a small pot pie in half? The sad truth is, once you crack the crust, there will be no stopping, which makes these calories worse than anything else you'll find in the freezer case.

Pick a better pie: Swanson's chicken pot pie has just 400 calories.

17. Ruby Tuesday Bella Turkey Burger

1,145 calories
71 grams fat
56 grams carbohydrates

We chose this burger for more than its calorie payload: Its name implies that it's healthy.

The truly healthy choice: Skip burgers entirely (few at Ruby Tuesday come in under 1,000 calories). Instead, order a 9-ounce sirloin (just 256 calories) with a side of steamed vegetables.

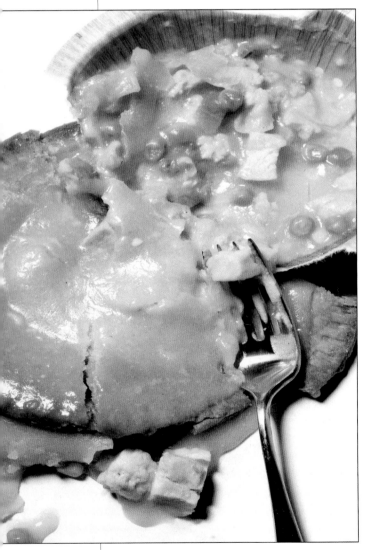

Breakfasts You Should Skip

It's never a bad idea to make breakfast your biggest meal of the day, but the bulk of the calories should come from high-quality protein (eggs), fruit, and whole grains, not refined carbohydrates. Almost all of these packaged products are brought down by two ingredients: white flour and added sugar.

Pop-Tarts Frosted Brown Sugar Cinnamon (1 pastry): 210 calories, 7 grams fat, 34 grams carbohydrates

Jimmy Dean Pancakes & Sausage Links Breakfast Bowl: 740 calories, 35 grams fat, 96 grams carbohydrates

Pillsbury Grands Cinnamon Rolls (1 roll): 310 calories, 9 grams total fat, 2.5 grams trans fat, 23 grams sugar

Colombo Classic Strawberry Banana Fruit on the Bottom Yogurt (8 ounces): 230 calories, 42 grams sugar

Pillsbury Grands Original Biscuit (1 biscuit): 180 calories, 8 grams total fat, 2.5 grams trans fat, 25 grams carbohydrates

16. Chipotle Mexican Grill Chicken Burrito

1,179 calories

47 grams fat

125 grams carbohydrates

2,656 milligrams sodium

Despite a reputation for using healthy, fresh ingredients, Chipotle's menu is limited to king-size burritos, overstuffed tacos, and gigantic salads, all of which lead to a humongous waistline.

Make over the menu: There are two ways to *Men's Health*ify a burrito at Chipotle: (1) 86 the rice and tortilla and request your meat, vegetables, and beans served in a bowl, or (2) bring a friend and saw the burrito in half.

15. Macaroni Grill Double Macaroni 'n' Cheese

1,210 calories

62 grams fat

3,450 milligrams sodium

It's like feeding your kid 1½ boxes of Kraft mac 'n' cheese.

Your best option: The 390-calorie Grilled Chicken and Broccoli.

14. Quiznos Classic Italian (large)

1,528 calories

92 grams fat

110 grams carbohydrates

4,604 milligrams sodium

A large homemade sandwich would more likely provide about 500 calories.

Cut the calories: Isn't it obvious? Order a small, or save half for later.

Gut Bombs to Go

In an age of supersize combo meals, 17-syllable coffee drinks, and 6-inch-long ingredient lists, it's hard to know what, exactly, you're eating, especially when you're in a hurry. Here are six items you should do without.

Worst Coffee

Starbucks Venti Strawberries and Crème Frappucino Blended Crème
- 750 calories
- 120 grams sugar

This drink has more sugar than three cans of soda.

Use this keyword: Order any blended drink "light" to cut the sugar in half.

Worst Doughnut

Krispy Kreme Caramel Kreme Crunch
- 380 calories
- 21 grams total fat
- 6 grams trans fat
- 46 grams carbohydrates

At about four or five bites per doughnut, it may provide more calories per swallow than any other food.

Damage control: Krispy Kreme's whole-wheat doughnut is the only one on the menu that contains fewer than 200 calories.

Worst Breakfast Sandwich

Dunkin' Donuts Sausage, Egg, and Cheese Croissant
- 690 calories
- 51 grams total fat
- 7 grams trans fat

Contains more trans fat than any breakfast food we've found. (Blame the croissant.)

A perfect portion: The Ham, Egg, and Cheese English

13. On the Border Grande Taco Salad with Taco Beef

- 1,450 calories
- 102 grams fat
- 78 grams carbohydrates
- 2,410 milligrams sodium

This isn't an anomaly: Five different On the Border salads on the menu contain more than 1,100 calories each.

The salad for you: The Sizzling Chicken Fajita Salad supplies an acceptable 760 calories. But remember to choose a noncaloric beverage, such as water or unsweetened iced tea.

12. Carl's Jr. Double Six Dollar Burger

- 1,520 calories
- 111 grams fat

Carl's Jr. brags that it's home to this enormous sandwich, but the restaurant chain also provides convenient nutrition information on its Web site, so ignorance is no excuse for eating it.

A simple solution: The Low Carb Six Dollar Burger has just 490 calories.

Muffin Sandwich packs a heavy dose of protein for a mere 310 calories.

Worst Minimart Snack

Hostess Fruit Pie, Cherry
- 480 calories
- 20 grams fat
- 33 grams sugar

Worst Airport Snack

Cinnabon Classic Cinnamon Roll
- 813 calories
- 32 grams total fat
- 5 grams trans fat
- 117 grams carbohydrates

This roll may give you a sugar lift, but a crash will soon follow.

Walk away: You're better off hoofing it over to Burger King for a regular Whopper, which contains 150 fewer calories but 13 more grams of protein. Just pass on the combo meal.

Worst Drive-Thru Combo Meal

Burger King Triple Whopper with Cheese, Fries, and Coke, King-Size
- 2,200 calories
- 115 grams total fat
- 11 grams trans fat
- 225 grams carbohydrates
- 117 grams sugar
- 2,590 milligrams sodium

Contains more carbs than 10 bread slices.

Create your own combo: The Angus Steak Burger, a garden side salad, and your choice of diet drink can fill you up for a justifiable 660 calories.

11. Lonestar 20-Ounce T-Bone Steak

1,540 calories

124 grams fat

Add a baked potato and Lonestar's Signature Lettuce Wedge, and this is a 2,700-calorie blowout.

Choose with your head: The golden rule of steak restaurants is this: Limit yourself to a 9-ouncer or smaller. After all, that's more than half a pound of meat. You won't walk away hungry.

10. Bob Evans Caramel Banana Pecan Cream Stacked and Stuffed Hotcakes

1,540 calories

77 grams total fat

9 grams trans fat

198 grams carbohydrates

109 grams sugar

Five Egg McMuffins yield the same caloric cost as this stack of sugar-stuffed flapjacks, which is truly a heavy breakfast, weighing in at a hefty pound and a half.

Order this instead: A Bob Evans Western Omelet starts your day with a reasonable 654 calories and 44 grams of muscle-building protein.

Restaurant Report Card

No one expects restaurants to serve only healthy fare. But they should provide options. So to separate the commendable from the deplorable, we calculated the total number of calories per entrée in 21 fast-food and sit-down chains. This gave us a snapshot of how each restaurant compared in average serving size—a key indicator of unhealthy portion distortion. Then we rewarded establishments with fruit and vegetable side-dish choices, as well as those offering bread made with 100 percent whole wheat. Finally, we penalized places for excessive amounts of trans fats and menus laden with gut-busting desserts. Did your favorite restaurant make the grade?

Fast-Food Restaurants

A+ Chick-Fil-A

Not a single entrée breaks the 500-calorie barrier, a feat unmatched in the fast-food world.

A Subway

An impressive selection of 6-inch sandwiches with less than 400 calories each earns Jared's joint a second-place finish.

A- Boston Market

Its expansive menu of healthy sides and nutritionally reasonable three-piece chicken meals gives diners plenty of choices.

B+ Taco Bell

It's okay to "make a run for the border," as long as you limit yourself to just two tacos or a single burrito.

B Wendy's

Although calorically comparable to McDonald's, Wendy's edges out the Arches with less trans fat and a range of healthy sides.

B- McDonald's

Burgers are reasonable, but other items, such as 1,000-calorie pancake platters, send McDonald's' numbers soaring.

C+ KFC

It's hard to have "fried" in your name and still make a decent grade. To halve calories, order your chicken without skin.

C Arby's

The array of sandwiches suffers from an abundance of creamy dressings, spreads, and melted cheese sauce.

C- Burger King

Thousand-calorie-plus burgers like the Quad Stacker give this chain a below-average score.

C- Domino's

Two slices of any Feast pizza contain from 460 (thin-crust vegetable) to 880 calories (deep-dish MeatZZa).

D Panera Bread

Healthy sides, whole grains, and free Wi-Fi can't offset oversized, calorie-loaded salads and sandwiches.

D- Pizza Hut

Massive pasta portions are nearly 1,000 calories, while personal pan pizzas average 660 calories.

Sit-Down Restaurants

A- Bob Evans

A massive menu of reasonable egg dishes and extensive sides ranging from broccoli to applesauce boosts Bob to the top spot.

B+ Fazoli's

Pasta portions are thankfully restrained and can be topped with chicken, broccoli, tomatoes, or garlic shrimp.

B Denny's

Abysmal burgers and the carb-loaded Grand Slam breakfast are offset by a range of lighter alternatives on the Fit Fare menu.

B- Ruby Tuesday

Most of the burgers hover around the 1,000-calorie mark, but seafood and chicken options offer a shot at redemption.

C Uno Chicago Grill

Any meal involving deep-dish pizza will likely break the 1,000-calorie barrier. (Go with a flatbread pizza.)

C- Chili's

Monster burgers and 2,000-calorie starters hurt. Order from the "Guiltless Grill" menu to keep your calorie intake below 650.

D P.F. Chang's

Most entrées begin in a wok with a puddle of oil and a scoop of sugar- and salt-laden sauce. Hunt for steamed options instead.

F On the Border

An average "Favorito" entrée contains 1,000-plus calories. Stick to two tacos and a side of grilled vegetables.

F Macaroni Grill

Even lunch portions and salads have more than 1,000 calories. Either split a pasta or order the 330-calorie Pollo Magro.

Freezer Burns

Here are some foods to avoid at all costs in the frozen food aisle.

Worst Frozen Pizza

Celeste Pizza for One, Pepperoni (1 very small pizza)
- 410 calories
- 21 grams total fat
- 4 grams trans fat
- 1,190 milligrams sodium

The 4 grams of trans fat come mostly from the imitation cheese.

Go thin to get thin: Palermo's Primo Thin Grilled Chicken Caesar has just 290 calories per serving.

Worst Ice Cream

Edy's/Dreyer's Peanut Butter and Chocolate Covered Dibs (1 serving)
- 510 calories
- 39 grams fat
- 23 grams sugar

These calorie-dense bites are made for mindless munching, which makes them all the more dangerous.

Waist management: Edy's Slow Churned Crunch Bar quells the ice cream urge with only 150 calories.

Worst Frozen Pasta

Bertolli Shrimp Scampi & Linguini (½ package)
- 550 calories
- 60 grams carbohydrates
- 1,200 milligrams sodium

Bertolli's pastas are consistently 200 more calories per serving than the competition's.

Swap the spaghetti: Most frozen pastas from Voilà! have less than 300 calories per serving.

9. Chili's Chocolate Chip Paradise Pie with Vanilla Ice Cream

- 1,600 calories
- 78 grams fat
- 215 grams carbohydrates

Would you eat a Big Mac for dessert? How about three? That's the calorie equivalent of this decadent dish. Clearly, Chili's customers get their money's worth.

Don't overdo it: If you want dessert at Chili's, order one single-serving Sweet Shot; you'll cap your after-dinner intake at 310 calories.

8. P.F. Chang's Pork Lo Mein

- 1,820 calories
- 127 grams fat
- 95 grams carbohydrates

The fat content in this dish alone provides more than 1,100 calories. And you'd have to eat almost five servings of pasta to match the number of carbohydrates it contains. Now, do you really need five servings of pasta?

Pick another noodle: P.F. Chang's Singapore Street Noodles will satisfy your craving with only 570 calories. Or try the Moo Goo Gai Pan or the Ginger Chicken & Broccoli, which have 660 calories each.

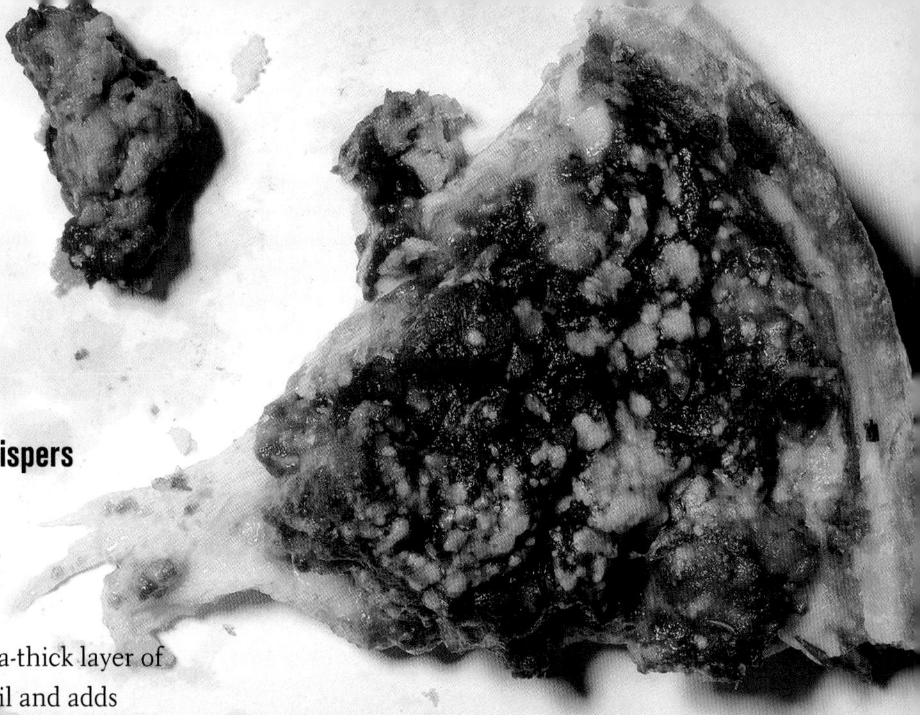

7. Chili's Honey Chipotle Crispers with Chipotle Sauce

2,040 calories

99 grams fat

240 grams carbohydrates

"Crispers" refers to an extra-thick layer of bread crumbs that soaks up oil and adds unnecessary calories and carbs to these glorified chicken strips.

Switch your selection: Order the Chicken Fajita Pita: At 450 calories and 43 grams of protein, it's one of the healthiest entrées you'll find in a chain restaurant.

6. On the Border Dos XX Fish Tacos with Rice and Beans

2,100 calories

130 grams fat

169 grams carbohydrates

4,750 milligrams sodium

Perhaps the most misleadingly named dish in America: A dozen crunchy tacos from Taco Bell will saddle you with fewer calories.

Lighten the load: Ask for grilled fish, choose the corn tortillas instead of flour (they're lower in calories and higher in fiber), and swap out the carbohydrate-loaded rice for grilled vegetables.

5. Uno Chicago Grill Chicago Classic Deep Dish Pizza

2,310 calories

162 grams fat

123 grams carbohydrates

4,470 milligrams sodium

Downing this "personal" pizza is equivalent to eating 18 slices of Domino's Crunchy Thin Crust cheese pizza.

Swap your slices: Switch to the Sausage Flatbread Pie and avert deep-dish disaster by nearly 1,500 calories.

More Burgers to Banish

Some are veiled in bacon. Others are slathered with ranch dressing. All of them will break the calorie bank.

Hardee's ⅔-pound Monster Thickburger: 1,420 calories, 107 grams fat

Denny's Mini Burgers (with onion rings): 2,220 calories, 179 grams fat

Chili's BBQ Ranch Burger: 1,110 calories, 71 grams fat

Jack in the Box Bacon 'n' Cheese Ciabatta Burger: 1,120 calories, 76 grams fat

4. Macaroni Grill Spaghetti and Meatballs with Meat Sauce

2,430 calories

128 grams fat

207 grams carbohydrates

5,290 milligrams sodium

This meal satisfies your calorie requirements for an entire day.

Downsize the devastation: Ask for a lunch portion of this dinner dish (or any pasta on the menu, for that matter) and request regular tomato sauce instead of meat sauce. You'll cut the calories in half.

3. On the Border Stacked Border Nachos

2,740 calories

166 grams fat

191 grams carbohydrates

5,280 milligrams sodium

2. Chili's Awesome Blossom

2,710 calories

203 grams fat

194 grams carbohydrates

6,360 milligrams sodium

1. Outback Steakhouse Aussie Cheese Fries with Ranch Dressing

2,900 calories

182 grams fat

240 grams carbohydrates

Even if you split these "starters" with three friends, you'll have downed a dinner's worth of calories before your entrée arrives.

Super substitutions: Front-load your meal with a protein-based dish that's not deep-fried. A high-protein starter helps diminish hunger without putting you into calorie overload. And remember: Appetizers are meant to be shared.

BY VIRGINIA SOLE-SMITH

Construct the Ultimate Diet Dining Room

Trying to eat (and weigh) less? Maybe it's time for a little redecorating

If a herd of dust bunnies has colonized under your dining room table because you eat most meals sprawled on your living room sofa, bent over your kitchen sink, behind the wheel of your car, or packed into a noisy restaurant, don't be surprised if you've got some extra junk in your trunk. "I analyze the dining environments of every one of my patients," says Dawn Jackson Blatner, RD, a spokesperson for the American Dietetic Association, in Chicago. "So many people try to rely on willpower alone and don't understand why their diets fail. You can't lose weight if you're in an environment that doesn't support healthy eating." Based on the newest research and the best expert advice, we've put together a 13-step plan to help you create one that does. So get ready to start losing: It's time to banish those bunnies for good!

1. Pull up a chair (and not in front of your PowerBook). Rule number one is simpler than Nicole Richie's job: "A meal is not a meal unless you have a table, a chair, and a plate," Blatner says. "If you eat on the go or standing in the kitchen, you rush through before your brain realizes you're full." Which means you shovel in more calories than you need.

2. Watch the clock. If your body were a grade school, your stomach would be in the slow learners' class: It needs about 20 minutes to figure out it's full. No wonder research shows that taking fewer than 9 minutes to eat your meal can cause you to scarf an additional 70 calories or more, Blatner says. "That could add up to 20 extra pounds per year!" But in an evil twist of nature, lounging at the table for more than 30 minutes can make you eat just as much. The longer you linger, the likelier you are to reach for seconds. The ideal amount of time to spend at the table? Twenty-nine minutes.

3. Dim the lights. "Bright lights encourage you to eat faster than you otherwise would because they make you feel stressed," says Brian Wansink, PhD, director of Cornell University's Food and Brand Lab and author of *Mindless Eating*. (Makes sense that most fast-food joints are as well lit as the Vegas strip.) But don't turn them off altogether: "A dark room will lower your inhibitions, which means you'll be more likely to have dessert," Wansink says. Try using medium-wattage incandescent bulbs (60 to 75 watts), so you can see well enough to eyeball your escarole but don't feel like you're in an interrogation room at Baghdad International Airport.

4. Repaint. Bright, warm hues such as red and orange are great for fall foliage, but for your dining room walls? Not so much. Just like bright light, these colors "make the environment more stimulating, so you'll want to eat and get the heck out," Wansink says. Blues and greens, on the other hand, encourage you to stick around longer (also bad). Go neutral with colors such as white, beige, and gray. If your walls are already scarlet and you'd rather eat paint than scan the Benjamin Moore selection at Home Depot, balance the brightness with softer lighting.

5. Hide the remote. An American Dietetic Association poll of 1,520 people found that a whopping 91 percent watch TV while eating at home. And if you dine tubeside, you're going to eat more. One Georgia State University study showed that college students consumed almost an entire extra meal's worth of calories on the days they channel surfed. "When you're distracted by the TV, you rely on external cues, like the end of the show, to tell you when to stop eating, instead of stopping when you feel full," Wansink explains.

6. Rock out at the gym, not at the table. A study in the journal Appetite found that participants took an average of 40.5 minutes to finish their meals with music playing, but only 29 without. (And they downed another 450 calories in those extra 11 minutes.) Doesn't matter whether you dig Kenny G or Green Day: Soft music makes you linger at the table, but you chew faster (and may eat more) when you listen to loud, fast songs. Unplug the stereo and have an actual conversation.

7. Turn off the AC. Heat is a dieter's BFF. When you're cold, "you fuel the furnace by eating," Wansink says. In other words, your body requires more energy to maintain your core temperature when you're chilly, and that energy often comes in the form of french fries.

8. Forget family-style. Except for a platter of fruit or vegetables. Just seeing food makes you likelier to eat it. One study in the journal *Nutrition* found that subjects who said they didn't want pizza were more inclined to eat a slice anyway when the pie was in front of them than when no food was on display. Keep calorie-dense foods in the kitchen and out of sight.

9. Minimize your menu. You eat as much as 40 percent more when you're given a variety of foods than when you get just one dish, according to research in the *Journal of Consumer Research*. That's probably because all the choices of color, smell, and taste distract you from noticing when you feel full.

10. Fire up the Viking. The temperature of your food can make as much of a difference as that of the room. "Hot food is more satiating, so you'll eat less of it," Blatner says. Take an extra minute to zap that leftover pizza in the microwave or add something warm (such as chicken) to a cold salad.

11. Pick petite plates. Eat your Edy's from a 17-ounce bowl rather than a 34-ouncer, and you'll ingest 30 percent fewer calories, according to a study in the *American Journal of Preventive Medicine*. When it comes to plates, use ones that are 8 inches instead of 12. And for flatware, swap your soupspoons for smaller dessert spoons. You'll slurp less.

12. Dust off the highballs and pour yourself a tall one! A study published online in the *British Medical Journal* found that we pour 32 percent more liquid into short, squat glasses than into tall, skinny ones. It's a classic optical illusion: Equal amounts of liquid appear more voluminous in thin glasses than in wide ones.

13. Enjoy your own company. It's sad but true: You eat less when you eat alone. In fact, according to a study in the journal *Nutrition,* a person consumes 44 percent more when he eats with at least one other person and 76 percent more with seven or more. Fellow diners—many of whom worship the breadbasket—set the pace of the meal, influencing how much you eat. When you do dine en masse, be the last one to start eating, and you'll keep calories down. And come armed with good stories: When you're flapping your gums, you can't stuff your face.

BY JEFFERY LINDENMUTH

Eat Half as Much and Feel Twice as Full

Enjoy big flavor—and a smaller belly—by harnessing the power of America's hottest culinary trend

Whether it's Spanish tapas, Chinese dim sum, or Greek mezes, small plates are huge news in American restaurants. And no one's walking away hungry. Why? Because big flavors can be just as filling as big portions. "Most places specializing in small plates create taste-rich sensations in microsize bites," says Brian Wansink, PhD, director of Cornell University's Food and Brand Lab and author of *Mindless Eating*. "And we've found that much of a man's eating satisfaction is derived from the flavor intensity and visual impact of a meal, not necessarily the amount served."

So forget mounds of mediocre food. Instead, downsize your dinner—and your gut—with these small but hugely satisfying dishes, courtesy of America's leading small-plate chefs.

SPICY GARLIC SHRIMP

The chef: Seamus Mullen
The restaurant: Boqueria, New York City

¼ cup olive oil
1 tablespoon red pepper flakes
4 cloves garlic, thinly sliced
16 ounces shrimp, peeled and deveined
Salt
Ground black pepper
1 tablespoon chopped parsley

In a small sauté pan, heat the oil until it starts to shimmer (just below smoking temperature); add the pepper flakes, and then the garlic. As the garlic begins to brown, season the shrimp with salt and black pepper, then place the shrimp in the pan with the garlic, swirling the pan gently. Sauté over medium-high heat for 1 minute, then stir in the parsley. Sauté for another minute, remove from the heat, and serve.

Makes 4 servings

Per serving: 249 calories, 23 g protein, 3 g carbohydrates, 16 g total fat, 2 g saturated fat, less than 1 g fiber

MINI BLUE-CHEESE STEAKS ON SALAD

The chef: Chris Santos
The restaurant: The Stanton Social, New York City

1 pound hanger or skirt steak, cut into 4 equal portions
Salt
Coarse ground black pepper to taste
1 teaspoon cooking oil

Salad

2 cups toasted, large, cubed pieces of baguette, crusts removed

1 bag mixed salad greens

2 pints cherry tomatoes

1 red onion, thinly sliced

¼ bunch chives, chopped

Vinaigrette

2 tablespoons red wine vinegar

1½ teaspoons tomato paste

⅛ to ¼ cup olive oil

½ cup Cabrales or other soft blue cheese

Preheat the oven to 500°F. Rub the steaks liberally with salt and black pepper. Heat the cooking oil in an ovenproof sauté pan until it begins to smoke lightly. Add the steaks to the pan and cook for 1 minute. Turn the steaks, then place the pan in the oven for 5 minutes. Remove the steaks from the pan and allow them to rest while you assemble the salad.

To make the salad, combine the baguette cubes, salad greens, tomatoes, onion, and chives. To make the vinaigrette, whisk together the vinegar, tomato paste, and oil. Toss the salad with the vinaigrette, and divide among four plates. Slice the steaks thinly and place on top of the salad. Garnish with the cheese.

Makes 4 servings

Per serving: 488 calories, 38 g protein, 22 g carbohydrates, 28 g total fat, 10 g saturated fat, 5 g fiber

VIETNAMESE CHICKEN SKEWERS

The chef: Michael Bao Huynh
The restaurant: Mai House, New York City

2 cloves garlic, minced

1 small red onion, minced

1 stalk lemongrass, inner leaves only, minced

1 tablespoon fresh ginger, peeled and minced

2 jalapeño peppers, split and seeds removed

1 tablespoon chopped cilantro

1 cup fish sauce

2 tablespoons sugar

Juice of 1 lime

2 boneless, skinless chicken breasts, cut into 1-inch cubes

Wooden skewers, soaked in cold water for 30 minutes

Combine the garlic, onion, lemongrass, ginger, peppers, cilantro, fish sauce, sugar, and lime juice in a saucepan. Slowly bring to a boil over medium heat, then remove from the stove and let cool. Toss the chicken in the marinade and let marinate for 1 to 2 hours. Preheat the grill. Skewer the chicken cubes and grill them for 3 to 4 minutes per side, until they're firm and lightly charred.

Makes 4 servings

Per serving: 112 calories, 16 g protein, 11 g carbohydrates, less than 1 g total fat, less than 1 g saturated fat, less than 1 g fiber

Complete the Meal

For a full meal, add a salad and a vegetable small plate to your main entrée. Each option has been infused with the biggest flavors from around the globe. Simply read down the columns to find the culinary companions that best match your main selection. (Each recipe makes 4 servings.)

American

Asian

Mediterranean

Salads: Start with: 4 cups loosely packed mixed greens

Add:

1 ripe pear, peeled and sliced

2 tablespoons crumbled blue cheese

2 tablespoons toasted walnuts

Toss with:

1 tablespoon balsamic vinegar

2 tablespoons olive oil

Pinch of salt and ground black pepper

Add:

1 orange, peeled and sectioned

1 carrot, grated

2 scallions, chopped

Toss with:

1 tablespoon rice vinegar

1 tablespoon peanut oil

2 teaspoons soy sauce

1 teaspoon minced ginger

Add:

¼ cup roasted red peppers

½ cup marinated artichoke hearts, quartered

2 tablespoons toasted almonds

Toss with:

1 tablespoon red- or white-wine vinegar

2 tablespoons olive oil

1 tablespoon Dijon mustard

Vegetables: Start with: A 2-pound mix of any of the following vegetables, cut into similar-size pieces: asparagus, zucchini, carrot, onion, cherry tomato. Brown in a 400°F oven for 15 minutes.

Add:

2 tablespoons olive oil

2 cloves garlic, roughly chopped

1 tablespoon chopped fresh thyme (or 1 teaspoon dried)

Add:

2 cloves garlic, chopped

1 tablespoon minced ginger

1 tablespoon low-sodium soy sauce

2 teaspoons sesame seeds

Add:

2 tablespoons fresh or bottled pesto (toss the vegetables in it before roasting)

Squeeze of lemon

CHICKPEAS WITH CHORIZO

The chef: Ken Oringer
The restaurant: Toro, Boston

¼ cup extra virgin olive oil, plus extra for drizzling

½ large onion

5 cloves garlic, minced

1 bay leaf

2 ounces Serrano ham or prosciutto, chopped

4 ounces ready-to-eat Spanish chorizo, sliced into ¼" rounds

3 tablespoons tomato paste

¼ cup dry white wine

1 cup chopped frozen spinach

1 cup canned chickpeas, in their liquid

Salt

Ground black pepper

2 hard-boiled eggs, quartered

In a large skillet over medium heat, heat the ¼ cup oil. Add the onion, garlic, and bay leaf and heat for 10 minutes. Add the ham and chorizo, and cook for another 5 minutes. Stir in the tomato paste and wine and cook for 10 minutes longer. Once the wine has evaporated, add the spinach and the chickpeas and their liquid. Simmer for 10 minutes. Season with salt and pepper, and turn off the heat. Remove the bay leaf and discard. Serve with the eggs and a drizzle of oil.

Makes 4 servings

Per serving: 438 calories, 20 g protein, 22 g carbohydrates, 29 g total fat, 7 g saturated fat, 5 g fiber

BRAISED SALMON WITH SOY AND GINGER

The chef: Susanna Foo
The restaurant: Susanna Foo Chinese Cuisine, Philadelphia

16 ounces salmon fillet

2 tablespoons extra virgin olive oil

1 tablespoon minced ginger

¼ cup mirin*

2 tablespoons soy sauce

2 tablespoons vodka

1 tablespoon butter

2 scallions (white parts only), chopped

3 or 4 sprigs cilantro

*Mirin is a Japanese condiment that's available in the ethnic-food sections of most supermarkets.

Cut the salmon into 1" squares. Heat the olive oil in a 12" nonstick pan over medium-high heat and add the salmon cubes and ginger. Sear together for about 1 minute, then pour the mirin, soy sauce, and vodka over the salmon. Lower the heat to medium and cook for about 3 minutes, until the fish turns pale. Add the butter and turn off the heat. Spoon the salmon onto a serving plate and top with the scallions and cilantro.

Makes 4 servings

Per serving: 359 calories, 24 g protein, 6 g carbohydrates, 22 g total fat, 5 g saturated fat, 1 g fiber

BY NANCY GOTTESMAN

Detour around Diet Roadblocks

Ten surprising reasons why you aren't losing when you should be— and what you can do about it

If losing weight were simple, Spanx would be just a screen name in an S&M chat room. But dieting is complicated: There are even ways to screw up without realizing it. For instance, who would ever think that working out in the a.m. or cranking the AC might be the reason you're not slimming down? Luckily, once you've I.D.'d these flubs, fixing them is nowhere near as hard as holding in your gut 24/7.

Roadblock #1: Always a Go-Getter, You Work Out at 6 a.m.

What's wrong with that? Morning workouts are great—if you go to bed at 10 p.m. In a study in the *American Journal of Epidemiology*, people who slept 7 or more hours a night were less likely to put on weight than people who didn't. Those who slept only 6 hours a night were 12 percent more likely to gain substantial weight—33 pounds on average over the course of 16 years! (People who slept a measly 5 hours had a 32 percent chance of gaining 30 or more pounds.) Other studies have linked lack of sleep to a higher body mass index (BMI) and have found that it negatively affects levels of the appetite-regulating hormones ghrelin and leptin.

Detour: Don't sacrifice your snooze time—not even for an extra-long run. And quality matters more than quantity, so taking a siesta later won't help. "In a 20-minute power nap you don't get into the deep-sleep stage," says Donna Taliaferro, PhD, associate professor of nursing at the University of Missouri-St. Louis, who conducts research on sleep and circadian rhythms. "You need to go through the cycles of sleep over a few hours to get the restorative rest that allows your body to work properly." Bottom line: You're better off sleeping through your workout every other day than stumbling to a sunrise Pilates class on too few Zs.

Roadblock #2: You're a Teetotaler (or a Sot!)

What's wrong with that? Alcohol may not be the diet kryptonite you thought it was. Research showed that people who have a single drink a couple of times a week have a lower risk of becoming obese than either teetotalers or heavy drinkers do. Those who consume more than four drinks daily, on the other hand, boost their odds of obesity by 46 percent.

Detour: Go ahead and have a drink, just avoid belly-busters such as a 245-calorie piña colada. Instead, raise a glass of heart-smart Merlot (123 calories per 5 ounces), Bud Light (110 calories per 12 ounces), Champagne (88 calories per 4 ounces), or sake (39 calories per ounce). Or mix a 100-calorie cocktail, such as vodka and diet tonic or tequila and club soda. "Just make sure you drink it with some healthy food, such as raw veggies with low-fat dip or whole-wheat pita and hummus," advises Dawn Jackson Blatner, RD, a spokesperson for the American Dietetic Association. Eating slows the rise of alcohol in your blood and lowers the odds that you'll drunk-order the deep-fried mozzarella sticks.

Roadblock #3: You Crank the AC

What's wrong with that? Al Gore wants you to lay off the thermostat to save the planet. Here's how it can save (the shape of) your own ass, too: In a study published in the journal *Physiology & Behavior,* researchers found that exposure to temperatures above the "thermoneutral zone"—the artificial climate we create with clothes, heating, or air-conditioning—decreases our appetite and food intake. "At a slightly uncomfortable 81 degrees, the people in the study experienced a 20 percent decrease in appetite and ate 10 percent less than at 72 degrees," says lead author Margriet S. Westerterp-Plantenga, PhD, a professor of food-intake regulation in the department of human biology at Maastricht University in the Netherlands.

Detour: Instead of cranking the air conditioner every time you feel a little warm, learn to endure slightly steamier conditions. Hitting the "off" button is well worth a little discomfort if it helps you lose the love handles.

Roadblock #4: You Jog Extra Miles to Make Up for Giant Meals

What's wrong with that? When it comes to dieting, success isn't 90 percent perspiration. You can't achieve lasting weight loss via exercise alone. But a study in the *Journal of Clinical Endocrinology and Metabolism* found that dieting can shrink your fat zones just as effectively as dieting plus exercise.

Detour: If you try the diet-only approach, you need a clear idea of how much you should be eating. Multiply your weight by 10, then add your weight again to that sum: that gives you the number of calories you need to maintain your current weight without activity. For example, 200 pounds × 10 = 2,000 + 200 = 2,200 calories. Eat more than that regularly, and your "loose-fit" pants won't anymore; eat less, and your muffin top will start melting away. But not so fast—before you burn your gym membership, read on about sarcopenia.

Roadblock #5: You Ignore Sarcopenia

What's wrong with that? Sarcopenia, in case you weren't paying attention to your medical TV dramas, is age-related muscle loss, and it can start in your thirties. If you don't take action now, you could begin to lose as much as 1 to 2 percent of your muscle mass by the time you hit 50. Less muscle means

you burn fewer calories and store more of them as fat.

Detour: The key to stopping muscle meltdown is to strengthen your back, shoulders, arms, and thighs. "When you increase lean muscle mass, you burn more calories, even when you're sitting down doing nothing," says Amy Campbell, MS, RD, education program manager for health care services at the Joslin Diabetes Center of the Harvard Medical School. Find a strength-building workout and start sculpting at least twice a week. And keep it up after you reach your goal weight: Studies show that if you don't exercise regularly (60 minutes of moderate physical activity a day), the pounds can creep back on.

Roadblock #6: You're Shooting for a Realistic Size

What's wrong with that? We all know size 29 jeans look like they were made for a 10-year-old, but, according to a study of 1,801 people published in the *International Journal of Obesity*, people who set unrealistically high weight-loss goals dropped more weight in 24 months than those who kept their expectations low.

Detour: The study authors concluded that having an optimistic goal motivated people to lose more weight. And the participants who failed to reach their magic number did not quit trying to drop the weight. Could aiming for Brad Pitt's bod really help you reach your goal weight healthfully? "If you're a driven person and a lofty goal motivates you," says Blatner, "it can work."

Roadblock #7: You've Been Popping M&M's Like They're Advil

What's wrong with that? You've heard the news: Cocoa can lower blood pressure; reduce the risk of heart attack, stroke, diabetes, and dementia; and possibly even prevent cancer. But the research isn't as delicious as it seems. The cocoa-bean products used in the studies are a far cry from the highly processed chocolate candy you find on the shelves of your local store. "Milk chocolate contains about 150 calories and 10 grams of fat per ounce," says Campbell.

Detour: The key here is small doses. Dark chocolate, which retains more of the bean during processing, generally has slightly less fat and fewer calories than milk chocolate—plus, it's richer, so less goes a longer way. We like CocoaVia's Crispy Chocolate Bar (90 calories, 5 grams fat) and Hershey's Special Dark Chocolate Stick (60 calories, 3.5 grams fat). If dark doesn't do it for you, opt for low-cal choices, such as a half-cup of Breyers French Chocolate Double Churn Fat Free Ice Cream (90 calories, 0 grams fat).

Roadblock #8: You Think "Water-Rich Diet" Means More Trips to the Cooler

What's wrong with that? Water in your glass is good, but water in your food can have serious slimming power. In an *American Journal of Clinical Nutrition* study, obese people ages 20 to 60 were told to either reduce their fat intake or increase their intake of water-rich foods, such as fruits and veggies. Although they ate more, people in the water-rich group chose foods that were more filling—yet had fewer calories—so they still lost 33 percent more weight in the first 6 months than the people in the reduced-fat group.

Detour: Fill up on food that's high in H_2O. Some good choices in addition to fruits and veggies: broth-based, low-sodium soups; oatmeal and other whole grains; and beans. For other filling options, consult *The Volumetrics Eating Plan: Techniques and Recipes for Feeling Full on Fewer Calories*, by Barbara Rolls, PhD.

Roadblock #9: You Give Up Junk Food Today but Put Off Joining a Gym until January

What's wrong with that? Tackling one goal at a time is supposed to help you succeed. But research published in the journal *Archives of Internal Medicine* bucks that conventional wisdom. In a study of more than 200 people who smoked, had high blood pressure, and weren't extremely active, one group was asked to quit the butts, cut back on dietary sodium, and increase physical activity all at once. Another group addressed one bad habit at a time. The group that tackled all their problems simultaneously had the higher success rate after 18 months.

Detour: Combining your goals may work for the same reason job negotiations do: When you ask for everything, you're more likely to get something. Put this thinking to the test by creating a healthy eating and exercise plan and throwing all your energy into following both.

Roadblock #10: You Never Think about Potassium

What's wrong with that? A Canadian study concluded that getting more potassium might help lower your weight and blood pressure. Levels measured in study participants were proportional to their diet and weight. "That makes sense," says Blatner. "The richest sources of potassium are beans, vegetables, and fruit, so the person with high potassium levels is consuming a lot of these foods, which are low in calories and are the most filling."

Detour: You should aim for 4,700 milligrams of potassium each day. Supplements may help you hit that target, but doctors don't recommend them for everyone. Try filling up on white beans (1 cup: 1,000 milligrams potassium), winter squash (1 cup: 494 milligrams), spinach (1 cup: 840 milligrams), baked potato with skin (926 milligrams), yogurt (1 cup: 600 milligrams), halibut (4 ounces: 566 milligrams), and OJ (1 cup: 473 milligrams).

BY MAUREEN CALLAHAN, RD

Power Up, Slim Down

Fuel your workout with the
19 best fitness foods

Choosing a bagel over a peanut butter sandwich isn't the kind of life-altering decision that, say, changing your e-mail address is. But your pick could have heavy fitness repercussions. Grab a lame prerun snack and you'll be dragging to the finish. Reach for the wrong food when you put down those weights and next time you pump iron, you could be crashing harder than a lead Zeppelin at a hot-air balloon festival. The simple truth is that what you eat influences your performance in key ways. That's why we pored over a stack of scientific studies and picked the brains of a half dozen experts—top-notch researchers, coaches, and sports nutritionists—to single out the top 19 foods for any activity, from running to rock climbing. Stock your pantry with these staples to perform and feel your absolute best.

Avocados

The cholesterol-lowering monounsaturated fat in these green health bombs can help keep your body strong and pain free. University of Buffalo researchers found that competitive runners who ate less than 20 percent fat were more likely to suffer injuries than those who consumed at least 31 percent. Peter J. Horvath, PhD, a professor at the university, speculates that the problem is linked to extreme low-fat diets, which weaken muscles and joints. A few slices of avocado a day are a great way to boost fat for people who are fat shy, says Leslie Bonci, RD, director of sports nutrition at the University of Pittsburgh Medical Center.

Bagels, Whole Grain

Never mind Dr. Atkins—carbs are the optimal workout food. "Not the simple ones, because they wind you up and drop you down,"

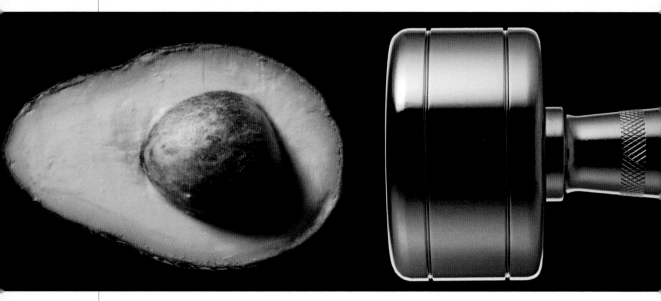

says Jackie Berning, PhD, RD, a nutrition professor at the University of Colorado at Colorado Springs and counselor to sports teams. "You want complex carbohydrates in their natural package, aka whole grains." A whole-grain bagel is an ideal pre-sweat-session pick: You'll digest it slowly because of all the fiber, which will deliver a steady flow of energy over time rather than one big burst.

Bananas

Thanks to bananas' high potassium content, peeling one is a speedy solution to that stitch in your side. While a lack of sodium is the main culprit behind muscle cramps, studies show that potassium plays a supporting role: You need it to replace sweat losses and help with fluid absorption. Bananas are also packed with energizing carbohydrates. One medium-size fruit has 400 milligrams of potassium and as many carbs (29 grams) as two slices of whole-wheat bread.

Berries

USDA researchers recently placed fresh berries on their list of the 20 foods richest in antioxidants. Just a handful of blueberries, raspberries, or blackberries is an excellent source of these potent nutrients, which protect muscles from free-radical damage that might be caused by exercise. Shop for berries by the shade of their skin: The deeper the color, the healthier the fruit.

Carrots, Baby

Close your eyes and they almost taste like crunchy candy. Carrots pack complex carbs that provide energy to muscles and potassium to control blood pressure and muscle contractions, Bonci says. And a half cup has just 35 calories.

Cereal, Whole Grain—with Fat-Free Milk

Looking for something to nosh before you hit the gym? Raid your cereal stash. The healthiest brands contain endurance-boosting complex carbs and muscle-building protein. Sixty minutes before a workout, fuel up with a 200-calorie snack: $3/4$ cup of whole-grain cereal with 4 ounces of fat-free milk. "When you eat something before exercising, you have more energy, so you can work out harder and perhaps longer. And you'll be less likely to overeat afterward," Bonci says.

Chicken Thighs

Skimp on iron and zinc and your energy will flag. Cooking up some juicy chicken thighs or turkey drumsticks is the best way to get more of both. Dark-meat poultry is significantly lower in fat than red meat yet has all the iron, zinc, and B vitamins that people need in their diets, says Seattle sports nutritionist Susan Kleiner, PhD, author of *Power Eating*.

Chocolate Milk, Low-Fat

There's way more to milk than just calcium. In fact, it's a damn near perfect food, giving you a lot of valuable energy while keeping your calorie count low, Kleiner says. The chocolate kind is loaded with calcium, vitamins, and minerals just like the plain stuff, but studies confirm that

Jumpstart Your Fat-Burning Engine

Monotony kills motivation. That's why this workout is the opposite of that—an explosive, weights-free workout of changeups and gear shifting that makes you leaner and more athletic.

In this workout, there's very little downtime, "so you'll improve cardiovascular fitness without compromising your strength or muscle," says Robert dos Remedios, CSCS, director of speed, strength, and conditioning at College of the Canyons, in Santa Clarita, California.

Here's your plan: Do 10 repetitions of each move, and proceed swiftly from one exercise to the next; your setup should take no more than 10 seconds. Complete all five exercises, rest for 1 to 2 minutes, and repeat the drill. Perform a total of three or four rounds.

---

milk with a touch of cocoa is as powerful as commercial recovery drinks at replenishing and repairing muscles.

Cottage Cheese, Low-Fat

Despite its frumpy image, this diet staple packs 14 grams of protein per half-cup serving, along with 75 milligrams of calcium and 5 grams of carbohydrates. That protein is crucial to healing the microscopic muscle tears that occur during exercise, says Amy Jamieson-Petonic, RD, health education manager at Cleveland's Fairview Hospital.

Cranberries, Dried

This packable fruit delivers a generous pre- or postworkout blast of carbohydrates (25 grams per $1/4$ cup). Plus, cranberries have proanthocyanins, compounds that help prevent and fight urinary tract infections.

Tuck Jump: Stand with your feet shoulder-width apart and your knees slightly bent. Jump straight up as high as you can and bring your knees toward your chest. Land on the balls of your feet with your knees slightly bent and quickly go into your next jump.

Power Skip: Don't worry: This looks much cooler than traditional skipping. You'll propel yourself as high as you can with each skip by driving your knee up into the air. As you punch each knee up, swing your opposite hand upward to get as much vertical lift as possible.

Stick Landing: Stand with your feet shoulder-width apart, hands beside your thighs. Jump and land with your knees bent and your butt and hips back. Try to land on the front two-thirds of your feet, with your heels just off the ground. Hold for 2 seconds before standing to perform your next jump.

Squat Jump: Stand with your feet slightly more than shoulder-width apart and your fingers laced behind your head. Bend at the knees to lower yourself until your thighs are parallel to the floor, then jump up as high as you can. Sink directly into the next squat without pausing.

Zigzag Bound: Think about lengthening your stride as much as possible. Drive one leg into the ground to push off forcefully and lift your opposite knee high in the air as you surge forward. Propel yourself upward, forward, and slightly laterally so that you bound forward and to the outside.

Running to the bathroom every 5 minutes definitely isn't the kind of workout you need.

Eggs

Don't skip the yolk. One egg a day supplies about 215 milligrams of cholesterol—not enough to push you over the 300-milligram daily cholesterol limit recommended by the American Heart Association. Plus, the yolk is a good source of iron, and it's loaded with lecithin, which is critical for brain health, Kleiner says. What does brain power have to do with exercise? Try catching a pop fly without it.

Flaxseed, Ground

"Flaxseed is full of fibers called lignans that promote gut health," Kleiner says. Because flax lignans contain both soluble and insoluble fiber, they keep you regular.

MUSCLE CHOW

SHAKE IT, BABY

Blend these ingredients for the perfect pre- or post-workout mix of protein, vitamin C, and carbs, says Leslie Bonci, RD. This may be the next best thing to an orange push-up pop.

½ medium banana
6 ounces low-fat vanilla yogurt
4 ounces orange juice
4 ounces water
1 ounce (2-tablespoon scoop) whey protein powder

Place the banana, yogurt, orange juice, water, and protein powder in a blender and mix well.

Makes 1 serving

Per serving: 370 calories, 35 g protein, 52 g carbohydrates, 2.5 g total fat, 1.5 g saturated fat, 2 g fiber, 160 mg sodium

"When you're trying to do an endurance sport, it can be disruptive to have digestive problems," she notes. A daily dose of 1 to 2 tablespoons of ground flaxseed tossed in your cereal nets you fiber without fuss.

Hummus

Complex carbohydrates, protein, and unsaturated fats—all the right elements to fuel activity—meet in one healthy little 70-calorie, 3-tablespoon package. Slip some to your wife or girlfriend, too. Hummus is often made with olive oil, which contains oleic acid, a fat that helps cripple the gene responsible for 20 to 30 percent of breast cancers, according to Northwestern University researchers.

Oranges

"They're portable. They're a fruit you can get year-round. And they're a rich source of vitamin C," Bonci says, "which helps repair muscle tissue." One orange has close to 75 milligrams of vitamin C, which is also key for making collagen, a tissue that helps keep bones strong.

Peanuts

No wonder Mr. Peanut never stops tap dancing. Soccer players kicked and sprinted just as well in the final minutes of a game as they did at the start when they added 2 ounces of peanuts a day to their regular diet, Horvath says. The extra fat may help improve endurance by giving muscles energy to burn up front so they can spare muscle glycogen stores later.

Potatoes, Baked

Sweat like a pig? Four shakes of salt (about 1,100 milligrams of sodium) and a small baked potato is the perfect recipe for electrolyte replacement. "The electrolytes, sodium and potassium, help maintain fluid balance in and around cells and make sure muscles contract as they need to," Bonci says.

Salmon

This fish is great for heart health, but here's an added twist: Studies are suggesting that monounsaturated fats and omega-3 fats might help lessen abdominal fat. It's too soon to understand the link, but this could be particularly good for people working to tone their core, Kleiner says.

Whey Protein

"Whey protein contains the ideal assortment of amino acids to repair and build muscle," Kleiner says. Plus, it's digested fast, so it gets to muscles quickly. Stir a scoop into a smoothie (see the recipe at left) for a delicious boost before or after your next workout.

Yogurt

Immune-strengthening probiotics are a fabulous feature, but the best thing about yogurt is that it will spike your energy without making your stomach gurgle in spin class. "It's liquidy in consistency and because you can digest it quickly, it's easy on the gut," Bonci says.

BY KIMBERLY DAWN NEUMANN

Maintain Your Motivation

Thirteen ways to stay on the
straight and narrow

Buy fish, vegetables, and a gym membership in an attempt to make good on your New Year's resolution to lose 12 pounds. Make healthy meals and work out five times a week for the first 3 weeks. Then two times a week for a month. Then, oh, never. Sound familiar? Maintaining your diet and exercise enthusiasm can be the trickiest part of the weight-loss equation. But before you give in to the Twinkies demon perched on your shoulder, check out these proven motivation boosters.

1. Have lots of sex. First off, it's pretty damn fun. But it can also keep you on the slim track. Having an orgasm releases the same endorphins in your brain that eating chocolate does—without the calories. And research shows that the more weight you lose, the better your sex life gets: A Duke University study found that even a 10 percent reduction in weight resulted in major improvements in all areas of the participants' sex lives, including arousal, feelings of attractiveness, and enjoyment of sexual activity (read: oodles of Os).

2. Make a promise. It's really hard to blow off a commitment you've made to lots of people. For example, "joining an athletic event to raise money means if you default on your training, you're not just letting yourself down but also the charity and everyone who sponsored you," says New York City–based Dan Hamner, MD, author of *Peak Energy*. Go to stepbystepfundraising.com and click on Athletic Events to find one near you. Choose something strenuous enough that you'll need to train seriously in advance.

(Triathlon, anyone?) Some groups, including Team in Training for the Leukemia & Lymphoma Foundation (teamintraining. org), even provide free coaching for participants nationwide.

3. Enlist Fido. Consider adopting a fuzzy friend if you don't have one already. Studies show that owning a dog can help you drop pounds. Why? Come rain, sleet, or snow, you've got to get your butt outside with pooch a few times a day (unless you really want urine-soaked carpets). What's more, most pet owners say they don't want to let down their exercise-starved doggy at walk time. It's another version of rule number 2.

4. Rock out. A recent study by the North American Association for the Study of Obesity found that people are more likely to stick to an exercise program if they listen to music while working out. So thank God for jogtunes.com. The site lets you select your workout pace, then download playlists of songs with beats per minute (bpm) that match your heart rate. For example, if your heart rate gets up to about 150 bpm when you exercise, songs such as the Killers' "Mr. Brightside" are perfect.

5. Get out your sexiest outfit. This is a common female trick, but it will work for you, too. You know that yogurt commercial where a woman takes a teeny-weeny yellow polka-dot bikini and hangs it on her wall to help motivate her to lose weight? She's one smart cookie. "I tell clients to take out an outfit they love and haven't been able to wear for a long time," says Christopher Warden, CSCS, a personal trainer in New

Eating His Way to the Top

How a sugar-free diet helped advertising's It man lose 250 pounds

Utter the phrase "larger than life" on Madison Avenue, and everyone within earshot will likely think of the same man: Peter Arnell. For more

than two decades, the 48-year-old brand inventor has uniquely reshaped the very concept of brand marketing, revitalizing the identities of companies such as Reebok, Banana Republic, and Samsung. But until a few years ago, his supersize reputation wasn't based solely on marketing genius.

"This is from when I weighed 350 pounds," says Arnell, holding up a size 60 suit jacket. He had already lost 50 pounds by the time he purchased it in 2001. A lifetime of skipping exercise and eating "Caesaresque" portions of knishes and tongue sandwiches had padded his 5-foot-9 frame with a blubbery 400 pounds. "It was embarrassing," says Arnell. "I used to leave meetings wondering what people were thinking of me."

Fed up, he sought help from Louis Aronne, MD,

York City. "Just pulling it out of the closet serves as a visual reminder of the goal they're trying to accomplish."

6. Lift the weight you've lost. A great way to keep yourself from sliding into what-the-hell eating mode when your weight loss plateaus: Use dumbbells that correspond to the number of pounds you've already dropped. You can't possibly forget how far you've come when you're straining to complete three sets of triceps kickbacks with a 25-pound weight. Feel how much

you're struggling to lift? That used to be on your gut!

7. Get gabbing. Reams of studies prove that support from other people can keep you motivated to lose weight. One study from the University of Kansas shows that dieters who get counseling over the phone lose just as much as those who get it face to face. So if you can't make that 5 p.m. Weight Watchers meeting, check out Bally's Built to Fit weight loss and nutrition program at ballynutrition.com, which offers

director of Cornell's Comprehensive Weight Control Program. The diet doc's advice was threefold: Arnell had to reduce his caloric intake to 1,800 calories a day, eliminate sugars and starches from his diet, and organize his meals around complex carbs such as vegetables and whole grains. Dr. Aronne hoped to stabilize Arnell's blood sugar levels, preventing the spikes in insulin that cause food cravings.

Of course, Arnell also had to exercise, working his way up to 45 minutes a day three days a week. And the diet and fitness plan worked. "People don't believe me when I tell them how much I weighed," says the 150-pound Arnell, who recently teamed up with Muhammad Ali to create the G.O.A.T. (Greatest of All Time) brand of vitamin-rich, low-calorie snacks for kids.

What Peter Arnell Eats to Keep Off the Weight

Breakfast 7 a.m.
½ cup All-Bran cereal with 4 ounces soymilk
20 ounces water

Snack 10 a.m.
10 oranges
small plate of seaweed

Lunch 2 p.m.
large plate of grilled vegetables with garlic
20 ounces sencha green tea
20 ounces water

Snack 4 p.m.
10 oranges
20 ounces sencha green tea

Dinner 7 p.m.
6 ounces seared tuna (no oil)
arugula salad with cherry tomatoes and capers
broccoli rabe (sautéed in garlic with no oil)
side of asparagus
shot of Italian espresso

weekly 15-minute phone sessions starting at $1 per minute.

8. Call on your inner cheapskate. You don't blow off the dentist, even though having your teeth drilled is about the most un-fun thing you can imagine. Why? Because you'll get charged whether you show or not. Consider buying a package of personal training sessions and scheduling all your appointments now. Who would throw away workouts that are already paid for?

9. Become a class regular. Join a group exercise class and make friends with your fellow regulars. Seeing your pals will inspire you to attend even when you feel like playing hooky. The guilt factor—always highly motivating—can help here, too. After all, in a place where everybody knows your name, they'll also know when you've missed a workout.

10. Get rubbed. A study from Ohio State University shows that people who accept their bodies are more likely to have better eating habits. And decadent as it may sound,

Need a Hand with Fat?

Here's Who You're Gonna Call

Certain things in life (tax preparation, brain surgery) just go better when you hire a professional. If you've tried the motivation tricks in this section and still can't shed a pound, it may be time to call in the big guns. Here's who they are and what they can do for you.

Diet Doctor (bariatric physician)

Who is he? An MD who is certified by the American Board of Bariatric Medicine and trained to spot medical causes of weight gain.

Try him if: You're overweight enough that your waist size is bigger than your chest, says Mary

Vernon, MD, president of the American Society of Bariatric Physicians.

What will he do to me? Ask for your health history and give you a physical exam, then run blood tests to see whether your glucose, insulin levels, and thyroid are normal. Once he's pinpointed the cause of your weight problem, he'll prescribe any necessary meds and work with you on a diet plan.

Best weight-loss tip: Kick processed carbs to the curb. They cause spikes in your blood sugar, which can lead to insulin resistance over time.

Cost: From $200 to $400 for the initial evaluation, then $30 to $50 for weekly follow-ups, plus the cost of any meds.

How to find him: Visit asbp.org and click on Locate a Doctor.

Registered Dietitian (RD)

Who is he? Someone with a bachelor's degree in nutrition or science who has passed a national certifying exam.

Try him if: You're confused about which kind of eating plan to follow.

What will he do to me? Ask you to write down everything you put in your mouth, so he can find out what you're eating, when, where, and why. Then he'll create a meal plan and show you how to incorporate healthier foods into your diet, control portion sizes, and cut back on junk food. "We tailor everyone's program to his specific needs," says Dawn Jackson Blatner, RD, a spokesperson for the American Dietetic Association.

Best weight-loss tip: Load at least half your plate with produce, a quarter with protein, and a quarter with grains (preferably whole), says Blatner.

Cost: From $15 for 15 minutes with an RD at your local hospital to $95 to $250 for an hour with one in private practice.

How to find him: Visit eatright.org and search for an RD certified in Adult Weight Management.

Weight-Loss Psychologist

Who is he? Someone with a PhD in clinical psychology who specializes in eating disorders and weight control.

Try him if: "You know what you're supposed to do to lose weight but just can't make yourself

do it," says Ed Abramson, PhD, a professor emeritus of psychology at California State University in Chico.

What will he do to me? Ask you to talk—a lot—to get to the root of your food issues and figure out whether you're overeating because you're bored, depressed, angry, stressed, or all of the above.

Best weight-loss tip: Go for a walk. "If you're stressed or depressed, it's hard to make the effort to lose weight," Abramson says. "But even mild physical activity will lift your mood and give you energy to do more."

Cost: About $100 per 50-minute session (covered if your insurance plan offers mental health benefits).

How to find him: Call your insurance company or state psychological association and say you're looking for a licensed psychologist who specializes in weight loss.

Weight Loss Coach

Who is he? Anyone who calls himself a weight loss coach. The best are certified by the International Coaching Federation, which requires at least 125 hours of training and a final exam.

Try him if: You need a kick in the pants to put

down the Fritos and get off the couch.

What will he do to me? Ask you to keep a food log to pinpoint which emotions are triggering you to down an entire box of doughnut holes and then teach you to counter the negative thoughts that lead you to the cupboard. He'll also help you find ways to overcome each skip-the-gym obstacle—whether it's reworking your schedule or learning to say no to people who eat up too much of your time.

Best weight-loss tip: "Refuse to beat yourself up for overeating," says Brooke Castillo, a weight loss coach in Shingle Springs, California. "That keeps you trapped in the negative thinking that made you eat in the first place."

Cost: About $100 to $150 per session.

How to find him: Visit coachfederation.org and click on Find a Coach.

getting a massage can help with that. Allowing themselves to be touched by another person—even when they aren't at their ideal weight—can help people become more comfortable with their bodies, says Mitch Klein, a licensed massage therapist in New York City.

11. Face your reflection. When you feel fat, you probably shun mirrors. Turns out you should do the opposite. A study in the *International Journal of Eating Disorders* found that mirror-exposure therapy— staring at your bod in the mirror and stifling the usual criticisms of your love handles—can improve body image, which, as we said in rule 10, can help keep you committed to healthy eating. Try it: Speak to your reflection without using any negatively charged words. For example, instead of moaning, "I have a huge gut," say, "Look at those biceps!"

12. Chart your progress. Weight loss is serious business. Treat it that way. Weigh yourself every morning—a study in the journal *Annals of Behavior Medicine* shows that people who do daily weigh-ins are more successful losers—and write the number down. (We like the Tanita HD-351 digital scale, which displays your current weight plus the number from your previous weigh-in; $64, amazon.com.) If you're even vaguely computer savvy, it's a snap to create a chart with a fever line that shows the pounds dropping away over time. When you get discouraged—say, you haven't lost a pound in a week—seeing your long-term progress will boost your motivation.

13. Score some free stuff. There's no motivation like saving money. And because insurance providers want you to stay healthy so you don't develop expensive diseases such as diabetes, some offer perks that make getting fit easier. Highmark Blue Cross Blue Shield, for example, gives its members discounts to certain gyms and free consultations with a dietitian. Check with your provider.

Shed Fat Fast

This workout combines cardiovascular drills with strength exercises to build muscle and burn calories. The only gear you need is a staircase or bench. See you at the top.

Sprinter's Step Drill: Stand facing the bench with your right foot on the bottom step and your right knee bent. Rapidly alternate your feet on and off the step so you're sprinting in place. Drive your knees up, and pump your arms as if you were sprinting. Continue for 30 to 60 seconds.

Pistol Squat: Stand with your back to the bench, lifting one leg straight out in front of you. Push your hips back, and bend your other leg to try to touch the bench with your butt. Once you've reached your lowest point, push your foot into the floor and stand back up. Do 6 to 10 reps on each leg.

Here are two ways to work the steps:

1. Alternate between the sprinter's step drill and the incline pushup for two sets of each move, and then alternate between the pistol squat and the upper-body shuttle.

2. Perform all four moves in a row, rest for 1 minute, then repeat the grueling circuit twice.

Complete the routine 3 days a week, resting at least a day between sessions.

Watch video demonstrations of 15-Minute Workouts at MensHealth.com/15minute.

Incline Pushup: Assume a pushup position, facing away from the bench or stairs. Place the balls of your feet on the third step. Brace your abs and keep your back flat. Bend your elbows and lower yourself until your chest is a couple of inches off the floor. Pause, then push back up. Do 10 to 12 reps.

Upper-Body Shuttle: Face the bench or stairs in a pushup position, with your fingertips just in front of the bottom step. Lift one hand onto the step, then bring up your other hand. Return your first hand to the floor, then the second. Walk your hands up and down for 30 to 60 seconds.

Burn Blubber, Not Biceps

Weight training is a key ingredient in any belly-off plan. Case in point: Ball State University researchers put overweight men on a 1,500-calorie-a-day diet and divided them into three groups—one that didn't exercise, another that performed aerobic exercise 3 days a week, and a third that did aerobic exercise and weight training 3 days a week.

The results: Each group lost nearly the same amount of weight—about 21 pounds. But the lifters shed 5 pounds more fat than those who didn't pump iron. Why? Because their weight loss was almost pure fat, while the other two groups lost just 15 pounds of lard and several pounds of lean body mass, a.k.a. muscle.

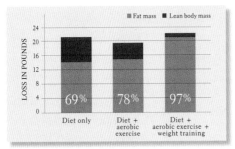

Push It to Lose It

Although conventional wisdom suggests lifting weights slowly, lifting weights quickly torches more calories, reports a study in the journal *Medicine & Science in Sports & Exercise.* Researchers measured oxygen consumption of nine participants as they slowly did four sets of 8 reps on a squat machine (2 seconds down, 2 seconds up), then again as they did the same

number faster (2 seconds down, up as quickly as they could lift). They found that explosive exercise combusted calories 11.2 percent faster, and the burn was also greater—by 5.2 percent—in the hour afterward.

Fast movements activate a type of muscle fiber that responds with greater calorie burn, says lead study author Scott Mazzetti, PhD. To rev up your reps: Allow 2 to 4 seconds to extend the muscle, then lift as fast as you can.

Get Some Oil, Slick

Start your sweat-fest with a shot of oil. Regular exercise combined with fish-oil supplements results in fat loss, reports the *American Journal of Clinical Nutrition.* Researchers had 65 overweight people take 6 grams daily of either fish oil or sunflower oil. Half the people in each group ran or walked three times a week for 45 minutes. After 12 weeks, the fish-oil eaters who exercised had lost 3.3 pounds on average; the others saw only minor weight loss.

Both exercise and fish oil increase the activity of fat-burning enzymes, so combining them leads to greater fat loss, says researcher Alison Hill, PhD. To boost your burn: Pop 2 grams of flavored fish-oil capsules 2 hours before your workout.

Go Light

Adding light therapy to your workout routine will boost your fat burn. Canadian researchers discovered that overweight adults who exercised for 90 minutes weekly on a light-box-equipped stationary bike lost 2 percent of their total body fat in just 6 weeks. A control group exercised at the same intensity but saw no change in body fat.

"Light is a natural stimulant, so the box may have triggered the people to be more active outside the gym," says study author Sharon Chung, PhD, who is working to identify the exact mechanism. To buy the same mountable light used in the study, go to litebook.com. Chung suggests using it for 45 minutes daily and when you exercise, as the participants did. Note that unlike the sun, a light box is UV-free.

Go for a Spin

Resistance-controlled bikes helped men burn 700 calories in just 50 minutes (100 calories more than men who rode ordinary stationary bikes), report Italian scientists. Think the classes are sissy? Spinning was originally designed to help professional cyclists improve their cardiovascular fitness.

Take 20

Try this move: the lounge. Chilling in the middle of a workout can burn more fat than exercising continuously, reports a *Journal of Applied Physiology* study. Scientists measured fat metabolism in seven men as they took three tests: pedaling on a stationary bike for 60 minutes; pedaling for 30, sitting for 20, and then pedaling again for 30; and sitting for 60 minutes. Subjects who took a break had three times the free fatty acids (compounds released when stored fat is used) at the 50-minute mark.

During a break, the body may redirect its excess energy into burning fat—so pausing revs up the fat-burning process twice. Not into time-outs? Interrupt cardio or weight sessions with easy spinning, stretching, or walking.

Sprint Away from Fat

In an Australian study, people who cranked out 20 minutes of high-intensity interval training 3 days a week dropped 10 percent of their body  fat, while those who exercised longer but at a lower intensity didn't lose any. Ignite your weight loss by performing the study's exercise-bike routine: Sprint for 8 seconds, then slow to an easy pace for 12 seconds. Repeat for 5 minutes. Go for longer as the sessions become easier. Why does this work? Sprints up your levels of catecholamine, a chemical that triggers fat burn.

Lift First, Run Second

We've long touted the fat-loss benefits of weight training. But now Japanese scientists have discovered that lifting weights before you run helps you burn more flab while you pound the pavement. In fact, men who performed a weight-lifting routine and then hopped on a stationary bike burned twice as much fat as those who only pedaled. Resistance exercise stimulates the release of fat-burning hormones, which trigger your body to use more lard for energy. For a weight-training workout designed to torch your midsection, check out "Fuel the Burn" on page 8.

Train Your Brain

Besides using up calories, exercise helps your brain stick to a diet. University of Pittsburgh researchers studied 169 overweight adults for 2 years and found that the participants who didn't follow a 3-hour-a-week training plan ate more than their allotted 1,500 calories per day. The reverse was also true; sneaking snacks sabotaged dieters' workouts.

"One healthy behavior without the other will not work. You need to diet and exercise to maintain long-term weight loss," says study author John Jakicic, PhD. Both actions serve as reminders to stay on track, reinforcing your weight loss goal and drive.

Try This Fitness Math

Anyone can lose 10 pounds. But the key to losing weight without losing muscle is to track your pound-for-pound strength, report researchers at Arizona State University.

"A stagnant bench press could make you feel like you're failing," says Mark Peterson, PhD, the study's lead author. "But you may be lifting more weight per pound of body mass, which means you're actually getting stronger." Divide the amount of weight you hoist by your scale's readout. If this number dips, you're probably losing muscle. Go heavier on basic exercises and add explosive moves to boost strength—and protect your hard-earned muscle.

Training
Tips

Do I need to eat before my morning workout?

To pump up the effectiveness of your workout, eat a simple carbohydrate that will digest quickly and give you the boost of energy you'll need. Try starting small: Even a few crackers, half a banana, or an orange will help.

I know breakfast is key to weight loss, but how soon after I wake up should I be eating?

The sooner the better. Your blood sugar is low when you wake up, so your body needs fuel to get going and to prevent you from overdoing it at lunch. Eat something within 1 to 2 hours of getting up, especially if you're doing anything that requires concentration (such as driving). Even a yogurt or a piece of fruit will do.

If I work out on an empty stomach, will I burn more fat?

It's not the fat burned during exercise that matters, it's the fat burned between your exercise sessions that really counts. Worrying about how much fat you burn during exercise makes as much sense as wondering how much muscle you're building while lifting. (You don't actually build muscle during training; you break it down to trigger growth.) Exercise is the catalyst for change, not the change

itself. During a high-intensity workout, your body burns carbohydrates and creatine instead of fat. But—and this is a great "but"—it stimulates your metabolism, which in turn attacks your fat stores between workouts. So go ahead and eat beforehand. You'll need the fuel to make it a worthwhile workout.

I crave carbs at night and end up eating hundreds of extra calories before bed. Help!

Low blood sugar or serotonin levels could be to blame; both can occur if you strictly limit the amount of carbs you take in during the day. Start your morning with a high-fiber, carb-rich breakfast that contains some protein, such as whole-grain cereal with milk and berries. Include grains at lunch and dinner, but keep portions modest (a small roll or ½ cup of pasta). Between meals, snack on dried fruit and nuts, which provide carbs, protein, and healthy fats.

What is nondairy creamer? Should I use regular cream instead?

Powdered or liquid creamers contain sodium caseinate, a substance derived from milk protein, but they typically lack the milk sugar lactose and aren't considered dairy. Plus, they're full of fattening corn syrup and saturated vegetable oils. Fat-free soymilk or regular milk is healthier. If you must use creamer, choose a low-fat, unflavored version, such as Nestle Coffee-Mate Original Lite.

Can you name some healthy between-meal snacks?

"Low-fat yogurt, 1 or 2 ounces of reduced-fat cheese and fruit, prepackaged carrots, and a handful of almonds are all great choices. Including at least some lean protein in snacks will improve satiety between meals," suggests Louis Aronne, MD, director of Cornell's Comprehensive Weight Control Program.

My blood sugar is high. What should I eat to gain muscle?

"Focus on lean meats and reduced-fat or fat-free dairy products for protein. Avoid sports drinks, because they're loaded with sugar. Likewise, skip juices in favor of whole fruit. Its soluble dietary fiber will help even out blood-glucose levels," says Mary Ellen Camire, PhD, a professor of food science in the department of food science and human nutrition at the University of Maine and a food-science communicator for the Institute of Food Technologists, a not-for-profit scientific organization.

Why do I weigh slightly less in the afternoon than I do in the morning?

On average, people gain 1 to 3 pounds during the day from food. If you're dropping pounds even though you're eating, it's most likely water loss. Do you sweat it out at the gym but never drain your water bottle, or otherwise skimp on fluids? Be sure to drink up to make it up.

I think my scale is lying to me. How can I find out?

Take the heaviest dumbbell you have around the house—at least 10 pounds—and weigh it. Does the scale's reading match? Estimate your weight based on the error, or replace the old clunker. (We like the Soehnle Comfort F5 scale; $130, soehnle.com.)

How can I combat the intense food cravings that sabotage my weight loss?

The best strategy to conquer a craving is to wait it out, because most cravings pass within 20 minutes. They're often psychological, not physiological. So to endure a craving, occupy your mouth with a piece of sugarless gum. A recent study found chewing gum helped reduce participants' hunger and diminished their cravings for sweets.

What's a realistic way to lose 20 pounds?

Don't become a slave to the scale. Although it's normal to lose 1 or 2 pounds a week on a successful program, monitoring your athletic performance can keep your eyes on what really matters: overall fitness. Aiming for improvements in strength, speed, flexibility, and blood pressure can make losing weight, and keeping it off, that much easier.

How can I stop pigging out after a workout? I get so hungry, I usually blow my diet.

You probably aren't eating enough before you exercise. Make sure you fuel up with at

least 200 calories' worth of protein, carbs, and a small amount of fat (try a tuna sandwich with light mayo on whole-wheat bread) an hour or two before hitting the gym. That way, your stomach won't bottom out on the treadmill.

What's the best fat-burning workout that I can do in 30 minutes?

When you're pressed for time, nothing beats a circuit—moving from exercise to exercise with little rest in between. Here's our favorite routine: dumbbell chest presses, dumbbell pullovers, squats with dumbbells, lunges with dumbbells, seated dumbbell shoulder presses, seated dumbbell biceps curls, crunches, and back extensions. Do a circuit of 8 to 12 reps per exercise, rest a minute, and then do another circuit. You'll get all the aerobic benefits of cardio and build muscle from head to toe.

I'm exercising and losing weight, but not in my gut. What am I doing wrong?

Sounds as if you're doing everything right. Men's bodies simply favor the midriff for fat storage. Natural selection made

it this way so that we'd have an easier time carrying our "energy reserves" as we went about hunting and gathering. Unfortunately, this also means that your belly will be one of the last areas to thin out.

But have faith: It will thin out if you continue to exercise, especially if you do both cardio and strength training (every pound of muscle you put on burns an extra 13 calories a day). And remember, it could be worse: Women store fat in their thighs and butts.

PART TWO

GET FIT

BY SCOTT QUILL

Push Harder

Update the classic pushup
for a whole-body overhaul

Guys tend to abandon the pushup for the bench press sometime around puberty, which is why you usually have to wait in line at the gym for a bench, but there's always plenty of floor space for the taking. Call it a natural rite of passage. After all, doesn't everybody agree that pressing a plate-loaded bar off your chest is far more manly—and effective—than pushing your body away from the floor?

"Think again," says Alwyn Cosgrove, CSCS, owner of Results Fitness, in Santa Clarita, California. "The pushup and the bench press both work your chest, shoulders, and triceps, but the pushup also trains your abdominals, lower back, upper back, and glutes." Read: Work more muscle, build more muscle. "You might say it's the ultimate multitasking exercise," says Cosgrove.

Besides the classic pushup, we've found six variations that will help you reach almost any goal—whether you want a stronger core, a leaner midsection, or, yes, a bigger chest. And the best part? No gym—or spotter—is required.

Break Your Pushup Record

Pick two pushups from the six movements here and substitute them for your regular chest workout. Twice a week, choose a new pair. Perform two or three sets of as many repetitions as you can do. This strategy shores up common weaknesses that prevent you from lasting longer. The result: In a month's time, you'll double the number of pushups you can do simply by performing the same movement in different ways, says *Men's Health* Muscle Guy Mike Mejia, MS, CSCS.

Push Harder for a Six-Pack

Unleash your abs with the first exercise you ever learned: the pushup. Not just a chest builder, the pushup also strengthens your core, and it's a good indicator of whether you're exercising enough now to avoid fat later. Canadian researchers found that guys who perform poorly in a pushup test are 78 percent more likely to gain 20 pounds of flab over the next two decades.

Strive for 30 reps, "but don't stop there," says lead study author Peter Katzmarzyk, PhD. "The higher the number of pushups you can do, the lower your risk of weight gain," he says. And as a result, the better your abs.

1. ROCK-SOLID CORE: MEDICINE BALL ARCHBISHOP

The secret to perfect pushup technique is keeping your body rigid. "Your abs and lower back usually fatigue first," says Mike Robertson, MS, CSCS, a strength coach in Indianapolis. That's when your hips sag, which increases strain on your back instead of building your chest and abs.

When you place your hands on a medicine ball or Swiss ball, the instability causes your core muscles to work 20 percent harder than when you do pushups on the floor, report New Zealand researchers. So you'll train the muscles of your midsection and hips to remain stable longer. As a result, you'll be able to do more pushups and work more muscle.

HOW TO DO IT

A. Place three to five medicine balls in a semicircle and assume the pushup position with both hands on the ball to the far left. Your chest should be over the ball and your feet should remain in place throughout the exercise.

B. Move your right hand to the ball at right and do a pushup. Bring your left hand to that ball.

C. Continue moving right and doing pushups until you reach the farthest ball. Then work your way back. That's one repetition.

Note: Place your hands directly beneath your shoulders.

2. A BIGGER CHEST: TRIPLE-STOP PUSHUP

Depending on where your weakness lies, pushups may challenge you most at the top, middle, or bottom position. "Pausing briefly at each point increases strength at your joint angle and 10 degrees in either direction," says Mejia. Bonus: Holding each position increases the time your muscles are under tension, stimulating growth.

HOW TO DO IT

A. Assume the starting position of a regular pushup.

B. Bend your arms to lower yourself halfway, then pause for 2 seconds.

C. Continue until your chest is just off the floor and hold again for 2 seconds. As you push yourself up, pause again for 2 seconds at the halfway point. Finally, when you straighten your arms, hold them that way—with your elbows unlocked—for 2 seconds. That's one repetition.

Note: Lead with your chest, not your hips. Keep your neck in line with your spine.

3. BOLDER SHOULDERS: SWISS-BALL PUSHUP PLUS

On the side of your shoulder blade and upper ribs lies a small, neglected muscle called the serratus anterior. When it's weak, you can't move as much weight in the bench press and military press. And because your rotator-cuff muscles must then pick up the slack to stabilize your shoulder joint, shoulder pain and injury often result.

Avoid pain and boost your bench press with the Swiss-ball pushup plus. The "plus" portion is when your shoulder blades glide away from each other at the top of the movement. When performed on the floor, the pushup plus activates your serratus anterior 38 percent harder than a standard pushup does, report researchers at the University of Minnesota. The Swiss-ball version works even better.

HOW TO DO IT

How can I ease my postworkout soreness?

Pop a multivitamin. A daily dose of vitamins and minerals before endurance exercise will speed your muscles' recovery. Athletes who took a multivitamin for 3 weeks prior to a 34-mile trail race (and for 2 days after) showed 11 percent faster recovery in their quadriceps than did runners who took a placebo.

Vitamins C and E, selenium, and glutathione help control inflammation and the muscle-damaging effects of free radicals, according to researchers at the National Institute of Sport and Physical Education in Paris. They used a multivitamin called Isoxan Endurance, which is comparable to Centrum Performance.

A. Assume a pushup position with your hands placed directly under your shoulders and on the sides of a Swiss ball. Spread your fingers, with your thumbs pointing forward.

B. Keeping your core tight, lower yourself until your chest grazes the ball, then push back up. At the top of the move, push yourself as far away from the ball as you can so your shoulder blades move away from each other.

Note: Brace your abdominals as if you were about to be punched.

MUSCLE CHOW

Fast and Filling

This recipe makes 25 to 30 walnut-size crunchy treats—delicious when they begin to melt. Just divvy them up into plastic sandwich bags and stick them in the freezer. Then, instead of reaching for a processed boxful of ingredients you can't pronounce, you'll be ready with a healthy, high-protein snack.

PEANUT-BUTTER BALLS

2 cups crunchy peanut butter

2 scoops chocolate whey-protein powder

2 extra-ripe bananas

2 tablespoons whole flaxseeds

Mix all the ingredients with a fork in a large bowl. Mold the mixture into walnut-size balls and place them in a container lined with parchment to separate the layers.

Refrigerate or freeze for at least 2 hours before serving or transferring to individual zipper-lock bags for a grab-and-go snack.

Makes 5 servings

Per serving: 710 calories, 35 g protein, 35 g carbohydrates, 54 g total fat, 9 g saturated fat, 10 g fiber, 521 mg sodium

4. BEACH MUSCLES: DUMBBELL UNDERHAND PUSHUP

In the classic pushup, your chest and shoulders move approximately 75 percent of your body weight; your biceps just keep your arms stable. But when you turn your palms forward, a large portion of your body weight falls directly on your biceps, says Houston-based trainer Carter Hays, CSCS. So you'll build all your mirror muscles—your abs, chest, and biceps—with just one movement.

HOW TO DO IT

A. Grab a dumbbell in each hand and get in pushup position with your palms facing forward. The dumbbells should align with the middle of your sternum, and your arms should be spaced about shoulder-width apart.

B. Without allowing your elbows to flare to the sides, lower your chest to the floor. (Your hands should touch the sides of your chest at the bottom of the movement.) Then push yourself back up.

Note: **Keep your legs straight, and keep your elbows close to your body.**

5. A LEANER BODY: EXPLOSIVE CROSSOVER PUSHUP

Explosive pushups, such as this one, allow you to generate maximum force by pushing your body off the floor. "The harder you push, the more muscle fibers you activate," says Cosgrove. And that means you'll burn more calories, both during and after your workout. What's more, the crossover portion of this movement forces your upper arms toward the center of your body, which is the main function of the pectoralis major, your largest chest muscle. The result: You work as many chest muscle fibers as possible.

HOW TO DO IT

A. Place your right hand on the floor and your left hand on the smooth side of a weight plate.

B. Lower your body.

C. Explosively push up and to the left so your hands leave the floor. Land with your right hand on the plate and your left hand on the floor. Reverse the move.

Note: Space your hands slightly wider than shoulder-width apart.

6. TOTAL-BODY MUSCLE: DUMBBELL PUSHUP ROW

"When most men perform rowing movements, they pull more with their arms than with their middle and upper back, which defeats the purpose," says Mejia. But in this pushup, your arms, abs, and shoulders are forced to work together to keep you steady while your back muscles draw the weight to your rib cage—so you can't cheat. The benefit? You'll simultaneously build your back and chest, which not only saves you time, but also helps prevent muscle imbalances of your upper body.

HOW TO DO IT

A. Get into pushup position with your arms straight and your hands resting on light dumbbells.

B. Squeeze your abs and glutes as you perform a pushup.

C. At the top, pull one dumbbell off the floor and toward you until your elbow is above your back. Slowly return the weight to the floor and repeat with the other arm.

Note: Forcefully contract your glutes.

BY ALWYN COSGROVE, CSCS

Maximize Your Time–And Muscle

Whether your goal is a bigger chest or tighter abs, your workout needs to yield great results fast. Here's how to get your best body in 1 hour

There's a workout that can help you look great at 20 and at 80. Every man I train uses some variation of it, and it's yours for free.

The biggest difference between this program and the one you're doing now is balance. Not stand-on-one-leg-and-curl balance, but the well-rounded-approach-to-training kind of balance.

What's that? You already hit the weight room and work the treadmill on training day? That's still incomplete, not to mention inefficient.

For starters, you need to stop thinking about going to the gym to "lift" or "do cardio." Instead, the perfect workout is actually a combination of six different yet equally important component parts.

Don't worry: This plan is easy to use, and we've carefully organized your gym time minute by minute, so you won't train longer than you do now. You'll just train more effectively and appropriately for your goal: a bigger, stronger, leaner body that works as great as it looks.

Fire Up Your Muscles

The strategy: Put your body in motion in ways that will recruit more muscle fibers in your workout, leading to bigger gains in the end.

The investment: 5 minutes

The drill: Junk your traditional warmup. If this were just about getting warm, you could sit in a hot tub. Instead, do calisthenics. They not only hot-wire nerve pathways that connect your brain to your muscles, but they

also help you move through full ranges of motion before adding weight. If the workout is the show, this is your rehearsal. See "Kickstart Your Workout" on page 73.

Target Weak Spots

The strategy: Troubleshoot problem areas to eliminate weak links and reduce injury risk.

The investment: 4 minutes

The drill: Do any of your joints or muscles hurt? If you answer "a little" or "only when I...," see a physical therapist. And train your glutes—your butt muscles—and your scapular muscles, which include the rhomboids, trapezius, serratus anterior, and pectoralis minor. You don't need to be able to pinpoint them on a dangling skeleton. Just remember that weakness in these areas signals "Danger: Work Ahead" for hips, knees, and shoulders. Use the exercises in "Injury-Proof Your Body," on page 74, to ward off trouble now. For years to come, your body will thank you every time you get out of bed.

HARD TRUTH
Number of free hours the average American has in a day

6

Train Your Core

The strategy: Sculpt a stable, injury-resistant core. Like a baseball team, a healthy body needs to be strongest right up the middle. Plus, women think a tight midsection is hot.

The investment: 8 minutes

The drill: The core—your abs, hips, and lower back—is the most important area of your body when it comes to injury prevention and overall performance. For great results, train it early in your workout, while you still have the energy and focus to put forth your best effort.

Build Your Biggest Muscles

The strategy: Lift more weight in less time to supersize the muscles you want to make bigger.

The investment: 30 minutes

The drill: Weight training is the most critical part of a muscle-building, strength-boosting workout. Streamline your routine with the alternating-set system. Do one exercise, rest for 1 minute, and then do another exercise. Alternate between moves until you've completed all your sets for each, then move on to a new pair. This strategy allows you to fit 15 to 20 sets into 30 minutes. It also provides sufficient stimulus for muscle growth, provided that 90 percent of those exercises are squats, deadlifts, dips, chinups, rows, and presses.

Accelerate Fat Loss

The strategy: Squeeze in a fat-burning cardio session to reveal rock-hard muscle.

The investment: 4 minutes

HARD TRUTH

Number of free hours the average American had in a day in 1990

4

The drill: You're no doubt familiar with interval training, in which you run hard, rest, and then repeat. That burns fat, for sure. But here's another option. Perform squats, chinups, or pushups for 20 seconds, rest for 10 seconds, and repeat, alternating for 4 minutes. This technique boosts your metabolism and your strength. What's more, Japanese researchers found that it provides the same cardiovascular benefits as a 30-minute bike ride.

Prepare for Tomorrow

The strategy: Reduce postworkout soreness as a means of maximizing your next training session.

The investment: 9 minutes

The drill: Spend a few minutes stretching and improving the quality of your fascia, the tissue that covers your muscle fibers. Injury, overexertion, or extended inactivity can cause fascia to knot up with adhesions. But when you use a foam roll to apply pressure to tender spots, the knots untangle and blood flows through those tissues more freely.

More Muscle in Less Time

The following routines show how to put your new workout strategies into action. As you become more comfortable with the movements, feel free to substitute exercises of your own.

Kickstart Your Workout

Perform these exercises at the beginning of your routine. They prepare your shoulders, back, hips, knees, and ankles to perform at a high level.

WARRIOR LUNGE

Stand with your feet together, then move your left foot forward about 12 inches and your right foot back about the same distance. Raise your arms straight overhead.

SUMO SQUAT TO STAND

Stand with your feet spread wide and angled out. With your knees flexed, bend at the waist and wrap your fingers under your big toes.

Keeping your head and chest up, bend both knees to lower your body. Shift your weight forward until the front of your right thigh feels stretched and your right knee is an inch or two off the floor. Hold for 3 to 5 seconds, then return to the starting position. Do 3 to 5 repetitions on each side.

Keeping your arms straight, drop your hips until they're near your ankles, and lift your chest and chin. Holding your toes, straighten your legs as much as you can without losing the natural arch in your spine. (In other words, if your back rounds, you've gone too far.) Move at a slow pace. Do one or two sets of 12 to 15 reps.

WORKOUT 2

Injury-Proof Your Body

Perform one or two sets of 8 to 10 repetitions of the following exercises.

GLUTE BRIDGE

Lie with your knees bent, with a rolled-up towel between them. Pull your toes toward your shins. Squeeze your glutes and raise your body.

Lower your hips to the floor, but don't touch it.

LATERAL TUBE WALK

Slip exercise tubing around your ankles and move it above your knees. Stand with your knees slightly bent and place your hands on your hips.

Sidestep to your right, then to your left.

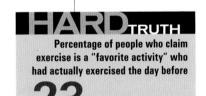

SWISS-BALL L

Lie on a Swiss ball as shown, with your chest off the ball.

Bend your elbows 90 degrees as you raise them to the level of your shoulders, so that your arms create a pair of Ls.

Next, rotate your forearms upward 90 degrees. Retrace the pattern to the starting position.

SWISS-BALL Y

Assume the same starting position as for the Swiss-ball L.

Glide your shoulder blades back and down, and lift your arms up and to the sides at 45-degree angles until you form a Y. Return to the starting position.

SWISS-BALL T

Use the same starting position as for the Swiss-ball L.

Pull your shoulder blades in toward your spine and extend your arms straight to the sides to create a T with your torso. Then reverse the move back to the starting position.

WORKOUT 3

Reclaim Your Flexibility

Stretch any muscles you trained in your workout, and stretch your hip flexors and chest every day.

KNEELING HIP-FLEXOR STRETCH

Place one foot on a bench behind you and your other foot flat on the floor. Lower yourself until your back knee touches the floor. Hold for 30 seconds, and then repeat on the other side.

LYING CHEST STRETCH

Lie faceup on a foam roll with your head supported, your arms bent 90 degrees, and your upper arms parallel to the floor. Your palms should face the ceiling. Hold for 30 seconds.

BY ALWYN COSGROVE, CSCS

Build Better Muscles in Just 5 Minutes

When your workout stops working, start here

No matter what kind of workout you do now, I can show you how to make it better. And all I need from you? An extra 5 minutes. Simply choose one of the bonus muscle builders that follow, and tack it on to the end of your current routine. It won't take long, and it'll yield great dividends, allowing you to customize your training to achieve almost any goal. Whether you want to build bigger arms, sculpt a rock-solid core, or eliminate back pain, it's just 5 minutes away.

Start today and you'll instantly improve your workout. Your body will soon follow.

Build Sleeve-Busting Arms

You can accomplish a lot in 5 minutes, and this arm-building routine is proof. To do this workout, simply pick any two exercises that target your arms: one for your biceps and another for your triceps. As an example, you might choose the EZ-curl-bar curl (biceps) and the dip (triceps). For either, select the heaviest weight that allows you to complete 8 to 10 repetitions, and then alternate between the exercises, doing sets of 5 or 6 repetitions without resting. It's not uncommon to do four or five sets of each.

And this means you'll be logging a total of eight to 10 sets of challenging arm work in just 5 minutes.

Perfect Your Posture

Sitting hunched over a keyboard for 10 hours a day trains your muscles and connective tissues to adapt to that position, adding a hunch to your posture. But you can unravel your slump with an exercise called the prone cobra, which helps counteract the damage of your daily grind.

MUSCLE CHOW

Round Out Your Diet

Buffalo meat is lean, free of growth hormones, and tasty. Mix up these high-protein meatballs in minutes, and store any extras in the fridge. (Microwave leftovers for 30 to 40 seconds for a muscle-building snack.)

BAKED BISON MEATBALLS

1 pound ground buffalo

2 eggs

½ cup toasted wheat germ

⅓ cup finely diced onion

2 teaspoons minced garlic

¼ teaspoon black pepper

1 tablespoon grated Parmesan

½ teaspoon McCormick Salt Free All-Purpose Seasoning

Preheat the oven to 400°F. Combine the buffalo, eggs, wheat germ, onion, garlic, pepper, Parmesan, and seasoning in a large bowl and mold into meatballs. Use an ice-cream scoop for uniform size. Coat a baking tray with cooking spray and place the meatballs on it. Bake for 15 minutes, turning once after 7 minutes.

Makes 16 to 20 meatballs

Per serving: 248 calories, 32 g protein, 9 g carbohydrates, 9 g total fat, 3 g saturated fat, 2 g fiber, 105 mg sodium

PRONE COBRA

Lie facedown on the floor and rest your arms at your sides, palms down. Contract the muscles in your glutes and lower back to raise your upper torso and legs off the floor. At the same time, rotate your arms outward till your thumbs point toward the ceiling. Hold this position for 60 seconds, rest for 60 seconds, then repeat two more times, for a total of three sets.

Banish Back Pain

"Lower-back problems often stem from tight gluteal muscles," says Nate Green, a personal trainer in Whitefish, Montana. His solution: a foam roll ($23, performbetter. com). "Your muscle tissue is like a rubber band. If it has a bunch of knots in it, you won't be able to stretch it very far," says Green. By using a foam roll to alleviate these knots, you'll make your muscles more pliable—and quickly relieve back pain.

KNOT-RELIEVER

Sit on a foam roll on the floor, with your feet up and your hands on the floor for balance. Now slowly roll your butt over it, stopping on the tenderest spots (these are knots) for 20 to 30 seconds, or until the pain subsides.

Pump Up Your Pecs

This workout is designed to trigger a growth spurt by maintaining tension on your chest muscles for a full 5 minutes. Use a timer; you'll need to know when to stop.

Set an incline bench at a 30-degree angle and grab a pair of dumbbells, choosing the heaviest weights that allow you to complete 10 repetitions of the dumbbell incline fly (below). You'll use this weight for both exercises 1 and 2. Do the moves in the order shown, following the instructions for each.

EXERCISE 1: DUMBBELL INCLINE FLY

Hold the weights above your chest, with your arms slightly bent. Without changing the bend in your elbows, lower the weights out to your sides. Reverse the motion to return to the starting position.

- Do one set of 8 reps.
- Don't release the weights; hold them straight above your chest, and rest for 15 seconds in that position.
- Do as many more repetitions as you can.
- Rest for 15 seconds, then move on to exercise 2.

The 5-Minute Six-Pack

If you do only crunches, you're shortchanging your abs. Why? Because in addition to flexing your trunk—as you do in a crunch—your core muscles also allow you to flex your hips, rotate your body, and stabilize your spine. So for the best results, you need to target each of these functions. To hit them all in about 5 minutes, do one set of each exercise here in the order shown, with no rest in between.

Plank

Assume a pushup position, but place your forearms on the floor. Brace your abs as if you were about to be punched in the gut, and hold for 30 seconds.

Side Plank

Lie on your left side and prop up your upper body on your left elbow and forearm. Then raise your hips until your body forms a straight line from shoulders to ankles. Brace your abs for 30 seconds. Then repeat on your right side.

Swiss-Ball Crunch

Lie on your back on a Swiss ball so that your hips and your lower and upper back rest on the ball. With your fingers placed behind your ears, raise your torso as high as you can by crunching your chest toward your hips, then return to the starting position. Do 15 reps.

EXERCISE 2: DUMBBELL INCLINE BENCH PRESS

Hold the weights above your chest with your arms straight. Bend your elbows to lower the weights to the sides of your chest. Pause, then push the weights up.

- Do as many repetitions as you can.
- Rest for 15 seconds with the weights held above you.
- Do as many more repetitions as you can.
- Rest for 15 seconds, then set the weights down and move on to exercise 3.

EXERCISE 3: WIDE-GRIP PUSHUP

Get into pushup position, but with your hands placed about twice shoulder-width apart.

- Do as many pushups as you can.
- Rest for 15 seconds, and then keep repeating until your 5 minutes are up.

Reverse Crunch

Lie on your back on the floor, with your knees slightly bent. Raise your knees to your chest by lifting your hips up and in. Lower your legs to the starting position. Do 15 reps.

Cable Woodchopper

With your right side toward the weight stack of a cable station, grab the rope handle of a high pulley with both hands. Pull the rope down and across your body until your hands are just outside your left knee. Reverse the move to return to the starting position. Do 15 reps, then face the opposite direction and do 15 more.

Reverse Cable Woodchopper

Now attach the rope handle to the low-pulley cable. Bend over and grab the rope with both hands, your arms nearly straight and just outside your right knee. Pull the rope up and across your body until your hands are in line with your left ear. Reverse the movement. Do 15 reps, then face the opposite direction and do 15 more.

Bench More, Save Your Shoulders

"One of the keys to both a bigger bench press and better shoulder health is the ability to stabilize your shoulder blades," says Bill Hartman, PT, CSCS, a physical therapist in Indianapolis. Here's the reason why: When you're able to squeeze your shoulder blades down and together—and hold them that way while you bench-press—you create a more stable surface from which to push the bar. This, in turn, allows you to lift heavier weights while at the same time reducing the stress on your shoulder joints.

Do the two exercises that follow in the order that they are shown. Hold each movement for 10 seconds, rest for 10 seconds, then repeat until you can't maintain a 10-second hold. As you improve, increase your hold time.

HANGING SCAPULAR RETRACTION

SERRATUS DIP

Grab a pullup bar with an overhand grip, hands just beyond shoulder-width apart, and hang at arm's length. Without bending your elbows, squeeze your shoulder blades down and together. (Your body will rise slightly.) Hold, then rest by relaxing your muscles without letting go of the bar.

Grab the bars of a dip station and lift your body until your arms are completely straight. Without bending your elbows, press your shoulders down as you push your torso up. Hold, then relax your muscles, which will cause your torso to lower relative to your shoulders, as if you were shrugging them.

pher Your Display

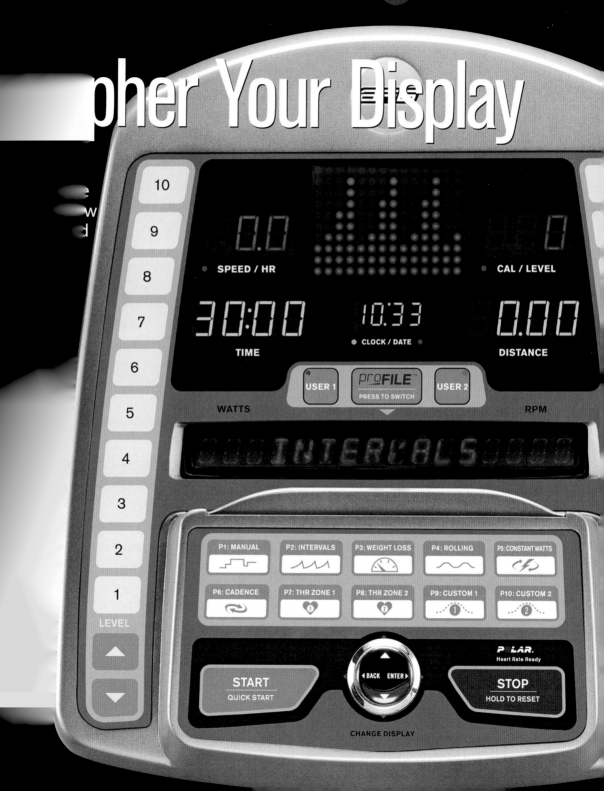

Between absorbing the latest on thesmokinggun.com and the dramas of a certain overchatty coworker, your brain has become bloated with useless knowledge. Oh, and then there's your cardio machine, blinking at you with unbridled enthusiasm. Welcome to the too-much-information age. But when it comes to fitness, paying attention to the minutiae is key to getting in shape and staying there. So we polled trainers and MDs to find out which details on the average machine's data-plastered dashboard you need to know to get a great workout—and the body that comes with it.

Your Machine: The Bike

Tweak your mph. To mimic your outdoor routine, pick a speed 5 to 10 miles per hour faster than your average speed on the road. With no wind or varied terrain to contend with, doing anything less is slacking.

Don't be a dork. No need to pay attention to watts or METS. These are measures of power (literally, how much electricity you'd produce if you were hooked up to a generator) and energy that are only useful to elite athletes.

Check your progress. Note your average speed (most bikes flash this stat on the large display area postworkout), suggests Tom Holland, MS, CSCS, owner of TeamHolland in Darien, Connecticut. Try to increase that average each pedal-fest. The most effective game plan: intervals. Alternate sprints at, say, 20 to 25 mph with recoveries at 15 mph.

Pedal faster. Keep your revolutions per minute (rpm) higher than 60. When you just slog along, you don't get into a good rhythm, and that can make you more liable to lose your form. Try this routine: Pick a range, such as 70 to 80 rpm, and try to stay within it for 5 minutes. Next, blast higher than 100 for 1 minute. Then recover at 60 to 80 rpm for 1 minute. Repeat three to five times.

Your Machine: The Elliptical

Test yourself. To gauge your progress, take this test every 4 weeks: See how many strides you can complete in 10 minutes within your target heart-rate zone. Or, if the machine has a built-in fitness test—as many brand-new models do—try that instead.

Let your rate rule. Elliptical machines feel so smooth and comfy, it's easy to doubt that you're actually getting a workout. Ignore the calories (which are okay as a benchmark but aren't entirely accurate because they don't take room conditions

AFG 4.0 AH

Cool feature: Hybrid upright/recumbent design goes easy on the joints without messing with your rep.
Price: $1,499
Get it: Visit advancedfitness-group.com for stores.

into account) and focus on stride rate (number of times per minute your legs go around). If you're not averaging at least 160, you're not racking up cardio benefits.

Cross-train smarter. Adjust the angle of incline based on the sport you're training for, suggests Emily Cooper, MD, founder of Seattle Performance Medicine, in Seattle. For hiking, set it at 7 to 10 percent to mimic trail conditions and make your glutes do the brunt of the work. For cycling, set it at 4 to 6 percent to work your hamstrings and quads,

Octane Q47

Cool feature: Adjustable stride length
Price: $3,599
Get it: Visit octanefitness. com for stores.

the pedaling muscles. For running, set it at 1 to 4 percent to target your quads and calves.

Take it in stride. The elliptical's sweetest feature is that you can adjust your stride—usually in half-inch increments from 18 to 26 inches. Generally, men should stay above 22 inches; taller people can go up to 26 inches.

Your Machine: The Treadmill
Pooh-pooh the fat-burning program. This setting is based on heart-rate ranges for less fit users, so for the average person who works out a few times a week, it will be far too easy. To truly fry fat, set it to "manual" and do this: Sprint for 2 minutes, then recover for 30 to 60 seconds. Repeat six times. During the sprint sessions, aim for

at least 85 percent of your maximum heart rate (220 minus your age times 0.85).

Angle for results. Your incline should always be set to at least 1 percent. Always, even during cooldown. Because there's less resistance on a treadmill than there is running on, say, the road, the incline will more accurately simulate actual running, according to Amy Dixon, exercise physiologist and group fitness manager for Equinox, in Santa Monica, California.

Go with the beat. Get your heart rate up to 10 to 15 beats per minute higher than it is when you run outside. Why? Your indoor heart rate is jacked, thanks to higher humidity and zero wind inside. The extra bmps will keep you at your normal exertion level.

Give good info. Most machines are calibrated to a 180-pound adult. If you tip the scale either way, you have to enter your weight for an accurate calories-burned reading, says Heather Guymon, exercise physiologist and certified personal trainer in Logan, Utah.

PEAK
performance

Test Your Fitness

Take our hard-body challenge. We've identified five performance standards and set the bar high. See how you measure up, then improve with our training program at MensHealth.com/challenge.

The 1-Mile Challenge

Why it matters: The mile is an iconic distance that has served as a solid measuring stick for fitness since grade school. It requires power, stamina, and determination. And although a 4-minute mile no longer impresses the world-class field of sprinters, a 6-minute mile remains the mark of a fit man.

How to do it: Go to a track or path that you know to be a mile. Set your timer and take off.

Out of shape: 10 minutes

Average: < 8 minutes

Fit: < 7 minutes

MH fit: < 6 minutes

The Single-Leg Squat Test

Why it matters: Strength is one thing; to have control of it is quite another. "The single-leg squat requires tremendous core control," says Micheal Clark, DPT, National Academy of Sports Medicine president.

How to do it: Stand on a bench. Hold your arms in front of you and flex your left ankle so your toes point up. Keeping your torso as upright as possible, bend your right knee and slowly lower your body until your left heel touches the floor. Pause for 1 second, then push yourself up. That's one repetition.

Out of shape: 0 reps

Average: 1 rep

Fit: 3 reps

MH fit: > 5 reps

The Vertical Jump Test

Why it matters: The vertical jump demonstrates your power and athletic ability, says Craig Ballantyne, MSc, CSCS, owner of TurbulenceTraining.com.

How to do it: Against a wall, extend your arm and mark your reach with chalk. Then jump as high as you can and make another mark. The space between marks is your vertical jump.

Out of shape: <16 inches

Average: 16–18 inches

Fit: 19–24 inches

MH fit: > 24 inches

The Chinup Challenge

Why it matters: Most workouts are "front" focused, but your back drives you in sports and protects you from injury, says Mike Boyle, MA, ATC, a strength coach.

How to do it: Start from a full hang, hands shoulder-width apart, palms toward you. Pull your chin over the bar, and then lower your body back down.

Out of shape: 0 reps

Average: 4 reps

Fit: 8 reps

MH fit: > 9 reps

The Pushup Test

Why it matters: The tug-of-war between a man and his weight is the best way to calculate his strength. Pushups gauge the amount of force you're able to generate with your chest, triceps, and shoulders while staying strong throughout your body's core.

How to do it: Assume the classic pushup position: legs straight, hands beneath your shoulders. Brace your abs. Keeping your body rigid, lower yourself until your chest touches the floor. Then push back up until your arms are extended.

Out of shape: <20 reps

Average: 20–34 reps

Fit: 35–49 reps

MH fit: > 49 reps

Recharge Your Routine

Four ways to beat boredom and lose your gut

It's not that Jamie Bamber has more willpower than the rest of us. He just has a built-in advantage: "Producers give me a date when I need to take my shirt off. It's an instant goal," says the 34-year-old star of *Battlestar Galactica*. "Everyone's going to see me, from the crew to the viewers. If I didn't have a date on the calendar, I wouldn't be as disciplined as I am."

When was the last time you set a date to show off your abs? It's time to pick one. Count ahead 6 to 8 weeks from today. By then, you should be ready to show friends, family, and women you don't know just how hard you've worked in the past 6 to 8 weeks. Prepare for the belly-baring now with this fat-blasting plan.

Escape the Cage

When Bamber's not being chased by adoring female fans who saw his body in *People* magazine's "Sexiest" issue, he's searching for the next great racetrack. "I don't know what to do in my mind when I'm on a treadmill," Bamber says. So he takes his cardio training outdoors, a strategy that West Virginia University researchers found makes you 52 percent more likely to exercise frequently. "The message is clear," says Paul Gordon, PhD, the study's lead author. "Don't force yourself to work out in a gym when you can better tolerate running outside." Gordon suggests finding a community trail in your area. It's free and safe, and you don't have to wait in line to use it.

Attack Hills

Sprinting raises your resting metabolism, which means you burn extra calories after your workout as well as during your run. Bamber makes his sprints harder—and more effective—by running uphill. Hill sprints can make you a faster runner in 6 weeks, according to a study in the *Journal of Strength and Conditioning Research*. And the faster you run, the higher your resting metabolism will soar. Try running hard for 10 to 15 seconds at a time on steep inclines and 20 to 30 seconds on moderate inclines, says Robert dos Remedios, CSCS, director of speed, strength, and conditioning at College of the Canyons, in Santa Clarita, California. Repeat this six to eight times in a workout, jogging lightly for about 60 seconds between sprints.

Run Wild

"I change my route and my pace as often as I can," says Bamber. "I just improvise."

For instance, when he's running on flat, relatively dull terrain, he'll spot a tree or stop sign a couple of hundred yards ahead and

Bamber's *Battlestar* shooting schedule gave him a fighting chance to get in shape.

sprint to it, and then slow to a jog until his breathing has returned to a normal rate. Then he charges toward his next mark. Try it yourself. Run sporadic intervals, with one thing in mind: As soon as you hit a mark, have a new one in sight. "This keeps your brain and body active," says dos Remedios. As a result, you'll always be working hard without having to check your watch constantly.

Train Harder

"I love the idea of going on an amazing hike up a mountain, but doing it at a trot," says Bamber. "The tricky footfalls keep my mind engaged." Is there a portion of your workout that you're walking when you could be running? Think about it. Raising your intensity may be more important for burning off belly fat than how often you exercise or for how long, report researchers at Smith College, in Massachusetts. Kick your workout into a higher gear.

PEAK
performance

Get Fit Fast

Running intervals, or sprints with intermittent rest periods, burns three times as much fat as running at slow, consistent speeds, according to research from the University of New South Wales, in Australia. We've developed a 6-week plan to rev up your body's natural fat afterburners.

Start by taking a baseline measurement of your endurance at high speeds. Head to a track, football field, or other measured area with room to run. Sprint for 45 seconds and record your distance. Rest for 60 seconds, then sprint again for 45 seconds. If you don't regularly run intervals or don't participate in intermittent sports, your second span will probably shorten by as much as 25 percent, says Craig Ballantyne, MSc, CSCS, owner of TurbulenceTraining.com. "A distance drop of only 10 percent between runs is excellent," he says. Use this plan to improve your endurance and burn fat, measuring your progress every week.

The Program

Alternate between workout A and workout B for a total of three sessions a week for 6 weeks.

Workout A: Jog for 2 minutes, do the exercises at right, then do the intervals below.

REPS	EFFORT	TIME	REST
1	50%	60 sec	60 sec
1	75%	60 sec	60 sec
3 or 6*	100%	30 sec	90 sec

Workout B: Jog for 2 minutes, do the exercises at right, then do the intervals below.

REPS	EFFORT	TIME	REST
1	50%	60 sec	60 sec
1	75%	60 sec	60 sec
3 or 6*	100%	45 sec	90 sec

*Do three of these high-intensity intervals the first week, and six each week after.

The Exercises

Prisoner Squat

Stand with your hands behind your head. Sit back at the hips and bend your knees to squat down. Squeeze your glutes and push back up. Do 10 reps.

Elbow-to-Instep Lunge

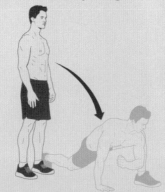

Step forward with your left leg and place your right hand on the floor. Press your left elbow down toward your left instep. Do 6 reps per leg.

Lunge

Take a large step forward with one leg. When your front thigh is parallel to the floor, hold for two beats and return. Repeat with your other leg. Alternate for 6 reps per leg.

Waiter's Bow

Pinch the skin of your lower back. Push your hips back and bow forward as far as you can while squeezing an inch of skin. Contract your glutes and stand back up. Do 10 reps.

Single-Leg Romanian Deadlift

Stand on one foot. Keeping the arch in your spine, push your hips back and lower your hands. Press your heel into the floor to return to standing. Do 6 reps with one leg, then 6 with your other leg.

Leg Swing

Swing your leg in front of you, then bend your knee and swing it behind you so your heel moves toward your butt. Do 6 reps with each leg.

BY SCOTT QUILL

Train with Attitude

Floyd Mayweather—
the cockiest man in sports—
shows how knowing exactly
what you want
can give you a
championship mind-set

The man you see here can run a 5-minute mile and bust out 40 pullups and 200 situps without breaking a sweat. But don't call it a workout. When Floyd Mayweather Jr. trains, it's a show.

I'm ringside for today's performance, starring "Pretty Boy Floyd" himself, with guest appearances by Paris Hilton and Tom Cruise.

As Mayweather explains, "There are stars, superstars, and supermegastars. Tom Cruise is a superstar. But I make stars starstruck. I'm a supermegastar."

Mayweather would repeat this speech—questioning Cruise's acting chops and Hilton's chops for doing, well, anything—at least three times during his interview and photo shoot for *Men's Health*. He's determined to flaunt his greatness, and trust me, it's not easy to look away.

Across Mayweather's T-shirt are the words "philthy rich," just in case, I suppose, the diamond boxing gloves draped around his neck, or the cash wedge he pulls from his pocket, or the Mayweather emblem in place of the Maybach logo on his Benz aren't proof enough.

For 2 hours, he's insisted how rich, famous, and talented he is, but I've come to realize the only things faster than Mayweather's mouth are his feet.

Mayweather, a 150-pound, baby-faced, self-proclaimed "greatest athlete ever," moves panther-fast as he swings his fists while taking verbal shots at musicians Pharrell Williams and Kanye West. At 30, he exhibits the antics of an arrogant, 15-year-old rich kid who needs the piss beat out of him.

Trouble is, no one can do it.

Mayweather has won titles in five weight classes, with an undefeated (38-0) record. In 2007, he squared off against Oscar De La Hoya for the junior middleweight championship, the fifth weight class Mayweather had fought in, and won.

At our photo shoot, 10 weeks prior to the fight, Mayweather had yet to officially begin his physical training, but you could bet his head was already in the game. His confidence, or cockiness—"call it what you want, but you can call me a winner," he says—is key to his success.

An athlete and an entertainer, Mayweather trains for performance and attention. But he has another objective that's even more ambitious: to motivate and inspire friends and family who watch him work out. And it's more important now that he do this than it's ever been.

Over the past few years, Mayweather's family has struggled with type 2 diabetes—it's struck his Uncle Roger, grandmother, and father. Lately, his mother has been ill, and as a result, her weight has ballooned, which puts her at high risk of the disease, too.

Mayweather desperately wants his mom to lose pounds. But he also wants the rest of the world to know what makes you healthy and what doesn't work. "How come you never see anyone go on TV and say, 'I didn't work hard, and I didn't get in shape'?" he asks. Sick of diet and fitness gimmicks, he has a business project in the works called Mayweather Fitness. He envisions it as a hybrid of an old-school boxing gym and a commercial health club, designed to help members kick up the intensity of their workouts to Mayweather level.

And to test-run this project, Mayweather intends to bring his own mother to his training camp to exercise until she's ready for her glamour shots.

"I want to keep everyone around me

Hard-Hitting Advice

Mayweather on sharing your wealth—and health. I don't drink or smoke, but I do buy a lot of Champagne for my friends when it's a special occasion. We've gotta keep them healthy, so only when it's a special occasion.

On carving million-dollar abs. I take pride in staying healthy and eating right. I don't care how much money you have if you wake up every morning and can't see your [penis]. You need to get that weight off.

On outhustling your competition. I do my homework on every opponent that I fight. I know that if my opponents run 5 miles every day, I have to run 7 miles. And when they up it to 7, I'm going to take it to 9.

On surrounding yourself with talent. Oscar [De La Hoya] has a lot more paper than I've got, but he's cheap. I pay my sparring partners well. It costs to have a good team, and every time I've fought, I've gotten good results. You pay for what you get.

On learning from losses. As an amateur, I was 84 and 6. I lost six fights by one point. But that was just a learning experience. Once I got to the professional level, I wasn't going to take an "L."

healthy and in shape," Mayweather says. "That's what 'keeping it real' is all about."

That's why his employees have 24-hour fitness gym passes: Every great star needs a rock-solid supporting cast.

And it's also why he's putting on a show today, at Barry's Boxing Center, a gritty gym in Las Vegas where stale sweat and the firing of quick jabs permeate the air.

Barry's is exactly like the gym in your basement, or the trendy, high-end health club down the street, in the sense that no matter where you train, the only way you'll stay fit and healthy for life is to stay motivated. For Mayweather, that means entertaining.

Watching him shadowbox, flex his abs, and punish the heavy bag is mesmerizing. But I'm blown away, almost literally, by his next act.

Mayweather explodes into a jump rope routine, tap dancing as he whips the leather so fast the temperature drops. He swings the rope between his legs, still jumping, like Iverson unleashing a crossover dribble. After a few minutes, he pauses for a sip of hot chocolate—as if to say, This is too easy—and then launches into his next tirade.

Mayweather can't decide where Paris Hilton fits within his celebrity-ranking system. "What's her talent? Being rich? Taking her clothes off and partying? That doesn't make you a star. I've got talent, baby."

Okay, Floyd . . . we get the point.

There's a science to showboating. Forget Floyd for a moment and imagine yourself doing a bench press while sexy, scantily clad

women walk by. This situation stimulates your sympathetic nervous system to a much greater degree than if you were lifting weights alone at home—meaning your nerve transmissions speed up.

As a result, your body increases energy production and muscle recruitment, says Matthew Rhea, PhD, the director of human movement at A.T. Still University, in Arizona. "So when someone else is watch-ing, you push yourself harder than you usually would."

In fact, in a study published in the *Journal of Strength and Conditioning Research*, Rhea and his colleagues discov-ered that men are able to bench-press an average of 41 pounds more in front of specta-tors than when they lift alone. "Both audience and competition improve perfor-mance," he says. "If the audience in our

Train Like the Champ

Give your workout a jumpstart with these drills from Shaun Hamilton, head coach of USA Jump Rope. Master them at home, then take your show to the gym, where training in front of a crowd can help you ramp up your intensity.

Boost Your Speed: The Jog Step

Begin with your right foot planted, your left foot slightly above the floor, and the rope behind you. Swing the rope over your head, jump, and land on your right foot. As the rope comes down, jump off your right foot—allowing the rope to pass under both feet—and land on your left foot, keeping your right foot suspended.

Work More Muscles: The Backward 180

Start just like the jog step. As the rope passes overhead, move your right hand to the left, so the rope swings next to your left side. As it hits the floor, jump and turn left 180 degrees. Move your right hand back to your right side, letting the rope pass over your head and behind you so you're now jumping backward.

Improve Coordination: The Crisscross

The trick here is to cross your arms at hip level. Jump rope normally for a bit. When the rope passes overhead, begin to cross hands. They should reach the opposite sides near your hips as the rope touches the floor. Jump, then keep your hands still while the rope rises. Start to uncross as the rope peaks the second time.

study would have been allowed to encourage the lifter, the effect would have been even greater."

This, in part, explains why Mayweather trains at a ferocious intensity with an audience. And it can work for you, too.

But Rhea warns that many injuries in the weight room occur when men are trying to show off and load more plates on a barbell than they can safely handle, or attempt an exercise routine that's too complex for their ability levels. So the key is to train with attitude, not with abandon.

Mayweather's show captivates him and everyone around him. His 20-year career has hinged on staying fit and healthy, and he knows you can't train consistently with a boring routine.

No, Mayweather's been forced to find new ways to keep his workout fresh, a hurdle every health-conscious man must leap over at some point. Rhea says that training with a workout partner can boost motivation. Challenging your friends to see who can improve the most in an exercise over a short period of time can even help you break out of a stale routine.

But perhaps the greatest benefit of an entertaining workout is the motivation to exercise when you otherwise might not train. For instance, say you're the type of man who wants to look especially great a few times a year—for the beach, a wedding, or maybe a reunion.

Most men—and professional fighters, for that matter—will slack off for months and then hack at the pounds they've packed on. In fact, fighters often cut weight for 12 weeks before a major event. But not Mayweather.

He hovers within 3 or 4 pounds of his fighting weight at all times by jumping rope, playing basketball, and doing body-weight exercises twice a week. Make no mistake: He trains as hard as any athlete on the planet for 6 weeks before every fight, but the rest of the time, he simply enjoys staying active, a strategy that's kept him within a few hard workouts of his peak condition year-round.

"I'm always in training, not just to be a better boxer, but because I still want to be able to move around exceptionally well when I'm 70 years old," says the fighter. "I won't be able to train like I do now when I'm 60. Actually, I might. My dad's 50, and he still moves like he's 21. So you never know."

And that's just it: You don't know. So stop wasting time sitting on the couch. Stop thinking you have months before you need to look and feel great. Stop waiting and start doing. Let the show begin.

BY JEFF O'CONNELL

To become fit for a king, *300* star Gerard Butler trained harder than most pro athletes for 4 months straight. But his biggest challenge came when the cameras stopped rolling

Build Character

As Gerard Butler rushes into his hotel lobby, he seems slightly disoriented. Maybe it's the chilly winds buffeting New York City. But more likely, it's the lingering effects of his just-completed session of eye-movement desensitization and reprocessing, a laser-light show of sorts that supposedly hot-wires the synapses of your gray matter. "It's normally used to treat post-traumatic stress disorder," the 37-year-old actor says. However, his hope is that it will help coordinate the analytical and creative lobes of his brain, enabling him to better manage his life.

Perhaps he should ask for a refund. Butler not only is 45 minutes late for our interview, but he also requires an additional 5 minutes to tidy up—his pug puppy is in heat—and then another 10 when his room key won't open the door. Once inside, he quickly apologizes for the clutter of brochures and tile samples, which he attributes to the overdue renovation of his Manhattan condo—the one he bought in early 2004 but has yet to occupy.

While all of this frustrates Butler enough to take a stab at laser-light therapy, at least he can justify his disorganized personal life as an occupational hazard. After all, his success as an actor depends on his ability to inhabit the mind of another person and then stay in character for months. And when you consider his larger-than-life roles in modern-day epics such as *Dracula 2000, Attila the Hun,* and *300*—in which he plays Leonidas, king of Sparta—you understand why he might run late for an appointment or take 3 years to remodel his apartment. Would a vampire heed deadlines? Would a king compare swatches?

To become King Leonidas, Butler, who by his own admission was in less-than-ideal shape when he was tapped for the starring role in *300*, spent 4 months transforming both his body and his mind. Early on, it became an all-consuming task. That's because the intense training required to build a warrior's physique—aesthetically and functionally—simultaneously cultivated a warrior's mentality. Or maybe it was vice versa.

Either way, it's the reason Butler enlisted the help of Mark Twight, a former world-class mountain climber who, based on personal experience, believes in training as if your life depends on it. In fact, Twight

would argue that a good workout should make you feel almost queasy upon hearing what lies ahead. For example, to hasten Butler's mind-body transformation, he created what he calls the "*300*-rep Spartan workout." (Trust us, 100 reps are plenty hard.) It goes like this: Without resting between exercises, Butler performs 25 pullups, 50 deadlifts with 135 pounds, 50 pushups, 50 jumps on a 24-inch box, 50 floor wipers, 50 single-arm clean-and-presses using a 36-pound kettlebell, and 25 more pullups. All this, in addition to utilizing other unconventional yet equally taxing training methods, such as tire flipping and gymnastics-style ring training. Sound like hell? It is. In fact, upon receiving his marching orders for a Spartan workout, one of Butler's costars told Twight, "It feels like you just killed my dog."

Five weeks before the cameras were to roll, Butler took on extra sessions with a Venezuelan bodybuilder named Franco LiCastro in order to exaggerate the physique he was after. "I wanted to look really strong," says Butler. "I've seen so many actors play these kinds of roles, and you see all this equipment on either a big belly or skinny little arms." It worked in more ways than one: On-screen, the bearded actor lords over the battlefield like testosterone incarnate, with the steely gaze, cobblestone abs, and broad, chiseled shoulders you suspect one would need to command 300 men to their slaughter.

"You know that every bead of sweat falling off your head, every weight you've pumped—the history of that is all in your eyes," says Butler of his dedication. "That was a great thing, to put on that cape and put on that helmet, and not have to think, Shit, I should have trained more. Instead, I was standing there feeling like a lion."

Of course, the downside to an extreme transformation is just that—it's extreme. Case in point: During production, Butler would often train with Twight, train with LiCastro, and then do his sword-and-shield work for hours on end. As a result, every joint in his 6'2" body ached by the time he set down his shield for the last time. And at some point along the way, he became overtrained, a state in which the stress of training has surpassed the body's ability to recover fully from it. As a result, once filming wrapped, Butler stopped working out as abruptly as he'd started. Understandably, his body—and mind—needed a break. But the upshot was that his no-holds-barred training regimen turned into an equally hard-to-shake layoff, one that would last 8 months. Neither approach is healthy long term.

According to Butler, it's all a result of his obsessive personality, which is at once an asset and a liability. As with most type A's, he's still learning to ride the positives while keeping the negatives from sending him off the rails. For instance, before he became an actor, Butler's keenly analytical mind led him to law school in his native Scotland, where he graduated with honors and became president of the Glasgow University Law Society. But that profession quickly took a backseat to his

Perform without a Net

"Spartans enjoyed that elitist feeling that nobody was as brave or skilled as them," says Gerard Butler. "If no one's worked as hard as you, why be bashful about being the best? Enjoy it. Stand up and own what you're good at."

1. Never say die. *300* tells of history's staunchest goal-line stand: 300 Spartan warriors fending off a million-man Persian army in the Battle of Thermopylae in 480 BC to save Greece, and perhaps even the seeds of democracy. Comicbook legend Frank Miller (*Sin City*) depicted the battle in a graphic novel, which hooked director Zack Snyder (*Dawn of the Dead*). "This is an incredible story to begin with," says Butler, "but Frank took it and turned it into a brilliant book. And Zack turned it into this masterpiece."

2. Train for victory. Start off by doing 100 reps using four to six different exercises, 10 to 25 reps per exercise. Build up from there until you can do 300 without rest. Feel free to swap in exercises such as jumping jacks, dumbbell curls, and Swiss-ball crunches, says Butler's current trainer, Manhattan-based Joe Dowdell, CSCS.

3. Learn a new move. "Lie on the floor holding a 135-pound bar straight overhead," says Twight.

"Keeping his legs straight, Butler touches his feet to one plate, lowers them to the floor in the center, and then raises them up to touch the other plate." That's one repetition. Try it yourself, but with an empty bar first, raising your feet until they're about 8 inches away from the bar (because there's no weight plate to touch).

4. Recover faster. To determine whether you're pushing too hard, begin measuring your heart rate upon waking. When your reading is three to five beats above normal, your ability to recover is compromised, says Bill Hartman, PT, CSCS, a physical therapist in Indianapolis. Downshift your training—and try to sleep more—until your heart rate returns to normal.

5. Stop smoking. Rather than having lights flashed into your eyeballs to quit the lung darts, you should start wearing the nicotine patch 2 weeks before your quit date. One study shows that this ups the success rate significantly. Wear the patch on your arm, rather than on your back or stomach, to improve absorption.

6. Strike a balance. To see Butler's current workout with Dowdell, go to MensHealth.com, keyword Butler.

extended trips to America, where he would work really odd jobs (leading guided tours at SeaWorld; traveling with a carnival full of ex-cons) when he wasn't being arrested for being drunk and disorderly.

An active, probing mind lacking an off switch, you see, is also an easily distracted one. I catch a glimpse of this when changing the tape during our interview. Seconds later,

Butler stops abruptly midsentence to ask if I just flipped it from side B back to side A—which, of course, would erase the first half of our conversation. (It was a new tape.)

Then there's his smoking. The actor has done it for years, knows cigarettes are as deadly as any sword, and wants badly to quit. In fact, the flashing-lights treatment that made him late is also intended to help

him kick the cancer sticks once and for all. Yet even for this *Men's Health* interview—here's Butler, firing up within the first 10 minutes. For what it's worth, the irony doesn't escape him.

We all struggle to balance the mundane tasks of our daily lives with our higher purpose, real or imagined. (Why worry about that oil change or checkup when you have a sales quota to meet or a screenplay to write?)

So imagine what it's like for someone whose career depends on transforming himself into another person for extended periods of time. "A more balanced life would be better for Gerry Butler. But the obsessive, all-or-nothing way I tend to go about things worked great for playing Leonidas, who knew he had no future," says the actor of his character's self-chosen fate. "But that's a short-term view of how to live in my world."

Which is why Butler seems as driven to regain control of his personal life as he is to sketch indelible portraits on-screen. After 8 months of not working out, Butler returned to the gym 4 days a week, adopting a more balanced approach to fitness. He's also finding that the nutrition knowledge he's picked up during his character transformations has begun to stick. "My diet is still never quite as scheduled as I wish it were, but now I try to eat vegetables and chicken instead of burgers and fries like I used to," he says. The reemergence of his six-pack suggests the newfound discipline is paying dividends.

Smoothing out the roller-coaster ride onto which Butler the actor takes Butler the man in between films, while still peaking when the cameras roll, may be his most challenging role yet.

Resist without Rest

Surely you've run nonstop for 15 minutes before. But have you ever performed 15 minutes of resistance exercise without rest? Try it with these challenging moves from Craig Ballantyne, MSc, CSCS, owner of TurbulenceTraining.com. "You'll be surprised how hard you can work without a gym," he says. Alternate between the Y squat and the Spider-Man pushup for three sets of each. Then perform the remaining three exercises consecutively (again, without rest), doing three sets of each.

Y Squat: Stand with your shoulder blades pulled back and your arms extended up and out so your body forms a Y. With your feet slightly more than shoulder-width apart, sit back at your hips to lower your body. Go as low as possible without allowing your back to round. Squeeze your glutes and push yourself back up to the starting position. Do 12 reps.

Spider-Man Pushup: Assume the classic pushup position with your legs straight and your abs tight. As you lower your body, bend your right leg and rotate your right knee outward until it's outside your right elbow. Don't drag your foot, and try not to allow your torso to rotate. Return to the starting position and repeat, pulling your left knee to your left elbow. Do 8 reps per side.

Wall Slide: Stand with your butt, upper back, and head against a wall. Raise your arms so your shoulders, elbows, and wrists also touch the wall. Maintaining these points of contact, bend your arms until your elbows are tucked in at your sides. You should feel a contraction in your shoulders and the muscles between your shoulder blades. Reverse the move. Do 10 reps.

Single-Leg Romanian Deadlift: Stand on your left foot with your right foot raised behind you, arms hanging down in front of you. Keeping a natural arch in your spine, push your hips back and lower your hands and upper body. Squeeze your glutes and press your heel into the floor to return to an upright position. Perform 8 reps per leg.

Spider-Man Lunge: Assume the classic pushup position with your hands directly beneath your shoulders, your legs straight, and your abs braced. Lift your right foot off the floor, bending your knee, and place the foot outside your right hand. Return to the starting position and lunge out with your left leg. Continue alternating legs for a total of 20 reps.

Take Two

You may not need more time to exercise, just a new strategy: Men can build significant muscle with only two workouts a week, according to Canadian researchers. The scientists, who studied beginners doing the same total body-weight workout either 2 or 3 days a week,

discovered that two sessions are as effective as three.

"They're also more manageable for people with busy schedules," says study author Darren Candow, PhD. One caveat: As your body becomes more accustomed to lifting weights, you may need 3 training days to stimulate further growth, he says.

Don't Ditch Those Dumbbells

Combining cardio and weights controls blood sugar levels better than either activity alone, reports a study in the journal *Annals of Internal Medicine*. Adults with type-2 diabetes who did 45 minutes of each activity three times weekly lowered their blood sugar levels further than those who did 45 minutes of either cardio or weight training. After 22 weeks, their levels had dropped by 0.97 percent (equal to a 15 percent reduction in heart attack or stroke risk), compared with 0.5 percent in the mono-exercisers. Why? Cardio burns glucose (sugar) for energy, while lifting increases the demand for

energy by upping muscle mass, leaving less sugar in the blood, says lead author Ronald Sigal, MD, MPH. Don't have 90 minutes to spare? Thirty minutes of each can do the same trick.

Break It Up

When you're too swamped to hit the gym, just put on your walking shoes in the a.m. According to an Indiana University study, a few short walks per day can keep you fitter than one sustained workout. Researchers asked 20 people with borderline high blood pressure to walk on a treadmill at $2^1/_2$ to 4 miles per hour for 40 minutes. On a different day, the subjects walked on the treadmill for four 10-minute periods over the course of $3^1/_2$ hours. The exercisers' blood pressure dropped significantly in each case, but the effect lasted 11 hours when they broke up the workout and 7 hours when they walked continuously.

"Blood pressure is reduced progressively after each short bout of exercise," explains study author Saejong Park, PhD. So when you don't have time for a sweaty run, stay healthy by fitting a few walking breaks into your day.

Don't Count on Starbucks

You may not get a caffeine lift at the gym, says a University of Nebraska study. During an 8-week endurance-training program, exercisers on decaf experienced the same fitness gains as those of daily caffeine users. Eighteen college students downed a 200-milligram caffeine pill an hour before three weekly workouts and took the supplement before breakfast on days off. Eighteen others took a placebo and trained on the same schedule. After the 8 weeks, time to exhaustion and body composition were equal in both groups. Apparently, the caffeinated exercisers adjusted to the stimulant, so there was no performance effect, says study author Moh Malek, CSCS.

Be a Night Owl

To break through to a personal best, hit the gym at night. Your body is primed for exercise in the evening, according to a University of South Carolina study. After testing swimmers at 18 different times over 3 days, researchers found that peak performance occurred at 11 p.m. It appears that our circadian rhythms—the physiological function that determines our normal sleep patterns—impact athletic performance. Swimmers covered 200 meters 6 seconds faster at night than during their morning pool sessions.

Relax in an Instant

Performing a single sprint—just 30 seconds of intense exercise—can clear your head, according to a new British study. After 22 men performed a single all-out cycling sprint, researchers found that each participant experienced less tension, anger, and confusion for about 75 minutes afterward. Short periods of exhaustive exercise fatigue the mind, resetting it to its baseline, says study author Dominic Micklewright, PhD, of the University of Essex. "This benefit can be gained simply by sprinting to catch a bus or running up a flight of stairs."

Get Milk

The best sports drink may come from a cow, according to a British study. When 11 men drank 2 percent milk, water, or Powerade after intense exercise sessions, researchers found that the milk drinkers remained hydrated four times longer than those who drank the other liquids. That's because milk contains higher levels of sodium and potassium, electrolytes that promote fluid retention, says the study author, Susan Shirreffs, PhD.

Relieve Your Pain

If the ache in your groin has you groaning, hit the gym: Exercise may help relieve chronic prostatitis, an inflammatory condition that causes severe pain in the pelvic area. Researchers reporting in the *Journal of Urology* had 97 men with prostatitis perform either 40 minutes of cardiovascular exercise or a placebo regimen consisting of stretching and mild

calisthenics, 3 days a week. At the end of the study, 40 percent of the cardio crew reported less pain, while the men who worked up less of a sweat noticed no improvement.

Lead author Gianluca Giubilei, PhD, says that exercise triggers an increase in endorphins, which may help fight the pain of chronic prostatitis.

Supercharge Your Workout

Squeeze in a quickie to build more muscle. Researchers at A.T. Still University, in Arizona, found that running wind sprints on the days between weight workouts can boost your lifting performance. "Both forms of exercise train the same energy system," says study author Matthew Rhea, PhD, the director of human movement at the university. So sprinting conditions your muscles and cardiovascular system in a manner similar to that of weight training. This, in turn, improves your "work capacity"—the ability to complete more sets and reps before fatigue sets in.

Give it a try: Run at your top speed for 15 seconds, then rest for 1 minute before your next sprint. Aim to do six sprints twice a week on days that you don't lift.

Hit the Floor

Stretching your legs could improve muscle performance, reports a *Clinical Journal of Sports Medicine* study. Scientists took flexibility and leg-strength measurements of 30 participants and asked them to stretch each leg

for 2 minutes 5 days per week. After 6 weeks, they found that the volunteers' flexibility had increased 35 percent, quad strength had increased 3.2 percent, and hamstring strength had increased 5 percent.

Stretching helps make your legs stronger by increasing your muscles' range of motion, making joint movement more efficient. That translates into more power, explains Carol Garber, PhD. Get tough: Broaden your muscle horizon with at least 15 minutes of yoga or Pilates twice a week.

Save Your Sight

Next time you're tempted to blow off exercising, consider how shortsighted you're being. Skipping workouts could lead to blindness, say University of Wisconsin researchers. After testing the eyesight of nearly 4,000 people over a period of 15 years, the researchers determined that couch potatoes were 70 percent more likely to develop age-related macular degeneration (AMD) than the gym faithful were.

"Exercise improves endothelial function—the ability of blood vessels to expand and contract—so it may protect the vessels in the eyes against AMD," says lead author Michael Knudtson, MS. Work out at least three times a week to insure your eyes.

Training

Tips

I get exhausted running a mile but can easily do 3 miles on an elliptical. Is my machine workout less effective?

In a word, yes. The elliptical claims to be a great fat-burning workout that's easier on your joints because your feet never leave the ground. But running wins in terms of total burn because your body is moving against gravity, and that takes more work than resting your body weight on pedals. If you're looking for max results in limited time, opt for running. However, if you're coming back from an injury and your doc okays it, the elliptical is a great way to ease back in.

How can I hit every fitness goal I set for myself?

Setting goals is an important way to measure your progress. But setting realistic goals is the only way to actually hit your milestones. Our rules:

For the first 2 weeks of a new regimen, strive to establish consistency and to change any bad habits. For instance, aim for a set number of workouts or cut out highly processed snacks from your diet.

Set your sights on your first performance-related fitness goal for the next month. Don't expect major physique changes just yet. You won't be discouraged as long as your performance improves.

The 3-month mark is when you'll start seeing some changes in the way you look. Take note.

After 6 months, you should be well on your way to achieving several long-term goals. Then you can reassess your goals for the next 6 months. Here's an example:

TIME	GOAL
2 weeks	Complete six to eight workouts
1 month	Increase your bench press by 10 to 15 pounds
3 months	Lose 3 to 4 inches off your waist
6 months	Lose 25 pounds, then reassess your goals

I hate cardio. Do I need to do it?

Sorry, suck it up. Studies show that just two short cardio sessions a week can improve heart health. The good news? If you're looking to increase your overall strength and size, that's all you'll need, as long as you train hard during each workout. Put this cardio game plan into action.

Maximize your cardio training. Stick with brief but intense workouts, such as intervals. On nonlifting days, do 30 to 45 seconds of near–all-out work followed by a recovery period of twice that time, and repeat this for a set, as you would in weight lifting.

If you're tired of running, try full-body cardio machines, such as the VersaClimber. This grueling climbing simulator works both your upper and your lower body through such a large range of motion that it accomplishes in 20 minutes what would take you twice as long to do on other cardio machines.

Is it better to do cardio after my weight workout rather than on days in between?

For maximum muscle, do your cardio directly after your lifting or on the following day—never prior to. "Cardio fatigues muscles, leaving them too tired to do strength training to the best of your ability," says Alwyn Cosgrove, CSCS, owner of Results Fitness, in Santa Clarita, California. "Doing cardio with a fatigued body doesn't matter because you're going for heart-rate response, not speed." (If running harder is one of your goals, however, your body will be positioned to run farther, faster if you wait at least a day after lifting weights.)

Yes, muscles undergo microscopic damage after a workout and need about 48 hours to repair themselves (becoming stronger and larger), but Cosgrove says the back-to-back days of stress won't interfere with your strength gains. Reports to the contrary have been widely exaggerated, he says.

What's the best cardio machine?

The rowing machine. Scientists at the University of Dublin found that men burn up to 50 percent more fat on rowers than on stationary bikes.

"It's simple math," says Paul Robbins, metabolic specialist at Athlete's Performance, in Arizona. "Rowers work the entire body, and the more muscles you use, the more calories you burn." But that doesn't mean you should use rowers exclusively. A better plan is to divide your time among multiple machines.

Next time you're in the gym, spend 10 minutes each on the treadmill, the Airdyne cycle (the one with handles that pump back and forth), the stairclimber, and the rower. "You'll work more muscles from more angles and send your metabolism into overdrive," says Robbins. "You'll also be less likely to crap out after 20 minutes."

Researchers at the University of Florida agree. In their study of 61 men and women, they found that people who mixed up their routines enjoyed exercising 15 percent more than those who did not. The former group was also 20 percent more likely to exercise regularly.

Why are my muscles sore 2 days after I exercise instead of the day after?

The condition is called delayed onset muscle soreness, and it's likely the result of microscopic tears in muscle tissue. We say likely because the whitecoats haven't nailed down a definite cause (or why it's delayed). What they do know is that it often

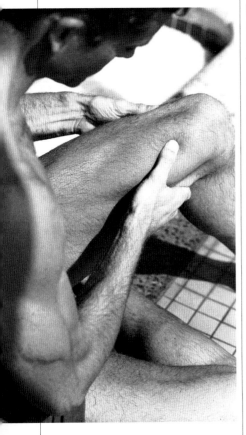

results from eccentric (i.e., lowering) movements, such as squats, so go easy on those if you are just starting out.

If the pain lasts longer than 3 days, see a doctor because you may have rhabdomyolysis, which is an excessive breakdown of muscle fibers, the contents of which can be toxic and cause kidney damage in high doses.

I've read that ointments such as Bengay and Icy Hot can be harmful if you use them too often. Is that true?

It's a myth that OTC drugs are always safer than prescription meds. Case in point: Bengay and Icy Hot both contain methyl salicylate, which can be toxic in large doses. In a rare event last summer, a teenage athlete was ruled to have died of an overdose after medical examiners found more than six times the safe amount of the ingredient in her body.

Used properly, these drugs aren't dangerous, but a few key warnings still apply: Don't use a product like Bengay with a heating pad or rub it on burned or cut areas; doing either can increase salicylate absorption.

Also, it's okay to use these ointments three or four times a day for up to 7 days, but if your aches don't go away after that, see your doctor.

I want to buy a home treadmill. How can I find a good one that's affordable?

Shop during the summer. Sales tend to lag when it's warm out, so you'll be able to find a better deal, says Jon Stevenson, cofounder of the exercise-equipment review site thetreadmilldoctor.com. Plan to spend no more than $1,600; how close you come should depend on your needs.

Are you a runner? You'll need

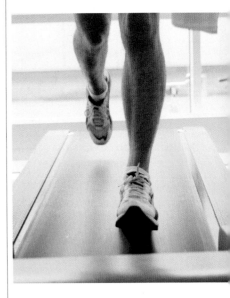

a sturdier machine with a longer, wider belt, such as the Sole F80 ($1,500), says Stevenson. Same goes if you're a heavy guy hoping to jog off what's jiggling.

On the other hand, if you want a treadmill for weight maintenance and basic fitness, you can spend significantly less. Stevenson recommends the Epic 425 MX ($800). "The motor is what you'd typically see in $1,500 models, and the design and engineering are first-rate," he says. Most of the savings, Stevenson says, comes from a less expensive frame.

Is there any difference between the StairMaster and the stairclimber (the thing that looks like an escalator)?

Both fry about 15 calories a minute, making them two of the best fat-blasting machines at the gym. And they tone the largest muscles in your body (buttocks, hips, thighs, and calves), giving the biggest bang for your calorie-cooking buck. But the stairclimber has a slight edge because it relies less on the spring action found in the StairMaster and more on your own effort and coordination.

Is using a roller more beneficial than stretching?

Think of foam rollers as a warmup for stretching, not a replacement. Run, roll, then stretch. A roller provides benefits similar to a deep-tissue massage: It increases muscle elasticity, decreases tension, and, in turn, lowers the risk of injury and boosts performance.

Spend 15 seconds rolling up and down each muscle you'd like to target, but stand warned: Just as it takes time to get past the preliminary pain of deep-tissue sessions, so too might the foam roller initially feel like a torture device. Once your muscles are loose, however, stretching will become easier and more effective.

MUSCLE UP

ESSENTIAL READING

BY BILL HARTMAN, PT, CSCS

Stretch to Get Strong

Start your workout with this 3-minute flex to build muscle quicker

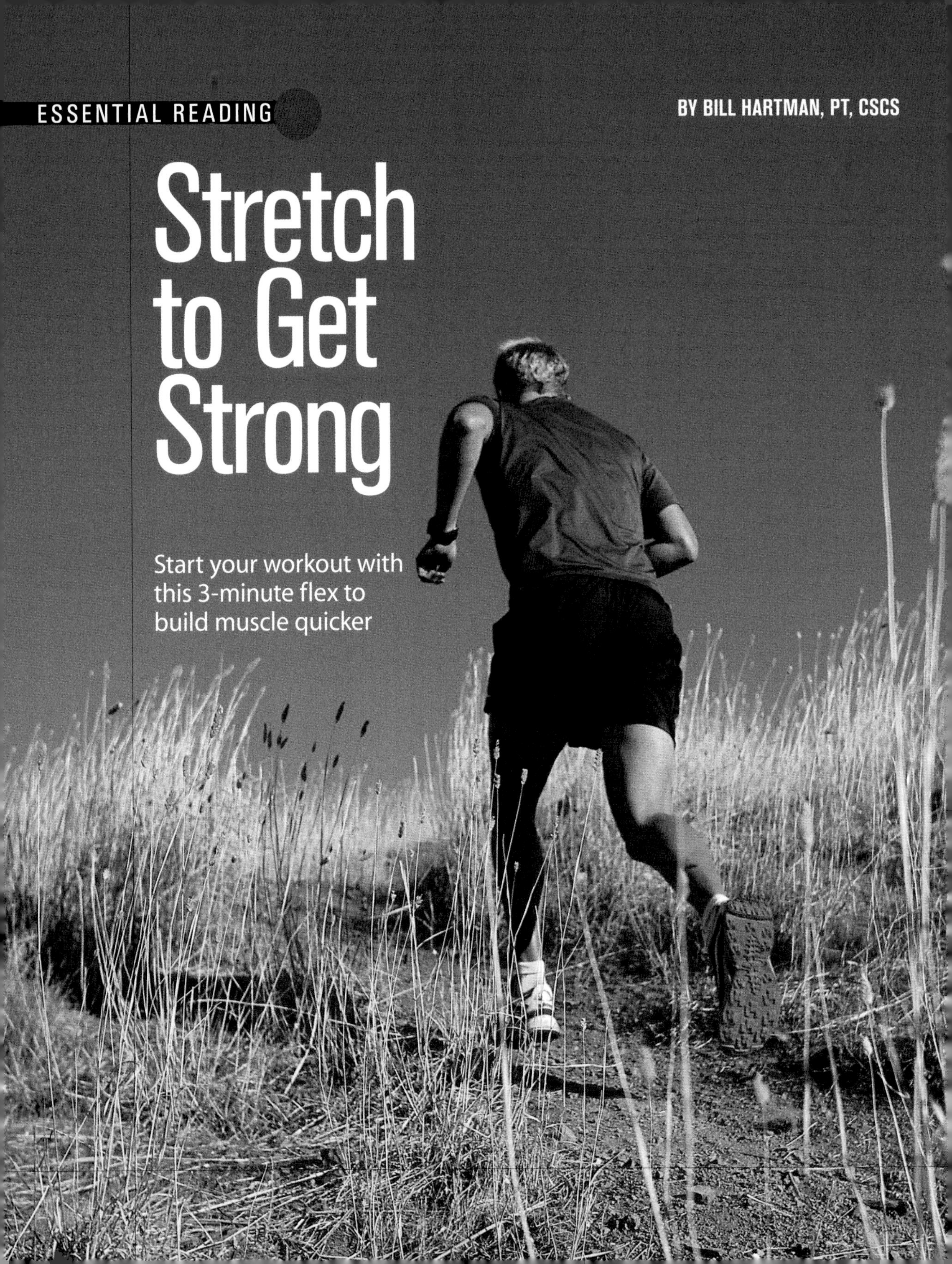

C an you touch your toes? If you fail this simple test (done the proper way, with legs straight), you've discovered a major flaw in your physique. That's because poor flexibility in this movement inhibits your ability to build muscle and makes you more susceptible to injuries, especially those involving your lower back. But don't worry: You can loosen up in just 3 minutes. So start the clock. Your physical therapy begins now.

Flexibility 101

If you fall short of touching your toes, as most guys do, you may think that tight hamstrings are the culprit. After all, that's probably where you feel the stretch most. But the problem could be elsewhere on the back side of your body.

You see, most men tend to think of their muscles in specific groups, such as "biceps" and "hamstrings." But the reality is that a thin film of connective tissue called fascia surrounds every bone, organ, and muscle in your body like a big sheet of plastic wrap. The fascia unites seemingly separate muscle groups, causing them to function together.

One of the best examples of this is the "superficial back line," a chain of fascia-linked muscles that run from the top of your head, down your back, and all the way to your toes. The fascia ties these muscles together in such a way that if one muscle is stiff, it can limit movement at any joint up or down the chain. So if you can't touch your toes, don't necessarily blame your hamstrings. The limiting factor could be the

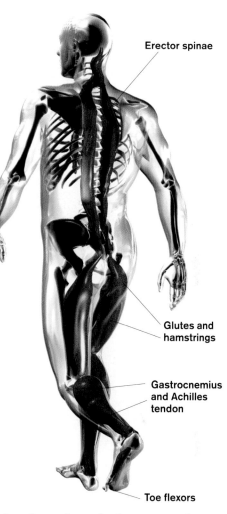

Erector spinae

Glutes and hamstrings

Gastrocnemius and Achilles tendon

Toe flexors

muscles of your lower back, in your calves, or even on the bottom of your feet.

Here's why this matters: Stiffness in your superficial back line prevents you from working your lower-body muscles through their entire range of motion—for instance, during a squat or a lunge. It also leads to poor lower-back posture when you're performing these movements. All of this results in a less effective workout and a higher risk of injury. Eliminate these problems with the four-step plan that follows.

Touch Your Toes in Four Easy Steps

Try this 3-minute flexibility plan. It's designed to diagnose and loosen your tight spots with simple exercises that you can perform at the gym, at home, or even at the office.

1. LOOSEN YOUR BACK

The erector spinae are back muscles that run from the top of your spine down to your tailbone. Stiffness of this muscle group limits the degree to which you can bend your spine and torso.

THE CAMEL-CAT

Get down on all fours. Your hands should be directly below your shoulders, and your knees directly below your hips. To create the hump-of-a-camel position, round your back by pushing it upward. Pause for one count, then push your lower back toward the floor to create the arched position of a cat. That's one repetition. After 10 repetitions, try touching your toes. No luck? Move on to step 2.

2. LOOSEN YOUR HIPS

This exercise stretches your hip muscles—the glutes and hamstrings—while removing tension from your calves, the next link in the chain.

HIP HINGE WITH HEELS ELEVATED

Place your heels on a 25-pound weight plate or a 2x4. Maintaining the natural curve in your lower back, bend forward at your hips and reach for your toes. Pause for one count, and then raise your torso back to the starting position. Do 10 reps, step off the weight plate, and retest yourself. Still reaching in vain? Go to step 3.

Note: Bend at your hips, not your back.

3. LOOSEN YOUR CALVES

By tweaking the exercise in step 2, you'll move the tension from your hips to your Achilles tendons and gastrocnemii, or calf muscles. This stretch often produces the most dramatic results.

HIP HINGE WITH TOES ELEVATED

Place the balls of your feet on a 25-pound weight plate or a 2x4, and perform the same movement as in step 2, again completing 10 repetitions. Then try touching your toes again. If you're still not there, head to step 4.

Note: You should feel this stretch in your calves.

4. LOOSEN YOUR SOLES

Most people don't realize that they have muscles on the bottom of their feet. They're called toe flexors, and they influence the flexibility of your entire lower body. Prepare to be amazed.

TENNIS-BALL FOOT ROLL

While standing, roll the bottom of your bare foot over a tennis ball. Work your entire sole over the ball for 60 seconds, and repeat with your other foot.

Now try to touch your toes one last time. If you haven't found success, go through the routine once more. Note that the steps in which you achieve the most improvement indicate your tightest muscles. These are the muscles you need to focus on.

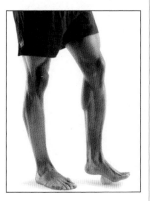

Note: **Start gently, and slowly increase the amount of pressure on the ball.**

BY DAN JOHN

Be a Dead (lift) Head

The best way to transform your body is simple: Pick up a heavy weight and put it down

In the late 1800s, a simple exercise called the health lift—the original lift—was believed to provide the only physical fitness a man needed.

The health lift was a very simple exercise. Pile heavy objects onto a machine, and then lift it. Workout completed, fitness and health improved—instantly.

Today we have another name for that exercise: the deadlift. And it's still king for developing total-body strength and muscle. But most 21st-century men avoid deadlifts because we've been told, rightly so, not to lift with our backs.

Sure, you can lift without your back, much like you can speak without your tongue. But it's not very efficient or effective.

The deadlift works wonders on your physique for the exact reason the move's opponents avoid it: It requires a team effort from hundreds of muscles, including those in your lower back.

As a result, you become more proficient at a basic human movement. Need to pick your kids up from the floor? Deadlift. Taking out the trash? Deadlift.

Make the original lift for optimal health and longevity a staple in your workout. Use our safe and effective plan to master this simple and time-proven move.

Do the Potato-Sack Squat

There's a subtle difference between deadlifts and squats when you're learning how to do them. Typically, when you hold the weight down in front of your body, the

move is a deadlift. When you hold it across your shoulders, it's a squat.

An exercise called the potato-sack squat is a sort of hybrid, and it helps you get comfortable using your back to lift weights. You can do this move with a dumbbell, luggage, or, yes, a bag of potatoes.

POTATO-SACK SQUAT

Stand holding a dumbbell—use a 20- or 30-pounder to start—with both hands under the top of the weight and your arms hanging straight down in front of your body. Keep your chin and chest up and your shoulders back. Next, lower your body until the weight touches the floor. Then stand back up.

Note: It takes longer to explain than it does to master. You should get the hang of it within 3 or 4 repetitions. Keep your back arched as you lift and lower the weight.

MUSCLE CHOW

A Strong Start

To fill out your shirtsleeves in a hurry, first fill a couple of pita pockets with eggs and vegetables. You'll have the energy you need for an intense, muscle-building workout.

BREAKFAST PITA

4 white mushrooms, sliced

1 tablespoon chopped onion

1 tablespoon chopped red bell pepper

Pinch of ground black pepper

1 egg

3 egg whites

½ small tomato, seeded and chopped

3 tablespoons water or 1% milk

1 whole-wheat pita, halved and toasted

½ avocado, sliced

Coat a skillet with cooking spray and place over medium heat. Add the mushrooms, onion, bell pepper, and black pepper. Cook for 3 to 4 minutes. Meanwhile, in a bowl, combine the egg, egg whites, tomato, and water. Whisk together until frothy. Pour the egg mixture into the skillet. Cook, stirring, for 3 to 4 minutes, or until the eggs are firm. Fill each pita with half the eggs and top with the avocado slices.

Makes 1 serving

Per serving: 399 calories, 25 g protein, 33 g carbohydrates, 21 g total fat, 4 g saturated fat, 11 g fiber, 417 mg sodium

Sit Back and Relax

Once you've done a set of potato-sack squats, try another set, but this time slide two 10-pound weight plates under your toes so the balls of your feet are on the plates and your heels are on the floor.

Doing the exercise this way stretches your hamstrings and calves, and, more important, trains your body to stay upright. Men have a tendency to let their weight creep forward over their toes, and that's when back injuries often occur. By keeping your weight on your heels and pressing into the floor every time you do the deadlift, you'll reduce your risk of injury.

Prepare for Bigger Muscle

This next move can help you attain all the hip and hamstring flexibility you'll ever need. You're going to do the potato-sack squat once more, this time on an elevated surface. Stand with each foot on a box that is about 6 inches high, or on a pair of 45-pound plates. An aerobics step will work, too.

Now perform the potato-sack squat. When you touch the dumbbell to the floor, your hips will drop deeper than they did before, so you'll expand your range of motion and your muscle-building potential.

Build Strength in Seconds

Now you're ready for the deadlift. Place two 45-pound plates on a barbell and do what comes naturally: Pick it up and put it down. Then see the workout plan on the opposite page to increase the amount of weight you can lift fast. Keep these cues in mind.

Bigger and Stronger in 4 Weeks

Here's a simple plan to make the deadlift work for you.

Week 1

(5 days a week)

Do the potato-sack squat (see page 123).

Perform two to five sets of 2 to 5 reps.

Week 2

(3 days a week)

Perform the potato-sack squat with your feet on weight plates or an aerobic step.

Do three sets of 5 reps in your first workout.

Do five sets of 3 reps in your second session.

Perform five sets in your third workout: Start with 5 reps, and then subtract a rep while using the next-heaviest dumbbell in each subsequent set.

Week 3

(2 days a week)

For your first workout, do three sets of the deadlift. Perform 7 reps in your first set, 5 reps in your second set, and 3 reps in your third set. Rest for 2 minutes between sets, and increase the weight by 10 pounds in each set. That's one "wave." Next, do another wave, but add 5 pounds to your starting weight.

In your second deadlift workout, perform 10 sets of 3 reps using the weight you lifted for 5 reps in the second wave of your first workout. Rest for 1 minute between sets.

Week 4

(2 days a week)

In your first workout, do the same progression you did in the first session of week 3, but perform two waves using one less rep in each set. So you'll do 6 reps, 4 reps, and 2 reps, resting for 2 minutes between sets. Increase your starting weight accordingly, and add 10 pounds every time you drop reps.

For your second workout, do the second session from week 3, but reduce your rest periods to 45 seconds between sets.

For an expanded version of this plan, go to MensHealth.com, keyword Deadlift.

- Keep your arms straight, elbows locked.
- Drive your chin toward the ceiling as you lift the weight.
- Press down on your heels.
- Elevate your chest.

Experiment by holding the barbell with an overhand grip (palms facing you) or an alternating grip (one palm forward, one palm facing you), with your hands placed shoulder-width apart or out toward the ends of the bar. Variations help you improve faster.

BY CRAIG BALLANTYNE, MS, CSCS

Pack on Size Fast

Break the muscle barrier with
eight strength-boosting exercises
you've never done before

The most popular exercise of all time could be holding you back. Sure, the bench press has helped you build your chest and arms. But the more often you return to the bench without mixing up your routine, the more muscle you might be missing out on. That's because your body adapts quickly to the same old routine, stalling your progress.

Simply trying any new exercise can rejuvenate your workout, igniting growth and curing boredom. But we'll spot you eight great new moves. These movements aren't particularly exotic. (Read: You won't be embarrassed to do them in a crowded gym.) They are, in fact, variations on classic, old-school muscle builders, including the bench press. And they are highly effective.

So swap a couple of these moves into your current lifting routine. Or scrap your old workout altogether and combine all eight exercises into one total-body training session. The result: more muscle built faster than ever.

Your All-New Workout

Do each pair of exercises as a superset, completing one set of each movement before resting. So you'll do 1a and follow immediately with 1b. That's a superset. Rest for 1 minute and then repeat. Do each superset three times before moving on to the next pair. Do this workout three times a week, resting a day between bouts.

SET	EXERCISE	REPETITIONS
1a	Dumbbell split jerk	6 per side
1b	Swiss-ball mountain climber	10 per side
2a	Front-loaded Bulgarian split squat	8 per side
2b	Dumbbell close-grip floor press	8
3a	Dumbbell swing	12
3b	Decline Spider-Man pushup	8 per side
4a	Single-leg deadlift	10 per side
4b	Underhand inverted row	15

SUPERSET 1

1A: DUMBBELL SPLIT JERK

The benefit: Strengthens your shoulders and develops explosive upper-body power for sports

Swap it for: The military press

Stand holding a dumbbell in one hand, just above shoulder height. Brace your abs as if you were preparing to withstand a blow to your gut. Next, in one explosive movement, press the weight overhead while moving your feet into a split position—one foot forward, the other foot back. Step back to the starting position and repeat. Finish all your reps with one arm before switching sides.

Note: Hold the weight so your elbow points down. Keep a slight bend in your knees.

MUSCLE CHOW

Protein Power

Shrimp is an unusually low-fat, low-calorie source of protein. But it's their great taste that makes them the second most popular seafood in Americans' diets (right behind canned tuna).

ROASTED SHRIMP 'N' VEGETABLE PASTA

1 pound large raw shrimp, washed, peeled, and deveined

1 cup white wine

½ teaspoon red-pepper flakes

¼ teaspoon ground black pepper, plus more for seasoning

4 cloves garlic, minced

½ box penne pasta

2 medium yellow squash, cubed

12–15 asparagus stalks, stemmed and cut into 2-inch pieces

12 grape or cherry tomatoes

Olive oil

1 tablespoon flaxseed oil

4–5 fresh basil leaves, chopped

4 teaspoons grated Parmesan cheese

In a large zipper-lock bag, add the shrimp, wine, red-pepper flakes, ¼ teaspoon black pepper, and garlic. Seal the bag and marinate in the fridge for 1 hour. Bring a large pot of salted water to a boil, add the pasta, and cook until al dente. Strain the pasta and keep warm. Meanwhile, preheat the broiler in the oven. In a baking pan, combine the squash, asparagus, and tomatoes, toss with a splash of olive oil, and season with black pepper. Place 6 inches from the broiler. Broil for 5 minutes, add the shrimp to the pan, and broil for 2½ minutes longer. Spoon the shrimp and vegetables over the hot pasta; add the flaxseed oil, basil, and cheese; toss.

Makes 4 servings

Per serving: 877 calories, 62 g protein, 107 g carbohydrates, 14 g total fat, 2 g saturated fat, 10 g fiber, 363 mg sodium

1B: SWISS-BALL MOUNTAIN CLIMBER

The benefit: Trains your core—abs, lower back, and hips—while stabilizing your shoulder joints

Swap it for: Any ab exercise

Assume the classic pushup position but place your hands on the sides of a Swiss ball, fingers pointing forward. Brace your abs and straighten your legs behind you. This is the starting position. Lift one foot off the floor and bring your knee toward your chest. Straighten your leg back out, move your other knee to your chest, and return that leg to the starting position. Keep alternating sides until you've completed all your repetitions.

Note: Raise your knee past waist height.

SUPERSET 2

2A: FRONT-LOADED BULGARIAN SPLIT SQUAT

The benefit: Builds lower-body strength and power and trains your core harder than standard split squats do

Swap it for: The leg extension

Stand a couple of feet in front of a bench, holding a dumbbell, weight plate, or medicine ball with both hands at your chest. Rest the top of one foot behind you on the bench. Keeping your back straight and your torso upright, lower your body until your front thigh is parallel to the floor. Push back up to a standing position. Do all your reps with one leg before repeating with your other leg.

Note: *Squeeze your glutes and brace your abs.*

2B: DUMBBELL CLOSE-GRIP FLOOR PRESS

The benefit: Boosts upper-body pressing power by minimizing momentum, and it's easier on your shoulders than a standard bench press

Swap it for: The bench press

Grab a pair of dumbbells and lie on the floor with your legs straight. Hold the weights with a neutral grip (palms facing each other), with your upper arms flat on the floor and your forearms pointing straight up. Squeeze your abs, pull your shoulder blades back, and press the weight up. Keep your elbows tucked in at your sides as you lower the weight.

Note: *Press the weight straight up.*

3A: DUMBBELL SWING

The benefit: Strengthens your hips and hamstrings in an explosive fashion, which can add inches to your vertical jump; improves overall conditioning

Swap it for: The leg curl

Stand with your feet more than shoulder-width apart. Hold a dumbbell with a hand-over-hand grip and your arms hanging down in front of you. Push your hips back and lower the weight between your legs until it's under your butt. Drive back up to a standing position and swing the weight up to chest height, keeping your arms straight. Go right into your next rep and continue at a swift pace.

Note: Keep your arms straight at all times.

3B: DECLINE SPIDER-MAN PUSHUP

The benefit: Strengthens your upper body and increases mobility in the hips and shoulders, which often become stiff in men

Swap it for: The standard pushup or the chest fly

Assume the classic pushup position but place your feet on a bench. Keeping your abs braced and your body in a straight line, slowly bend your elbows until your chest is a few inches from the floor. As you go down, bring your right knee to your right elbow. Straighten your leg back out as you use your chest, shoulders, and triceps to push yourself back to the starting position. Alternate legs.

Note: Resist the urge to let your hips sag.

4A: SINGLE-LEG DEADLIFT

The benefit: Strengthens your entire lower body and improves balance

Swap it for: The lunge

Stand with your feet slightly more than shoulder-width apart. Raise one foot and extend it behind you, just off the floor. Contract your glutes, brace your abs, and keep your spine naturally arched. Focusing on your balance, lower yourself until your torso is parallel to the floor. Initiate the movement by pushing your hips back. Push back up to the starting position, and complete all your reps before switching legs.

Note: Pull your shoulders back and stand tall.

4B: UNDERHAND INVERTED ROW

The benefit: Builds your back and biceps and bolsters your grip

Swap it for: The arm curl or the seated row

Set a bar at hip height in a Smith machine or squat rack. Lie underneath the bar with your heels on the floor and grab the bar with an underhand grip (palms facing you), your hands 1 or 2 inches more than shoulder-width apart. Keeping your body in a straight line, pull your chest up to the bar using your back muscles. Slowly lower yourself until your arms are straight.

Note: Keep your core tight throughout the move.

BY DAN JOHN

Build a Firm Foundation

This innovative muscle maker will revolutionize your workout—and transform your body

A young man once told me that squats hurt his knees. So I asked him to demonstrate a squat. He tucked his head into his chest like a turtle, brought his knees toward each other, and bowed forward. I told him, "Squats don't hurt your knees; what you're doing hurts your knees."

As a national masters champion weight lifter and someone who's been doing this exercise since the Johnson administration, I've heard all the arguments against squats, such as how they're bad for your knees and back. And I've seen many men prove those accusations right by butchering the move.

Any properly executed squat, however, may be a more effective muscle builder than all other exercises combined. It requires the synchronized recruitment of muscle fibers throughout your body. And because squatting is one of the most natural human movements, such as walking or using the remote, it's perfectly safe. And new research shows that squats burn up to three times as many calories as previously thought. So it's a powerful fat-burning tool as well.

Ready to carve rock-solid muscle and harness whole-body strength, power, and athleticism? Use the plan that follows. It's simple, and I've used it with thousands of athletes—so I know that it works.

Step 1. Squat with Your Elbows

First, do three consecutive vertical jumps, then look down. This is roughly where you want to place your feet every time you squat.

Set your feet and bend your hips and knees to lower your body as far as you can. Then, when you're in your deepest position, push your knees out with your elbows. Try to keep your feet flat on the floor and allow your butt to sink below knee height.

Relax in this position for 2 or 3 seconds, then descend a bit deeper and drive your knees out with your elbows once more. For most men, this small elbow maneuver will simplify squatting forever, because it makes you drop your torso between your thighs rather than fold at the waist.

Stand up, and move on to step 2.

Step 2. Do the Doorknob Drill

You may think of the squat as a lower-body exercise, but proper upper-body

---

MUSCLE CHOW

A Strong Spin on Salad

Build muscle by swapping your lettuce salad for quinoa (pronounced KEEN-wah). It's an easy-to-cook grain with as much protein as milk.

QUINOA SALAD

½ cup uncooked quinoa
1 bunch parsley, chopped
¼ cup finely chopped onion
½ cucumber, peeled and chopped
2 plum tomatoes, diced
1 tablespoon extra virgin olive oil
Juice of ½ lemon or lime
Ground black pepper

Cook the quinoa according to the package directions. Allow it to cool for 30 minutes. In a bowl, toss the cooled quinoa with the parsley, onion, cucumber, tomatoes, oil, lemon juice, and black pepper to taste.

Makes 1 serving

Per serving: 506 calories, 14 g protein, 72 g carbohydrates, 20 g total fat, 3 g saturated fat, 9 g fiber, 36 mg sodium

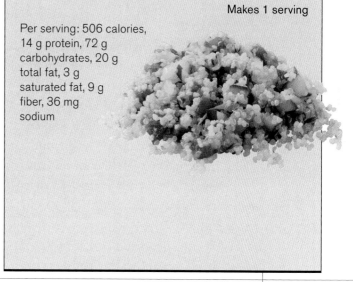

The Workout

Throw down a 100-pound goblet squat in just 6 weeks using this plan. Your upper body stays rigid, so your glutes, quadriceps, and hamstrings do most of the heavy lifting. One hundred pounds may not sound all that impressive, but wait till you try it. Once you're able to bang out a few sets of 10 with triple-digit weight, you'll realize the full-body benefits of squats.

Weeks 1 and 2

Hone your technique. Five days a week, perform two or three sets of 5 to 20 repetitions of goblet squats. Use a light dumbbell, or even a heavy book.

Week 3

Do squats 3 days a week, resting for at least a day between sessions. You'll improve your technique and increase strength and muscle endurance.

Day 1: Perform a "rack walk-up." Grab the lightest dumbbell you can find and do a set of 5 goblet squats. Return the weight to the rack and grab the next heaviest dumbbell. The exchange should take you no more than 20 seconds. Do another set, then continue moving up the rack until you find a dumbbell that's challenging to lift but still allows perfect technique.

Day 2: Do the reverse of day 1: a "rack walk-down." Start with your second-heaviest dumbbell from day 1, and complete a set of 5 reps. Move down the rack, lifting a lighter weight for each set of 5. Aim for a total of 10 to 12 sets, resting for no more than 20 seconds between sets.

Day 3: Combine your workouts from day 1 and day 2. You'll start by moving up in

alignment is essential. Perfect your posture with this drill.

Stand an arm's length away from a doorknob and grab the handle with both hands. Set your feet as you did in step 1.

Now imagine that you're walking into a bar full of swimsuit models. Your natural reaction will be to immediately lift your chest, which in turn will tighten your lower back. Your latissimus dorsi muscles will naturally spread a bit and your shoulders will move back slightly.

Holding the doorknob, and keeping your chest up and arms straight, bend your hips

and knees to lower your body, and lean back. Then stand up.

By staying tight through your chest, shoulders, and core muscles, you distribute weight more evenly throughout your body. As a result, you'll be able to handle greater loads with less risk of injury.

3. Behold the Goblet Squat

Named for the way in which you hold the weight—in front of your chest, with your hands cupped—the goblet squat may in fact be the only squat you need in your workout.

Start with a light dumbbell, between 25

weight, performing sets of 5 repetitions. When you reach your heaviest weight, work back down the rack. Rest for 2 days before your next squat workout.

Week 4

Same as week 3, but perform 3 reps with each dumbbell, using heavier weights than in your last workout.

Week 5

By now you should feel comfortable performing the goblet squat. You'll focus on building muscle and strength. Again, rest for at least a day between workouts.

Day 1: Do two sets of 20 repetitions using a dumbbell

that challenges you in the last 5 reps. Rest for 2 minutes between sets.

Day 2: Choose a weight that makes it difficult to complete 10 reps. Do three sets of 8 reps, resting for 60 seconds between sets.

Day 3: Perform a rack walk-up. Do 3 reps with each weight, and stop when you feel your technique beginning to falter.

Week 6

This week's theme is simple: If you can pick it up, you can squat it.

Day 1: Do the regular rack walk-down, performing 3 reps per set with a heavy weight.

Then do it again, this time starting with a slightly heavier dumbbell. Rest for no more than 20 seconds between sets and for 30 seconds between walk-downs.

Day 2: Do a couple of light warmup sets of goblet squats, then do the rack walk-up twice. Do 3 reps per set and rest for up to 30 seconds between sets.

Day 3: Do a few easy sets to warm up. Then find the heaviest dumbbell you can lift—aim for three digits—and perform the goblet squat.

and 50 pounds, and hold it vertically by one end. Hug it tight against your chest.

With your elbows pointing down, lower your body into a squat. Allow your elbows to brush past the insides of your knees as you descend. It's okay to push your knees out.

Return to a standing position. Your upper body should hardly move if you're using

your legs, hips, and lower back as a unit.

Don't worry if this isn't perfect the first time. Most men mess up when they think about the move. Just let your elbows glide down by rubbing past your knees, and good things will happen.

HARDTRUTH
Percentage of Americans who did not stick to their fitness goals in 2006

71

BY JOE KITA

Get Strong to Get Big

America's top strength coach shares his five best strategies for explosive gains

Standing in one of Southern California's typically well-appointed athletic clubs, Robert dos Remedios folds his arms, furrows his brow, and points his stubbled chin at various men in the gym.

"Look at that guy on the leg-extension machine," he says. "You never isolate muscles like that in the real world. . . ."

"See that kid in front of the mirror doing dumbbell curls? He wants to get big, but he should train to get strong. He'd get double the benefit in half the time. . . ."

"And how about all those people on the treadmills watching TV? Do you think they're really out of their comfort zones?"

That there's more designer water in here than sweat gripes him. "I don't want to sound negative," dos Remedios says, "but most people don't understand training fundamentals or what it means to train hard."

To learn what it means to train really, really hard, travel a few miles from that posh club to the gym at College of the Canyons, in Santa Clarita, California. One minute, members of the football squad are snatching mammoth dumbbells off the floor with one hand, pushing them overhead, and then stepping up onto makeshift boxes. The next, they're doing torturous variations of pushups and bridges, all designed to promote strength and explosiveness.

"Let's go, guys!" screams one player with agony on his face and a puddle beneath his chest. "This is what makes you the best!"

Coach Dos, as he's known to these athletes, is the squad's director of speed,

strength, and conditioning. He strides through the suffering with his arms crossed, like a captain overseeing his galley slaves. "Push the pace! Push the pace!" he bellows. "You're personally offending me! Let's get something out of this!"

They crumple to the floor in exhaustion when they're finished, 30 minutes later.

"By training like this, not only are you going to look strong, but you're also going to be strong," says dos Remedios. "And you're going to see your performance improve. Follow these principles and you'll become stronger, bigger, and leaner."

Those aren't idle promises. The football team at this obscure community college north of Los Angeles is 67-7 since 2001. It's one reason the National Strength and Conditioning Association and coaches across the country chose dos

Remedios, and not some strength guru at some big-time program, as the 2006 Collegiate Strength Coach of the Year.

How 41-year-old dos Remedios molds what he calls "lumps of clay" into prized Division 1 and even professional athletes in less than a year with no money is the basis of this article and his new book, *Men's Health Power Training*. His principles can work for you, but you'll need an open mind, a willingness to recast your fitness goals, and, of course, the guts to withstand some torture.

Remedios, pointing to a shirtless specimen walking off the field after an evening workout. "Look how cut he is. But he's not doing hundreds of crunches, curls, and seated calf raises. His body is a product of athletic conditioning."

Instead of focusing just on getting big, dos Remedios wants you to concentrate on getting strong. That way, you sculpt the body you want along with a valuable bonus: functional fitness.

Swap this for that. If you're doing any of the single-joint exercises listed below, try replacing them with the corresponding compound exercises. For example, if you're doing 25-pound biceps curls, you'll probably be able to handle 50s for bent-over rows. You'll build strength and burn more calories, and the extra weight will create added muscle stress and trigger more testosterone production. The result: Your biceps will grow faster than they would with simple curls.

The Five Iron Rules of Training

Dos Remedios—whose name, incidentally, means "of the remedy" in Portuguese—bases his program on five bedrock strength-training principles.

1. STRIVE FOR STRENGTH, NOT SIZE

Like most men, you want a mighty chest, big biceps, and washboard abs. But instead of training like a bodybuilder and relying on single-joint exercises designed to isolate specific muscles, start training like an athlete. You'll finally build the body you want as you also improve your performance, minimize injury, burn fat, and feel more motivated.

"Look at the body on that guy," says dos

SINGLE-JOINT EXERCISE	COMPOUND EXERCISE
Biceps curl	Bent-over row
Calf raise	Clean pull
Leg extension	Lunge or stepup
Crunch	Cable woodchopper

The 7-Minute Warmup

Before starting a workout as intense as dos Remedios's, muscles and tendons need to be warm and pliable. He knows you're a busy guy, so here's how to start them cooking in just 7 minutes.

Aerobics (2 to 5 minutes): Light jogging, jumping rope, or doing jumping jacks

Mobility circuit (2 to 3 minutes): Mobility movements are dynamic flexibility patterns. This means they help improve range of motion by elongating muscles. Set a barbell in the squat rack and follow the patterns outlined in the accompanying photos.

Bar warmup (1 to 2 minutes): Using only an unweighted Olympic bar, perform 5 reps of each of the following movements: body-weight squat jump, push press, front squat, and bent-over row.

2. EMBRACE PROGRESSIVE OVERLOAD

"Progressive overload" means spending more time in your discomfort zone. "It's the most basic of all strength-training principles," dos Remedios says, "but it's the one people understand least. The human body is amazing. The more work you do, the more you will be capable of doing over time." He's talking about manipulating loads and volumes during strength and cardio workouts for continuous progress.

More time in your discomfort zone equals less time in the gym. This is why dos Remedios usually trains for just 35 to 45 minutes a day, and why his athletes are in the gym for only 30 to 40 minutes two or three times a week.

Cycle your workouts. You won't make much progress doing three sets of 10 for the rest of your life. To build strength, it's smarter to alternate 3-week cycles within 12-week training periods, an approach called periodization. Say, for example, you're accustomed to bench-pressing 150 pounds for three sets of 10 in every chest workout. Your periodized plan might look something like this.

Weeks 1–3: Three sets of 10 with 150 pounds for a total volume of 4,500 pounds ($3 \times 10 \times 150$)

Weeks 4–6: Four sets of 5 with 175 pounds, for 3,500 pounds

Weeks 7–9: Three sets of 8 with 160 pounds, for 3,840 pounds

Weeks 10–12: Five sets of 4 with 185 pounds, for 3,700 pounds

Notice how the weight you're lifting and your total volume cycle and progress over time while ensuring that your muscles have plenty of time to adapt. This produces more strength and size as the load on your muscles keeps increasing.

3. BALANCE YOUR MOVEMENTS

Strength requires balance. But on our visit to that SoCal athletic club, dos Remedios counted three times as many push-based strength machines as he did pull-based ones. "If you're bench-pressing three sets of 10, you also need to be doing some exercise, such as horizontal pullups or standing cable rows, where you're pulling for three sets of 10," he says. "If you're not, structural problems develop."

Yin-yang your gym time. Dos Remedios has identified eight key movements that are fundamental to strength, sports, and everyday living. They are listed next to their counterparts below. Perform the exercises with their complements. You don't have to do all of these movements every time you step into the gym, but they should be equally represented across your entire training plan.

HORIZONTAL PUSH	HORIZONTAL PULL
Bench press	Bent-over row
Pushup	Horizontal pullup
Dip	Standing cable row
VERTICAL PUSH	**VERTICAL PULL**
Shoulder press	Chinup/pullup
Push press	Lat pulldown
KNEE-DOMINANT	**HIP-DOMINANT**
Squat	Good morning
Lunge	Back extension
ROTATIONAL CORE	**STABILIZED CORE**
Russian twist	Plank
Windshield wiper	Side bridge
Cable woodchopper	Barbell rollout

4. BECOME UNSTABLE

In life, we usually reach or step with one arm or one leg at a time. Then we hit the gym, and we immediately plant both feet or grab a bar with both hands. This "bilateral bias," as dos Remedios calls it, often results in a dominant limb negotiating more of the weight than its weaker counterpart. This can lead to physical imbalances, performance flaws, and eventual injury.

PAINkiller

When I lift weights, it feels like I have shinsplints in my forearms. What gives?

"Muscles such as the biceps, back, and chest often become stronger than the forearms, relatively speaking, making them prone to fatigue during heavier lifts. Use hand squeezers to address the imbalance," says Nicholas A. DiNubile, MD, an orthopedic surgeon specializing in sports medicine and the author of *FrameWork: Your 7-Step Program for Healthy Muscles, Bones, and Joints.*

"Say you can bench-press 400 pounds," says dos Remedios, who was once an offensive lineman at the University of California at Berkeley. "You probably think you're pretty strong. But I guarantee you won't be able to lift two 200-pound dumbbells the same way. That's because each arm is now required to work independently."

Training with one arm or leg at a time creates instability. Muscles, especially those in the core, compensate by firing. So you're not only working to move the weight, but you're also working to stay balanced.

Do more unilateral exercises. When dos Remedios devises programs for his athletes, he works from an extensive menu of exercises. For example, he may have them bench-press on Monday but then do different horizontal-pushing exercises (say, a single-arm dumbbell incline press, or

pushups) for the next two workouts. "When we finally get around to bench-pressing again, everybody's stronger because of the carryover," he says. To apply the same principle to your workout, use this chart for occasional substitutions.

BILATERAL	UNILATERAL
Barbell squat	Forward lunge
Bench press	Dumbbell alternating bench press
Pushup	Side-to-side pushup
Lat pulldown	One-arm lat pulldown
Good morning	Single-leg Romanian deadlift
Back extension	Single-leg back extension
Shoulder press	Dumbbell one-arm push press

5. DO IT ALL EXPLOSIVELY

To dos Remedios, it's not enough to just lift a weight. He wants you to explode with it—that is, raise it as fast as you can while still retaining control. This is also known as speed-strength conditioning, and it has great influence on power, endurance, and metabolism. Be forewarned: This training style will gas you like never before.

Light the fuse. Olympic barbell and powerlifting exercises, such as squats, clean and jerks, and snatches, are the best moves for explosiveness. Here are some alternatives.

Body-weight squat jumps: Stand with your hands behind your head, squat until your thighs are parallel to the floor, and jump as high as possible. Rest for 3 to 5 seconds and repeat 10 to 12 times.

Dumbbell squat press: Stand with your feet shoulder-width apart, holding dumbbells at your shoulders. In one continuous movement, squat until your thighs are parallel to the floor. Stand while driving the weights overhead. Lower back to the squat position and repeat for two or three sets of 8 to 10 reps.

Get Bigger Easier

Gaining size quickly while becoming more athletic is a tall order. Follow the lead of these NBA stars to take your body—and your game—to new heights

143

When Indiana Pacers president Larry Bird sent Stephen Jackson and Al Harrington to the Golden State Warriors in exchange for Troy Murphy and Mike Dunleavy Jr. in January 2007, he was trading athleticism and headaches (in Jackson's case, at least) for height and marksmanship. Yet the trade's aftermath only made Bird reach for more extra-strength Excedrin. The Warriors made the playoffs for the first time since 1994 and saddled the Dallas Mavericks with a shocking first-round defeat. Preseason favorites, the Pacers staggered to fourth place in the Central Division.

The Indianapolis media needed only to look up to assign blame. "We took a lot of hits," says Murphy, having fortified his 6'11" frame with 22 new pounds of lean beef over the summer. "After the trade, the Warriors did well and the Pacers didn't, so that reflected on us," he says. "It's on our shoulders to change that. That's what we're doing here."

"Here" is the Peak Performance Strength & Conditioning Center, set discreetly in an expansive loft space in Lower Manhattan. At first glance, it seems like a strange place to undergo penance for a lost season. The gym's sleek interior is filled with the latest machines and training gadgets, not to mention enough hard-bodied actors and models to stock a Hollywood premiere. On any given day, you'll find Gerard Butler hoisting kettlebells, John Leguizamo tattooing a heavy bag, and Claire Danes torturously dragging a sled yoked to her waist.

Dowdell (left) added bulk to Dunleavy (at left on top photos)

Today, two of Indiana's starting five take turns pulling that same apparatus across the floor. They're here to bulk up, but this isn't your father's mass-gaining regimen of bench-pressing and slurp-till-you-puke weight-gain shakes. For nearly 2 hours, the players work their way through a battery of exercises reflecting owner and cofounder Joe Dowdell's blend of functional training and old-school iron pushing. The pace is relentless. One moment, the guys are performing an Olym-

pic lift, the hang pull; the next, it's medicine-ball tosses. Suddenly they're jumping off smaller boxes and exploding up onto much taller boxes. Then come defensive slides, with Dowdell pulling against tubing wrapped around their waists. Later, they flash for passes in the same rigging. Murphy seems to traverse half the gym in one step.

Next stop is the power rack. "Look at that—the bar is bending!" yells Dowdell over his shoulder, laughing, as Murphy descends below parallel with 275 pounds loaded on his back, normally a biomechanical nightmare for a human skyscraper.

Shawn Windle, CSCS, Indiana's head strength coach, selected Dowdell to work with Murphy and Dunleavy for 5 months in the off-season. "The goal for Murphy was to pack on some serious size and strength," says Dowdell, adding that Dunleavy presented different challenges. Extremely skilled for 6'9", he has lacked, to date, the strength and athleticism to justify having been picked third overall in the 2002 NBA draft. A gifted

shooter, he also needs to bang bodies with power forward while defending freakishly athletic wing players. So his focus wasn't just on bulking up, although he did gain 12 pounds over the summer. "I wanted to improve my strength—mostly in my legs—and improve my flexibility and add some muscle. At the same time, I was looking to become quicker and more agile," says Dunleavy. Sweat dampens his T-shirt, courtesy of the slide-board drills he's doing to improve his lateral agility. "A lot of players gain weight in the off-season, and it makes them slower. I feel great." For both players, improved athleticism was the ultimate off-season acquisition.

Dowdell trained the players using free weights, high-tech machines, metal chains, elastic bands, sleds, kettlebells, sandbags, slide boards, Swiss balls, medicine balls, foam rollers, weighted vests, wooden boxes, an assortment of strangely angled bars, and a lifting platform called the Power Plate, which vibrates to supposedly make more muscle fibers fire. (The research on vibration training's effectiveness, while intriguing, remains inconclusive.) The men trained 4 days a week, and each session included multijoint exercises, such as the squat and deadlift, using moderate to heavy resistance. Exercises targeting more specific areas were divided according to a 4-day split routine: lower body on Mondays and Thursdays, upper body on Tuesdays and Fridays. "In addition to the strength training, we did some plyometrics training on all 4 days, with the drills varying from low to high intensity," says Dowdell. "We'd wrap each session with core exercises."

Even if you don't have access to all the equipment Dowdell employs, you can still apply his principles to your own workouts with a bit of planning and improvisation.

Pick up the correct weights. Most men equate mass building with grabbing the heaviest weight they can lift from the dumbbell rack and then squeezing out several shaky reps before that hunk of iron comes crashing to the floor. Dowdell recommends finding the heaviest weight you can lift cleanly for one and only one repetition, a weight referred to by exercise scientists as your one-rep max (1RM). This will require trial and error, but once you find this weight, rack it. You don't need it anymore. Instead, find the weights that represent 75 to 85 percent of that super-heavy 1RM.

So to calculate your best weight to lift in any exercise, multiply your one-rep max by 0.75 (to 0.85).

Use more than one set of joints at a time. Dowdell hates leg extensions, because movement occurs only at the knee joints. He loves squats, because the hips and knees bend simultaneously to execute the lift. "Bigger moves like the squat release more of the key hormones that increase strength and muscle and decrease body fat," says Dowdell. Find several of his favorites in "Reengineer Your Body" on page 212.

Here's an even more fundamental reason to base your mass-gaining workouts around these moves. "Muscle strength and power improve more when you use multijoint lifts, because those lifts involve larger muscle masses than single-joint lifts do," says David Pearson, PhD, a professor of exercise

Five Ways to Double Your Strength in Just 3 Weeks

If you want lightning-fast results in the gym, you need to behave like lightning—that is, never strike the same place twice. "Variety is everything," explains Chris Jordan, fitness director at the Human Performance Institute, in Orlando, Florida. "If you keep changing your workouts, your muscles will have to adapt constantly, and performance will never plateau." We know, constant change sounds like a tall order when you have about as much time for a workout as you do for a power lunch, but these changes need not be drastic. "Simply altering your grip or your stance can stimulate new growth," says Jordan. Indeed, researchers at Arizona State University found that men who varied just the reps and resistance of their bench press every workout gained twice as much strength as men who did so every 3 weeks. Here are five uncommon variations on common exercises that can lead to huge gains.

Lateral raises: Perform them standing on one foot. In addition to working your shoulders, you'll strengthen the muscles of the lower legs and ankles, which is essential for any sport that emphasizes agility. Plus, people who balance-train also suffer fewer ankle injuries, according to a study at the University of Wisconsin.

Seated cable rows: Switch to an underhand (palms up) grip on a straight bar. "You'll place more emphasis on your biceps," says John Loeber, a clinical exercise physiologist in New York, plus you'll spread the work from your upper back to your middle back.

Bench press: Place equal emphasis on lifting and lowering, taking 3 seconds to ease the weight back down to your chest. Researchers at the University of Texas found that men who did "negative" sets gained twice as much strength as those who did not.

Biceps curls: Use a 4-foot-long body bar instead of a dumbbell. "The longer the bar, the more muscles you use to control it," says Loeber. "If you grab it with a single-hand or an off-center grip, the result will be a stronger forearm and grip."

Lunges: Transition between reps with scissor jumps. Australian researchers found that men who incorporated explosive movements into their training improved their 3-K times by 3 percent, which is the difference between an 8-minute mile and a 7:45 mile.

---

physiology and director of the strength research lab at Ball State University.

Rest for 60 seconds between sets. "Research suggests that rest periods of 45 to 90 seconds should be used when lifting for hypertrophy, or building muscle," says Pearson. Dowdell achieved his best results with the Pacers last summer by using 1 minute.

Fuel your body for growth. No matter what you do in the gym, your body must have the building blocks it needs to grow. Never is this more true than before and after you train, because muscle fibers break down during the workout. It's only during recovery that regeneration and growth take place.

Here are examples of good pre- and

Step Up to the Plates

The double-plate press is a surefire route to ripped abs and sculpted shoulders. 2001's World's Strongest Man Svend Karlsen uses two 25-pound weight plates for this exercise. Try starting with a pair of 5s or 10s.

The benefit: Builds your chest, biceps, shoulders, and abs, and strengthens your grip. Try it at the end of an upper-body routine or chest workout, or in place of cable crossovers.

How to do it: Stand holding two weight plates together, smooth sides out, close to your chest. Your fingers should point forward. Squeezing the plates, extend your arms straight out in front of you. Pause, then return to the starting position. Start with four sets of 8 reps.

Improve your gains: Squeeze the plates together as hard as you can throughout the movement. This is most difficult when your arms are extended. Mix it up by pressing at a slight upward or downward angle. It's harder to squeeze your hands together when pressing down—so watch your toes!

postworkout meals, given to Dunleavy by the Pacers strength team. Choose one 30 to 45 minutes before your workout, and then another within 20 minutes of finishing your workout.

1 protein shake

1 scoop whey-protein powder mixed with 16 ounces Gatorade

1 container Boost or Carnation Instant Breakfast

1 peanut butter or turkey sandwich on whole-wheat bread

12 ounces low-fat chocolate milk

Increase your body's capacity to do work. There was a reason Dowdell had the players dragging sleds and doing farmer's walks. Actually, several reasons. Murphy needs to muscle around bodies on the oppos-

ing team. Dunleavy needs to have his legs remain under him after three grueling quarters so that he can still drain three-pointers. But these exercises were also instrumental when it came to building muscle. "I was training their bodies to be able to do more work, which is a key factor for gaining mass," says Dowdell. "These moves also increased their ability to recover during workouts."

"Pushing the sled and doing similar drills have noticeably increased my strength on some of the other exercises I normally do," says Murphy. "I definitely see a correlation. My squat has gone up, my bench has gone up—everything has gone up, everything has gone up faster—and I think it's because of this. That's what I did differently this year."

Improve other aspects of your game

while upsizing your body. Murphy can't jump through the roof, but he can now leap up and slap his palm against the 11'6" ceiling in Dowdell's office, thanks to the 5 inches he added to his vertical jump over the summer. And remember, there are now 22 additional pounds of baggage at liftoff. "Improving lean body mass while simultaneously decreasing body fat allows for significant improvements in athleticism," says Windle.

Sleep for 8 hours a night. The secretion of human growth hormone, the most powerful anabolic substance in your body, peaks at night. The off-season manual given to Pacers players includes guidelines on effective slumber. Our favorite: "Get out of bed if you can't sleep. Don't just lie awake for long periods of time." Why? The longer you think about falling asleep, the harder it is to do so.

The tale of the tape suggests that these strategies worked big-time. But when push comes to shove, Murphy will be pushing on 300 pounds' worth of Shaq, not some sled, and Dunleavy will be chasing Kobe Bryant around.

Still, the early signs bode well for the players. On his first day in camp, Murphy e-mailed that he was "horsing" teammates around the court—pushing them off the low block, shielding them from the glass, buckling their knees on screens. His improvement didn't escape the watchful gaze of Indiana's new head coach, Jim O'Brien. "[Murphy] is in remarkable shape, and he's looked very mobile defensively," he told the *Indianapolis Star* early in training camp.

Time to Pull Your Own Weight

It seems better suited to a construction site than a gym, but sled training can build your body, too.

Sled work has a growing following in the strength-and-conditioning community. The sled, you pull. Its cousin, the Prowler, you push, although you can grasp handles or attach straps to pull it, too. If your gym doesn't offer these devices, try elitefts. com. (The Prowler costs $350.)

Last summer, Joe Dowdell, CSCS, used sleds and Prowlers to bulk up and enhance the athleticism of two Indiana Pacers ectomorphs, Troy Murphy and Mike Dunleavy Jr. The results: better workouts, more muscle, greater endurance, and heightened explosiveness, especially in the hips, legs, and lower back.

Speaking of construction, a wheelbarrow can be used to reproduce both moves. To mimic the Prowler, load the wheelbarrow with weight plates, sandbags, heavy-duty knapsacks, or some other load. Keeping your chest up, push it across a flat surface, working to prevent it from tipping. To mimic sledding, remove the wheel assembly so the shell can slide on the ground. Run a rope through the holes in the shell (you may have to drill them) and drop weights inside. Grab the rope ends—which should have a good 15 feet of slack—and use your hips, glutes, and legs to yank the weight toward you.

Dunleavy's conditioning has improved so dramatically that he is penciled in as the team's starting shooting guard, with Danny Granger taking over at small forward.

"I'm excited about this season," says Murphy, sizing up his team's chances. "Expectations are low for us, but I think we're going to sneak up and surprise a lot of people."

BY JOHN BRANT

Fight Age with Muscle

The latest research is changing how doctors look at muscle mass

> "The sixth age shifts Into the lean and slipper'd pantaloon,
> With spectacles on nose and pouch on side,
> His youthful hose well sav'd, a world too wide For his shrunk shank."
>
> —WILLIAM SHAKESPEARE, *As You Like It*, 2.7

Just as most men believe they possess a keen sense of humor, most men also assume they are reasonably strong. Their muscle mass—the aggregate of muscle tissue they have built over a lifetime, enabling them to support their bones, fill the legs of their jeans, and lift the heavy end of a sofa—is at least adequate, relative to other men their age. Before my meeting with Gianni Maddalozzo, PhD, an exercise physiologist at Oregon State University, I was one of those men. After our meeting, I still think I have a pretty good sense of humor.

Maddalozzo's research focuses on the study of osteoporosis and muscle strength in adults ages 40 to 80. Most of his subjects suffer from advanced sarcopenia, the loss of muscle mass that occurs naturally—and inevitably—with age. Sarcopenia, in other words, is the scientific term for a phenomenon that Shakespeare identifies with the sixth age of man: the gray, traditionally enfeebled years of the "shrunk shank."

Compared with sarcopenia, other sneaky scourges of the middle years, such as arterial plaque buildup and prostate enlargement, announce their presence with a fanfare of symptoms. But sarcopenia creeps by in imperceptible increments, stealing a fifth of a pound of muscle a year, from ages 25 to 50, and then it picks up a dreadful, yet still mostly silent, velocity. The condition subsequently bleeds a man of up to a pound of muscle a year, a loss he is unlikely to notice until it's too late. "You haven't gotten any thinner, because the pounds of muscle are typically replaced by pounds of fat," explains Maddalozzo. "But sarcopenia is progressing all the time. One day you trip and fall and suffer a fracture of your hip. Then, when you try to rehab after hip-replacement surgery, you discover that you have virtually no muscle mass to build on."

While listening to the professor, I reflexively probe my thigh, sounding the depth and texture of my quadriceps muscle. By serving up a hypothetical untrained victim, I tell myself, Maddalozzo has provided a worst-case scenario. I, by contrast, have trained plenty in my lifetime: For the past 35 years, since my college football and lacrosse days, I may not have darkened a weight-room door, but I run 20 miles a week, and my body weight remains under control, as does my total cholesterol, blood pressure, and resting pulse rate. I had smugly assumed that my skinny butt was covered when it came to exercise. But now I know that I had only been drifting in a state of muscle-mass denial.

These midlife realizations brought me to

the Bone Research Lab at the university's campus in Corvallis, where Maddalozzo has offered to assess my state of muscular fitness and prescribe an anti-sarcopenia strength-training regimen.

Despite (or perhaps because of) its universal, inexorable nature, sarcopenia, until recently, did not get much respect. Indeed, until 1988, the condition lacked its own scientific name. "Historically, the scientific community has taken muscle for granted," concedes William Kraemer, PhD, a professor of kinesiology at the University of Connecticut. Perhaps more tellingly, sarcopenia's proven antidote—resistance training—will never make a dime for a pharmaceutical company. Scientists such as Kraemer, Maddalozzo, and a cadre of others are at the forefront of a movement that is redefining the importance of muscle mass in terms of overall health, not simply performance or vanity.

Recent research shows that diminished muscle strength and mass are empirically linked to declines in the immune system and the onset of heart disease and diabetes, not to mention weaker bones, stiffer joints, and slumping postures. Muscle mass has also been shown to play a central role in protein metabolism, which is particularly important in the response to stress, and decreased muscle mass correlates with a decline in overall metabolic rate. (Muscle mass burns more calories at rest than fat does.) Further research is expected to show measurable links between diminished muscle mass and cancer mortality. The thinking about muscles and resistance training, in short, is reaching critical mass, and a major shift in the American fitness paradigm is under way. Along with this increasing emphasis on resistance training, there is an increasing awareness about the nutritional factors that can complement muscle growth, namely increasing daily intake of protein.

"In the last 20 years, we have come full circle," says Wojtek Chodzko-Zajko, PhD, a professor of kinesiology and community health at the University of Illinois and a fellow of the American College of Sports Medicine. "We used to discourage older adults from lifting heavy weights. Now we're telling them they can't maintain overall health without it. After age 50, you can't get by just doing aerobic exercise." Although it's not explicit yet in the government's overall health guidelines, agencies such as the Centers for Disease Control and Prevention now recommend a couple of rounds of resistance training a week. "Muscle function can improve—sometimes robustly—with resistance training, even after the onset of sarcopenia," says Robert Wolfe, PhD, a professor of geriatrics at the University of Arkansas. "But it is far more effective to begin resistance training before the process gains momentum. Intervention in the middle years is necessary."

The muscles of most men reach maximum size (or, strictly speaking, attain the maximum number of fibers per muscle) at age 25. From that lamentably early peak, a long, gradual decline ensues. Over the next 25 years, the muscles lose approximately 10 percent of their fibers. Then, starting around age 50, things go to hell. The body's production of testosterone, human growth hormone, and DHEA ebbs, and the motor cells of your nervous system, which spider out from the spinal cord to control the contraction of muscle fibers during physical activity, deteriorate rapidly. As the motor cells die, so do the fibers to which they're attached, especially type II or "fast-twitch" fibers, the ones employed for short bursts of anaerobic power. For instance, if your biceps consist of 90 fibers when you're 50 years old, by age 80, that number will be closer to 50 fibers, most of them feeble type I "slow-twitch" fibers.

It's through the study of sarcopenia that a greater appreciation of muscle mass is

HARD TRUTH

Percentage of weight-lifting injuries that are chronic in men who exercise 6 hours a week

41

evolving. Two seminal works, "Starvation in Man," an article published in the *New England Journal of Medicine* in 1970, and *Hunger Disease: Studies by the Jewish Physicians in the Warsaw Ghetto*, a book published in 1979, show that the depletion of muscle mass is the cause of death in human starvation. This is because essential organs and tissues such as the brain, heart, and liver rely on a steady supply of amino acids to synthesize new proteins and maintain function. Normally, dietary protein supplies these amino acids. Under duress, however, these organs maintain homeostasis by drawing protein from the muscles. Our skeletal muscle mass, besides powering all of our movements, also serves as a reservoir for our vital organs. And like all reservoirs, this one can run low—or, in the case of starvation, run dry.

Less dramatic maladies also demonstrate a deep relationship with sarcopenia. "Not surprisingly," observes Wolfe, "individuals with limited reserves of muscle mass respond poorly to stress." A 2000 study in the journal *Annals of the New York Academy of Science* examining lung-cancer patients undergoing chemotherapy, for instance, showed that the levels of body protein predicted the recurrence of cancer. In 2004, a study in the journal *Annals of Medicine* demonstrated a clear link between diminished muscle mass and cardiac failure. And a 2006 study in the *Journal of the American College of Surgeons* found that survival from severe burns was lowest among individuals with reduced muscle mass.

In 2005, results from the Mediterranean Intensive Oxidant Study, which examined the causes of osteoporosis in men, found that bone density and mineral content had a direct correlation to skeletal muscle mass. "The stronger and thicker your muscle tissue, the more force that tissue exerts on the bone," explains Maddalozzo. "And increased force, both during exercise and normal daily functioning, results in the bones growing stronger and denser. That significantly retards osteoporosis and, as a man ages, the rate of hip fractures." A man with a full reservoir of muscle mass enjoys dual protection: stronger bones combined with enhanced strength and agility.

Muscle mass has also proved to play a key role in more common, but no less deadly, conditions such as cardiovascular disease and diabetes. A study of scientific literature published in the journal *Circulation* in 2006 cites articles showing that sarcopenia has been linked to insulin resistance (the main factor in adult-onset, or type 2, diabetes), elevated lipid levels in the blood, and increased body fat, especially "visceral adipose tissue," which gathers around the heart and other vital organs and is a primary risk factor of heart disease. In fact, researchers concluded that long-term adaptation to resistance training lowers cortical response to acute stress; increases total energy expenditure; relieves anxiety, depression, and insomnia; and demonstrates beneficial effects on bone density, arthritis, hypertension, lipid profiles, and exercise tolerance in coronary artery disease. "As the dates on

Nourish Your Muscles

The key to fast and sustained muscle growth is timely servings of protein.

Eat less, tone up. To lose body fat and increase muscle tone, use these tips from Gianni Maddalozzo, PhD, an exercise physiologist at Oregon State University:

Consume 10 calories per pound of body weight a day, divided into five or six meals.

Consume 1 gram of protein and 2 grams of carbs per pound of body weight per day.

Fat should total 10 to 20 percent of total daily calories.

Eat 35 grams of fiber per day. Include at least three pieces of fruit per day.

Eat more, bulk up. To gain muscle size and strength, Maddalozzo advises following the aforementioned diet, but consuming 15 calories per pound of body weight.

Never skip breakfast. After 8 hours without food, your body will start breaking down muscle for fuel. Keep your metabolism stoked by eating every 3 hours, for a total of four to six small meals a day.

Snack on protein. To keep your muscles goosed, Maddalozzo recommends eating a low-fat protein-rich food at each meal or snack, such as cottage cheese (1 cup, 28 grams of protein), lean steak (3 ounces, 26 grams of protein), chicken breast (3 ounces, 27 grams of protein), turkey breast (3 ounces, 28 grams of protein), tuna (3 ounces, 25 grams of protein), wild salmon (3 ounces, 19 grams of protein), black beans (1 cup, 15 grams of protein), or yogurt (8 ounces, 11 grams of protein).

Drop acid, lift weights. Although researchers at the University of Texas have shown that downing a fortified drink with 6 grams of amino acids before a workout leads to superior muscle-mass gains, Maddalozzo recommends getting protein from natural sources and eating or drinking a combination of proteins and carbs within 60 minutes of finishing your workout. Researchers at Vanderbilt University showed that this speeds muscle recovery. Suitable snacks that nail this combo include a bagel with peanut butter, 12 ounces of low-fat chocolate milk, or an Endurox R4 Recovery Drink. Maddalozzo's preference is a smoothie fortified with 30 grams of whey protein.

these studies indicate, we are just seeing the tip of the research iceberg," says Wolfe. "In the years ahead, we are likely to see the proof of even closer relationships between muscle mass and disease states."

The case against overreliance on cardiovascular fitness—a case striking close to my heart—was made best in a study conducted at East Tennessee State University more than a decade ago. Researchers studied 43 healthy individuals who were 55 or older. Twenty-three of the subjects worked out three times a week for 30 minutes per session, confining their exercise to the treadmill, stair machine, and stationary bike. The other 20 subjects performed 15 minutes of aerobic exercise and devoted the rest of their sessions to training their major muscle groups on weight machines. After 4 months, bone density and lean muscle mass increased significantly in the group combining aerobic and strength training, but it did not improve for the group confined to aerobic activity.

Maddalozzo and I leave the bone lab and stroll across campus. He nods hello to students, whose endocrine systems sluice with testosterone and growth hormone, the juices goosing youthful muscle development. From a modest distance, Maddalozzo, at age 52, might pass as one of them. He carries a well-toned 150 pounds on a 5'9" frame, with just 10 percent body fat.

Despite the sunshine, the professor's

hospitality, and the presence of so many attractive young people, my mood continues to darken. I experience a moment of classic middle-age angst, as if I were approaching a sigmoidoscopy or a periodontal exam. I worry, in short, that I've seen the light too late. My "muscle intervention" threatens to be as penitential as it sounds. According to Wolfe, Kraemer, Chodzko-Zajko, and other experts, resistance training must be conducted at a high intensity, at 70 percent or more of the maximum perceived effort, in order to produce the cellular and metabolic changes that yield stronger, thicker muscles and the resultant health benefits. "A little bit of training—swinging a 5-pound dumbbell around—just won't cut it," says Kraemer. "That's not enough to catalyze growth and engage the systems."

The premise of all strength training is the concept of overload and recovery. Muscle fibers are made up of long strands of protein, and overloading the muscles to the point of failure during weight training causes microtears in myofibrils, the tiny proteins that force the muscle cells to contract. This activates satellite cells located on the outside of the muscle fibers to accumulate at the point where the damage occurs (much in the way that white blood cells gather at the site of skin lacerations). In effect, resistance training triggers an alarm that the muscle is falling apart, and the substance the body uses to fix it—the glue, as it were—is protein.

That's why scientists such as Maddalozzo also emphasize a muscle-friendly diet that

The Busy Man's Workout

The beauty of this workout is its simplicity and speed: It's one set of eight exercises that you can burn through in 30 minutes. Designed by Gianni Maddalozzo, PhD, who has studied muscle for 15 years, the workout is aimed primarily at novices, and the goal is not to get buff or to boost athletic performance (although those aren't bad side effects), but to improve health. The eight exercises should be done twice a week, performing 8 to 15 repetitions to the point of volitional fatigue, which is when you can't do a rep without cheating (by using momentum, for example). Do the entire set at each workout, with 1 minute in between exercises and 1 to 2 days of rest between sessions. Go to BestLife Online.com/muscle for more details.

Squat: Virtually every muscle in the lower body helps at some point during this lift. Squats build a solid foundation in the hips, trunk, legs, and postural stability for almost any task or movement.

Deadlift: The original test of strength: Who could lift the heaviest rock or dead animal? Especially effective for strengthening the lower back, which is key for good posture.

Lunge: Uses all the muscles of the squat, plus the hip flexors. Also good for strengthening the butt and the quads. Do them on the beach to develop extra power.

Stepup: Good burner for the thighs and hips. Boxes should be 12 to 18 inches high, or high enough to create a 90-degree angle at the knee.

Front lat pulldown: Works the latissimus dorsi muscles, which run along the sides of the back. The lats help you reach, pull, and extend, and they play a major role in activities ranging from golf to driving a car.

Dumbbell incline bench press: The classic chest exercise strengthens the pectoral muscles. The bench should not be tilted more than 30 degrees.

Biceps curl: A single-joint exercise for strengthening your guns. The bar should be lifted smoothly with no jerky movements.

Triceps pushdown: Trains the muscles that actually comprise more of your arms than your biceps and are susceptible to atrophy and jiggle. Don't cheat by moving your elbows.

---

will complement—and, to a certain degree, compensate for—the bare-bones, let's-get-through-this strength-training programs that most people are likely to follow. "Unless you eat the right diet, you won't get the best benefit from strength training," says Fred Hahn, a trainer in New York City. "You absolutely must have an adequate intake of protein for your body to adapt to the stress."

In Wolfe's 2006 study in the *American Journal of Clinical Nutrition*, "The Underappreciated Role of Muscle in Health and Disease," he argues that the present recommended daily allowance of protein, 0.36 grams per pound of body weight, was established using obsolete data and is woefully inadequate for an individual doing resistance training. He, along with many

Press Pause for More Muscle

This stop-and-go routine adds resistance throughout your range of motion by interrupting momentum at various power points. By pausing, you recruit more muscle fibers, making each repetition harder. As a result, you'll strengthen weak spots and spur new muscle growth.

Do the pushups and split squats without resting between moves. Rest for 60 seconds, and then repeat the superset. Next, do the dumbbell row and sumo squat as another superset. Perform this workout three times a week.

SUPERSET 1

Stop-and-Go Pushup

Assume a pushup position. Brace your core and lower your chest to the floor. When you're halfway down, pause for 2 seconds before continuing. Then, when your chest is 2 inches from the floor, pause again for 2 seconds before pushing halfway back up. Hold for 2 more seconds, then straighten your arms. Do 8 reps.

others, recommends an amount between 0.8 and 1 gram per pound of body weight. (See "Nourish Your Muscles" on page 155.)

Strength training conforms to all the puritanical dictates that I, along with countless other men my age, spent our youths repudiating: You have to keep track, you have to keep improving, and it hurts. The weight room occupies the basement of a nearby classroom building. The room is clean and airy, with neat rows of machines and free weights, just a few small mirrors, and at this hour, to my relief, no students.

Still, my heart sinks. I have never liked gyms of any description. They all seem like places of confinement, regimentation, and pain. Despite the dawning of a new age of muscle awareness, this still seems true.

To steel myself, I recall some of strength training's well-documented, no-nonsense health benefits: bone density . . . resting energy expenditure . . . protein metabolism . . . blood lipids. The promises we heard about running in the 1970s and '80s we now hear about weight training. In fact, some experts, such as Greg Anderson, an elite

Stop-and-Go Split Squat

Stand with one foot 3 feet forward and hold a barbell across your shoulders. Rise on the ball of your back foot, then bend at the knees. When halfway down, pause for 2 seconds. Pause again when your back knee is just off the floor. Push halfway up, pause again, and return to the starting position. Do 6 reps with each leg.

SUPERSET 2

Stop-and-Go Dumbbell Row

Holding dumbbells, lie facedown on a bench set at 45 degrees. Pull the dumbbells up toward your torso. When your upper arms align with your torso, pause for 2 seconds before continuing, until the dumbbells are at your sides. Hold for two beats, then lower halfway and pause again. Return to the starting position. Do 10 reps.

Stop-and-Go Sumo Squat

Stand holding a barbell across your shoulders, feet wide apart with toes turned out. Bend at the knees to lower your body. Halfway down, pause for 2 seconds before continuing until your thighs are parallel to the floor. Pause for two beats, then press halfway up and pause again before returning to the starting position. Do 10 reps.

trainer in Seattle, maintain that weights and diet are all you need; you don't have to do traditional cardio at all.

Of course, I'm not the only former countercultural desperado who has to be dragged off the running trail and into the weight room. Recognizing that resistance training is less convenient and, by and large, requires more concentration than aerobic training (you can't linger over erotic fantasies as you do while laying down the miles at lunchtime under a canopy of Douglas fir), various researchers are trying to determine rock-bottom minimum workouts for muscle-mass maintenance.

Maddalozzo's strength-training program, which he teaches others and practices himself, is one of these new programs: It's two 30-minute sessions a week, comprising one set of eight full-body, multijoint exercises. (See "The Busy Man's Workout" on page 157.) Each exercise consists of 8 to 15 reps, at 60 to 80 percent of "maximum perceived effort," with the final rep performed to the point of voluntary failure. "I work 60 hours a week, and I have two kids at home," says Maddalozzo. "I don't have the time or interest to spend hours in a gym."

"We'll start with the squat," he says, leading me across the floor to a bare barbell. "That's the fundamental lower-body exercise. You need basic leg strength for your running and also for general functioning, for movements such as getting in and out of a chair."

Getting in and out of a chair? "How much weight?" I ask coolly.

Maddalozzo hesitates. "Before we talk about weight," he says, "let's see a squat with no resistance." I reach for the barbell, but he stops me. "We don't even need that for now. Let's just see you do a squat."

I squat, or at least I give my version of a squat. I begin by pushing out my knees, and then I bend from the waist with my shoulders curled forward. "Not like that," says Maddalozzo. "You need to keep your back flat and your shoulders square, and drop your buttocks." He demonstrates the proper form with striking ease and fluidity.

I try to copy the motion, but I am dealing with decades of scar tissue from a torn ACL,

compensating behavior, avoidance, and, I admit, increasingly active sarcopenia. My shanks have undeniably shrunk.

I try a third time, imagining myself as a baseball catcher crouching behind a batter.

Maddalozzo brightens. "Good," he says. "That's perfect."

It hardly feels perfect. Bands of pain shoot through the decimated muscle fibers of my tight, weak hamstrings. I force myself to squat lower, and in so doing, I briefly lose my balance. I touch the mat to right myself. My quads begin to tremble. A cool breeze combs the room, but I start to sweat. With some gruesome noises from my knee joint, and another bolt of pain, I stand, a lean and sneakered pantaloon, summoning as much dignity as possible.

"I guess I should begin with a pretty modest weight."

Maddalozzo gives an encouraging smile. "Just by repeating the proper motion a couple of times, you're starting to redirect your neural pathways," he says. "You're on your way. Let's go try some lunges."

Don't Waste Your Time

If you belong to a gym, it's likely that most of what you're doing there is nearly useless—and might be ruining your chances of getting fit. Here's a no-nonsense look at the often nonsensical world of fitness clubs

A state-of-the-art health club recently opened in Rochester, Minnesota, where I live. A gleaming cathedral of exercise, it cost $22 million to build and features an expansive climate-controlled fitness floor beneath three-story ceilings and a soaring wall of windows. Like most American health clubs—a $17.6 billion industry made up of more than 29,000 clubs and 42.7 million members—the facility reserved its nerve center to house its greatest treasure: hundreds of futuristic and impossibly sleek cardio- and strength-training machines. Walking these aisles is like entering the showroom of a Mercedes-Benz dealership.

You can't help but touch the things, to rub their cool slate-gray exteriors and to squeeze their padding. The mechanical housing has become more unisex, the digital readouts more technical, and the end result is an impressive ability to make you forget that this is the same basic collection of machines that have anchored the floors of health clubs for almost four decades. There are leg-extension, leg-press, leg-curl, and upper-body workstations in the aisles for building muscle, and treadmills, elliptical trainers, and stationary cycles in the aisles for developing cardio fitness.

On a recent afternoon, it thrummed with activity: Men and women logged obedient noiseless reps on a range of machines; runners banged out the miles on treadmills; and one gal raced away on an elliptical machine, legs neither running nor swinging, but doing something inexplicable in a feverish Road Runner–like blur. It's a vision of exercise utopia that is mirrored in gyms across the country. Except that a growing chorus of critics find fault with it: The man jackknifed into the leg-extension machine could be risking knee injury; the exercisers slaving away on other stationary machines are building individual muscles in place of whole-body strength; the people slogging away on the treadmills with their eyes glued to TV screens seem like automatons.

No wonder the attrition rate for gym members hovers at 35 percent a year, according to the International Health, Racquet & Sportsclub Association (IHRSA), and the latest estimates show that almost half of exercisers give up on a new routine

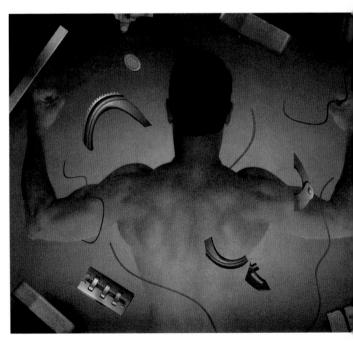

Functional Training 101

Use these online resources to keep up with the latest workouts, find local training communities, and score the best gear.

The Functional Path Training Blog, functionalpath training.typepad.com: A lively portal to conversations about smarter ways of training from Vern Gambetta, the godfather of functional fitness and the author of *Athletic Development: The Art & Science of Functional Sports Conditioning.*

The Male Pattern Fitness Blog, malepatternfitness. com: Lou Schuler, author of *The New Rules of Lifting*, provides incisive commentary on the latest research, science, trends, and culture from the fitness world.

CrossFit, crossfit.com: CrossFit, a back-to-basics workout approach, posts different full-body workouts every day, with video to boot. Ideally, you want to do Cross-Fit's fun and grueling workouts in classes with other members and a trainer, and this site can direct you to the nearest gym.

Exuberant Animal, exuberantanimal.com: The silly name belies one of the most cutting-edge training philosophies around. Seattle-based trainer Frank Forencich offers dozens of play-based exercises, which are growing in popularity.

Perform Better, perform better.com: Find essential training gear you will not find easily at most gyms, including kettlebells, medicine balls, resistance bands, squat stands, climbing ropes, chinup stations, and jump ropes—all at reasonable prices.

Beacon Athletics, beaconathletics.com: Pick up the best agility training gear and educational materials, as developed by fitness instructor Steve Myrland, former conditioning coach for the San Jose Sharks.

within a year. It seems fair to ask whether health clubs are partially responsible for the obesity epidemic, a trend that has followed the rise of the industry. Perhaps the first development has not been caused by the second, but it certainly hasn't been helped either. With all the fancy equipment and with all the desire out there to look good, why can't we keep the weight off? Why can't we stick to our gym workouts? Is it our fault? Or does the fault lie elsewhere?

"The health-club culture tries to create a dependency on machines," says Vern Gambetta, a trainer with 38 years of experience training professional and recreational athletes, and the author of *Athletic Development: The Art & Science of Functional Sports Conditioning.* "If you have a limited amount of time to work out, you're better off ditching the machine to do different kinds of body-weight and whole-body exercises. You'll get more caloric burn for your time spent." Critics also charge that a traditional machine-centric regimen has other downsides. In general, it relies excessively on the discipline of the exerciser, it promotes training muscles in isolation (as opposed to how muscles really work, in a chain of movement), and it can stress vulnerable joints more than is necessary. At issue is not

The 10 Machines You Must Avoid

Defenders of stationary equipment argue that machines are designed to limit what you can do wrong. But seated machines often put heavier loads on the back and joints than is necessary, and they almost always miss the mark when it comes to replicating the movements found in everyday life, according to the book *Ultimate Back Fitness and Performance*, by Stuart McGill, PhD, a professor of spine biomechanics at the University of Waterloo, in Ontario. For this list of exercises, we consulted McGill; Nicholas DiNubile, MD, author of *FrameWork: Your 7-Step Program for Healthy Muscles, Bones, and Joints*; and trainer Vern Gambetta, author of *Athletic Development: The Art & Science of Functional Sports Conditioning.*

Seated Leg Extension

What it's supposed to do: Train the quadriceps

What it actually does: It strengthens a motion your legs aren't actually designed to do, and can put undue strain on the ligaments and tendons surrounding the kneecaps.

A better exercise: One-legged body-weight squats. Lift one leg up and bend the opposite knee, dipping as far as you can, with control, while flexing at the hip, knee, and ankle. Use a rail for support until you develop requisite leg strength and balance. Aim for 5 to 10 reps on each leg. (If you are susceptible to knee pain, do the Bulgarian split squat instead, resting the top of one foot on a bench positioned 2 to 3 feet behind you. Descend until your thigh is parallel to the ground and then stand back up. Do 5 to 10 reps per leg.)

Seated Military Press

What it's supposed to do: Train shoulders and triceps

What it actually does: Overhead pressing can put shoulder joints in vulnerable biomechanical positions. It puts

only the very meat and potatoes of how you work out, but also the best way to get the most out of your time at the gym.

There is potential for pain in any workout. The key to preventing injury is to find your weak links and then modify your exercise to fortify your weak links, while also not putting stress on them, says Nicholas DiNubile, MD, an orthopedic surgeon specializing in sports medicine and the author of *FrameWork: Your 7-Step Program for Healthy Muscles, Bones, and Joints.* The three most common strength-training-related injuries Dr. DiNubile sees are rotator-cuff problems, knee issues, and lower-back pain. While these are not exclusive to machine-based training, the nonfunctional movements that some machines require, undue stress on the shoulders, and the movement doesn't let you use your hips to assist your shoulders, which is the natural way to push something overhead.

A better exercise: Medicine-ball throws. Stand 3 feet from a concrete wall; bounce a rubber medicine ball off a spot on the wall 4 feet above your head, squatting to catch the ball and rising to throw it upward in one continuous motion. Aim for 15 to 20 reps. Alternative: Standing alternate dumbbell presses. As you push the right dumbbell overhead, shift the right hip forward. Switch to the left side.

Seated Lat Pull-Down (Behind the Neck)

What it's supposed to do: Train lats, upper back, and biceps

What it actually does: Unless you have very flexible shoulders, it's difficult to do correctly, so it can cause pinching in the shoulder joint and damage the rotator cuff.

A better exercise: Incline pullups. Place a bar in the squat rack at waist height, grab the bar with both hands, and hang from the bar with your feet stretched out in front of you. Keep your torso stiff, and pull your chest to the bar 10 to 15 times. To make it harder, lower the bar; to make it easier, raise the bar.

Seated Pec Deck

What it's supposed to do: Train chest and shoulders

What it actually does: It can put the shoulder in an unstable position and place excessive stress on the shoulder joint and its connective tissue.

A better exercise: Incline pushups. Aim for 15 to 20 reps. If this is too easy, progress to regular pushups and plyometric pushups (where you push up with enough force that your hands come off the ground), and aim for 5 to 8 reps.

(continued)

coupled with heavy loads and less-than-perfect form, can cause problems—especially in men over 40 whose joints are getting creaky—and are not especially meaningful.

Researchers, for instance, have known that the leg-extension machine (the unit in which you sit with your shin behind a padded bar attached to a weight stack and then straighten your leg in front of you) trains you to do just one thing: become very strong at the leg-extension machine. In one of the few studies on this subject, researchers from the University of Kentucky studied 23 patients with knee pain to see what made them stronger: a stepup test or doing leg extensions. While they found that both groups eventually became stronger at doing

Seated Hip Abductor Machine

What it's supposed to do: Train outer thighs

What it actually does: Because you are seated, it trains a movement that has no functional use. If done with excessive weight and jerky technique, it can put undue pressure on the spine.

A better exercise: Place a heavy, short, looped resistance band around your legs (at your ankles); sidestep out 20 paces and back with control. This is much harder than it sounds.

Seated Rotation Machine

What it's supposed to do: Train abdominals and obliques

What it actually does: Because the pelvis doesn't move with the chest, this exercise can put excessive twisting forces on the spine.

A better exercise: Do the cable woodchopper, letting your heels turn freely with your torso. Aim for 10 to 12 reps.

Seated Leg Press

What it's supposed to do: Train quadriceps, glutes, and hamstrings

What it actually does: It often forces the spine to flex without engaging any of the necessary stabilization muscles of the hips, glutes, shoulders, and lower back.

A better exercise: Body-weight squats. Focus on descending with control as far as you can without rounding your lower back. Aim for 15 to 20 for a set and increase sets as you develop strength.

leg extensions, only the group doing the stepup test actually became stronger at stepping up and doing functional activities. The reason: The seated leg-extension machine has nothing to do with how we use our legs, which are meant to hold us upright against gravity while we walk, climb, or descend.

In fact, Chris Powers, a biokinesiology researcher at the University of Southern California, determined that although the thighbone rotates under the kneecap as we walk, using a leg-extension machine actually causes the kneecap to rotate on the thighbone. The mechanics of the leg-extension machine simply doesn't simulate what happens in functional activity (such as walking, running, or going down steps). "The leg-extension machine puts a lot of

Squats Using Smith Machine

What it's supposed to do: Train chest, biceps, and legs

What it actually does: The alignment of the machine—the bar is attached to a vertical sliding track—makes for linear, not natural, arched movements. This puts stress on the knees, shoulders, and lower back.

A better exercise: Bodyweight squats. See "Seated Leg Press."

Roman Chair Back Extension

What it's supposed to do: Train spinal erectors

What it actually does: Repeatedly flexing the back while it's supporting weight places pressure on the spine and increases the risk of damaging your disks.

A better exercise: The bird-dog. Crouch on all fours, extend your right arm forward, and extend your left leg backward. Do 10 seven-second reps, and then switch to the opposite side.

Roman Chair Situp

What it's supposed to do: Train abdominals and hip flexors

What it actually does: The crunching motion can put undue stress on the lower back when it is in a vulnerable rounded position.

A better exercise: The plank. Lie facedown on the floor. Prop up on your forearms, palms down. Rise up on your toes. Keep your back flat and contract your glutes, abdominals, and lats to keep your butt from sticking up. Hold this pose for 20 to 60 seconds.

strain on the knee ligaments and the patella," says Tim Hewett, PhD, a professor in the departments of biomedical engineering and pediatrics at the University of Cincinnati. "I would never consider letting our athletes use a leg-extension machine."

Paul Juris, EdD, executive director of the Cybex Institute, the research and education arm of the leading stationary-equipment manufacturer, says "maybe" to the criticism that leg-extension machines impose pressure on the knee, but adds that shear forces exist in a host of exercises, such as lunges and squats. "On the leg-extension machine," he says, "I can mitigate those forces by moving the pad higher up the shin, raising the weight, and then using only the top 15

(continued on page 170)

The Freethinker's Workout

Build all-body strength, develop true fitness, and improve your coordination with this functional workout that will make you feel—and look—better than ever.

Designed to bypass the parts of your gym that promote passivity and stagnation, this ground-based workout—created by athletic-development coach Vern Gambetta, a leading voice in the functional-fitness movement with 38 years of experience—will keep you on your toes, both figuratively and literally. Gambetta, the

former director of athletic development for the New York Mets, as well as the former conditioning consultant for the U.S. soccer team, says that newcomers to functional training are often surprised at the demands of a complete body-weight workout. Try this 60-minute workout three times a week. Start out with humility and focus on developing greater control over your body weight. Then crank up the speed. Warm up for each session by jumping rope or dribbling a basketball for 5 minutes.

Part 1
Build leg strength and total body conditioning with aerobic intervals.

On a running track (or on a treadmill, if need be), run easy for 30 seconds, then harder (at 70 percent effort) for 30 seconds. Keep changing your pace up and down for 15 minutes.

Alternate days: 20-minute reverse pyramid interval session.

Using a heart monitor, start with 3 minutes at 70 percent effort, followed by 3 minutes at an easy pace. Repeat for 2 min-utes at 70 percent effort, followed by 2 minutes easy. Finish with 10 minutes at a steady rate of your choosing.

Part 2
Sharpen coordination and stabilize joints with agility and mobility drills.

Body-weight lunge and reach: Step forward into a lunge while reaching your arms overhead. Then step back and repeat three to six times, alternating legs. Next, do the same laterally, so that you face forward but your center of gravity shifts as far to each side as possible.

Shuffle run: On an empty basketball court or aerobics floor, shuffle laterally the length of the floor and back.

Carioca run: Do the shuffle run, but alternate steps over and under your leading leg.

Zigzag run: Taking three steps to the right and then to the left, work your way down the length of the court. Return to the starting line treading in the same pattern, but run backward like an NFL cornerback.

Lateral bounding and hopping: Pick a sideline and hop on one leg for one-quarter of the court, then switch to your other leg for another quarter of the court, then hop on both legs for a quarter. Return the same way, but move backward.

Touchdown running drill: Run 5 yards, then 10 yards, then 15 yards, and then 20 yards (or one-quarter, half, three-quarters, and the full length of a basketball court). Each time you reach an end point, crouch, touch the ground, and then return to the baseline, crouch, and touch the ground.

Railing step-over, step-under: Find a railing that's waist high and step over it carefully, lifting one leg at a time. Turn, pivot at the hips, and then dip under to go back to where you started. Aim to do a total of 10, or as many as you can do with good form.

Part 3

Build functional upper-body strength with pushing and pulling exercises.

Incline pushups: Place a bar in the squat rack at waist height, grip the bar, and do three sets of 20 pushups. If this is too easy, lower the bar or do regular pushups on the ground. If that's too easy, raise your legs or put them on a Swiss ball.

Incline pullups: Place a bar in the squat rack at chest height or lower, hang from both arms with your feet in front of you, and do three sets of 20 pullups. As the work gets easier, lower the bar.

Chinups: Do three sets of 5 to 10 reps. If this is too hard, lower the bar and let your feet rest on the floor behind you until you build up your strength.

Overhead medicine-ball throws: Stand 3 feet from a concrete wall, hold a rubber medicine ball overhead, and bounce it off the wall in rapid succession for 15 to 20 repetitions.

Medicine-ball chest passes: With a partner, play catch with a medicine ball by pushing it with two hands from your chest. If you have no partner, bounce a rubber medicine ball off a concrete wall from about 3 feet away. Alternative: Chest pass the ball from one end of an open basketball court, chase it down, and throw it toward the other end, never letting it reach the opposite wall. Do 15 to 20 repetitions.

Part 4

Increase athleticism and leg strength with stepping and squatting drills.

Platform stepdowns: Stand on a 12-inch box (or higher), step down with one leg to touch only your toe to the floor, then step back up. This is about descending with control. Do 20 stepdowns for each leg.

Body-weight lunges: Do three sets of 20.

Body-weight squats: Do three sets of 20. Go as low as you can with good balance to build body control.

Dumbbell squats: Hold dumbbells hammer-style on each shoulder, dip to chair-seat height, and return to the starting position. Do three sets of 10.

Lateral resistance-band walk: Place a heavy, short, looped resistance band around your ankles. Step sideways for half the length of a basketball court, and then back again.

percent of the machine's range of motion." It's a thoughtful response, but it undercuts the primary selling point of machine-based training, which is that using a machine is always safer than other forms of training. When it comes to promoting strength that is not meaningful, the leg-extension machine is one of many. See "The 10 Machines You Must Avoid" on pages 164–167 for others.

The leg press is equally disconnected from the reality of human anatomy. Doubters can Google the sight of 77-year-old televangelist Pat Robertson leg pressing what he claims to be half a ton, while former secretary of state Madeline Albright, who is 70, has stated that she is good for up to 400 pounds on a leg-press machine. Either these two septuagenarians are as strong as linebackers or something's wrong here.

"There are no motor-control requirements on a leg-press machine," explains Stuart McGill, PhD, professor of spine biomechanics at the University of Waterloo, in Ontario. "You just push. In real-life tasks, you have to balance on one leg, you have to sidestep, and you have to get all the muscles to coordinate together. These are very different patterns." Machines such as the leg press and the leg extension give off a faulty assumption that muscles are to be strengthened one at a time—in isolation—rather than in the ever-changing alliances in which they must actually produce and reduce force in real life. According to Cybex's Juris, we need to isolate muscles to get at hidden weaknesses, that, thanks to our body's desire to protect its weakest link, we won't otherwise find.

"If you have a weakness in a particular portion of your musculature, the body will compensate to protect that weakness," says Juris. "The only way you can target that weakness is by isolating a joint." Critics see the targeting of isolated muscle weakness as hubris, plain and simple. "How are you going to isolate every one of those weak areas anyway?" asks Gambetta. "That's a reductionist view of the body. I take a holistic view of the body." Gambetta calls "compensation for weakness" the beauty of the body. "The body is not a machine," he says. "The body is smart."

Many critics also say that health clubs perpetuate the false divide between strength and cardio. "This dichotomy is artificial," says Gambetta. His argument is based on the perceived importance of VO2 max, the term for your maximum oxygen absorption potential and the holy grail of most sessions spent on a treadmill, stairclimber, rower, stationary cycle, or elliptical trainer. "VO2 max is a popular yardstick for health because it is measurable," says Gambetta, "but it is just one of many factors related to endurance performance." If it's the steady elevation of heart rate you're after, any strength program based on whole-body movements will have your heart rate elevated as readily as the most popular elliptical trainer. It's hard to understand how we came to the point where a healthy person with two good knees can find himself stepping off an elliptical trainer and climbing onto a commercial-grade Total Gym, a newly marketed device otherwise known as a gravity machine. Aren't we all living on a gravity machine?

When he passed away on August 28, at the age of 80, Arthur Jones died having accomplished nothing less than fundamentally rewriting the way we exercise. In the late 1960s, Jones designed the multistation Blue Monster (later renamed the Nautilus), the first user-friendly strength-training machine. His invention "led to the 'machine environment' that is prevalent today in health clubs," according to his obituary in the *New York Times*. The consensus within the health-club industry was that Jones's legacy was for the better, both for the physical health of Americans and for the financial health of modern health clubs. Joe Moore, president of IHRSA, says, "Many of the innovations he came up with in the 1970s are still incorporated into strength training on machines of all brands." Nautilus vice president of product development Greg Webb said in the *New York Times*, "The idea of a health club changed. It became big business. Arthur Jones started that."

If that is the case, it might trouble some to know that our machinery-based approach to fitness, far from having been distilled through years of careful academic study of biomechanics, was in fact set in motion by a ninth-grade dropout and amateur anatomist

who carried a Colt .45, rode the rails, imported and hunted exotic animals, married six different women who were between the ages 16 and 20 when they married him, and "lived on a diet of cigarettes, chocolate, scrambled eggs, and coffee," according to the *New York Times*. There's no doubt that Jones's invention brought resistance training to the masses, but his claim that he created a "thinking man's barbell" is more marketing than truth. In fact, most strength machines are designed for bodybuilding and require relatively little expertise for either the user or the trainer, and therein lies both their appeal and their flaw.

If you are a bodybuilder—that is, if you have strength trained for years and dieted so rigorously that your body-fat percentage is in the single digits—then it potentially makes sense to train individual muscles in isolation. The other case in which machine-based training makes sense is in rehab, when the body has become so disabled that it must be rebuilt brick by brick. But most of us are neither crippled nor on the verge of entering the Mr. Olympia competition, so why do we train as if either is the case? The answer is a combination of the gyms' desire to maximize profits and our own desire to find workouts that don't involve work.

"The club owners bought into what the equipment industry told us," says Michael Scott Scudder, a former club owner and a leading consultant to the industry since 1991. And what the equipment makers ultimately told the gym owners was that if you stocked enough machines, you could do without as much one-on-one attention from trainers. "I don't think fitness happens best in isolation," says Steve Myrland, manager of Myrland Sports Training and a former strength coach for the University of Wisconsin and the San Jose Sharks. Various studies back this up, showing that people who exercise in groups

maintain greater motivation to train than those who work out alone. "This is hard stuff, and it's a lot easier to share hard stuff than do it yourself. At the clubs, you are going to be turned loose on the machines, and a machine is like an isolation booth."

The desire to retain customers also has led to a modern gym environment that some critics believe sends mixed messages. "The problem with our gyms is that they misrepresent the fact that you are fundamentally there to do work," says Jack Berryman, PhD, a professor of medical history at the University of Washington and a historian for the American College of Sports Medicine. "The modern gym is a techno holiday with gadgets and lights. They're trying to entertain people." And this can be detrimental to exercisers who are trying to stick with their workouts. Performance psychologist Jim Loehr, EdD, author of *The Power of Story* and chairman and CEO of the Human Performance Institute, in Orlando, Florida, advises busy corporate executives on how to become more successful at sustaining their commitment to fitness. He has found that a primary component for making exercise sustainable is to stop tuning out during workouts. "We don't want you disengaged while you are working out," he says. "We tell ourselves that exercise is so painful that the only thing you can do to get through it is to watch TV. Watching television and working out is a form of multitasking. To me, however, real value lies in paying attention. It is an engagement practice, it gets your mind off work, and it aligns what you're doing with what you're thinking."

Perhaps the best evidence against traditional health clubs is that these days most elite athletes rarely step foot in one. They work out in environments designed for functional training. Evolving on the sidelines of the fitness industry for the last decade or so, functional training, or FT, has become the buzzword within the fitness industry, and many observers feel that it can cure some of the ailments plaguing health clubs.

An FT approach to fitness stresses the training of movements over muscles, the irrelevance of strength without mobility, the neurological foundation to strength and athleticism, and the use of simple tools to gain complex results. The main purpose of FT is to bridge the gap between absolute strength and functional strength, to achieve peak performance, and to prevent injuries, says Gambetta, one of FT's early proponents. In general, FT discourages the use of machines in favor of free weights, body-weight exercises, and certain devices used in physical therapy, such as medicine balls, Swiss balls, wobble boards, and resistance bands.

The proliferation of FT-based approaches has touched various sports and all levels of athletes. For instance, there's Bill Knowles, director of iSport Training, in Vermont, who has trained various Olympic athletes, and Greg Roskopf, founder of Muscle Activation Techniques, who has worked as a biomechanical consultant for the Denver Broncos, the Denver Nuggets, and the Utah Jazz.

Core-training gurus such as Paul Chek and Mark Verstegen have built up extensive client lists with athletes from all the major professional sports. Boutique FT clubs are cropping up all over the country, such as Conrad's Body Tribe, in Sacramento, California; Exuberant Animal, in Seattle; and Myrland's Morning Movement Mayhem, in Madison, Wisconsin. In 2001, Gregg Glassman founded CrossFit, a back-to-basics functional-training program that's popular with the military and law enforcement; it now has close to 200 affiliates, with outposts in almost every state.

HARD TRUTH

Most pushups ever performed in 1 hour

3,416

Health clubs themselves are also adapting. "Most IHRSA clubs can now offer functional training," says Moore, but you will have to seek it out. "Aerobics areas often have smaller classes that utilize free weights, dumbbells, and different types of balance mechanisms." While men have traditionally avoided large classes, more and more are participating in small group exercises, says Richard Cotton, the American College of Sports Medicine national director of certification. "There's a trend of groups of two or three signing up for a session together," he says, "especially if they are transferring from a machine-based regimen to a functional-training approach, because learning the proper form is essential. Some guys worry that they'll lose bulk, but that's a misperception. You can still make strength and mass gains, and the advantage is that your body will be in better balance."

Michael Rogers, a professor of human performance at Wichita State University who has studied functional training in older adults, concurs: "Many young men strength train purely for appearance," he says, "while older men are looking for exercises that will improve function in their daily lives, whether it's a golfer strengthening his swing with a resistance band or a triathlete training his core on a stability ball. They realize it's more meaningful to work out to enhance an aspect of your life." In recent years, manufacturers such as FreeMotion and Hammer Strength Ground Base have built cable-based strength machines and special functional machines to build whole-body strength. Many allow ground-based training that does not conform to a factory-set plane of movement. In fact, my gym has some of these new machines, and a lot of health clubs have them, so there are some good choices to be made in many gyms if you know what to look for. But the essence of training smarter doesn't require a high-end piece of gear, but rather the ability to absorb

PAINkiller

I have patellofemoral pain syndrome. Is a knee brace enough?

"No, it's not. You need to strengthen your quads and glutes, which control thigh rotation and, thus, knee alignment. Single-leg squats are great for this, assuming you can do them with good form," says Michael Fredericson, MD, an associate professor in the department of orthopedic surgery, division of physical medicine and rehabilitation, at Stanford University.

a small set of principles. Gambetta, who created the Freethinker's Workout, recommends using these guidelines to make the best decisions in the gym.

Train on your feet. Sitting is an unnatural body position for strenuous work. Once you sit, you lose your body's natural anchor: the muscles of the back, butt, abdominal core, and legs. Ground-based training immediately puts an end to a host of outdated stationary-machine and free-weight lifts, including the bench press, military press, incline press, and chest press, and leg extensions, leg presses, leg curls, preacher curls, and so on. You'll find that staying on your feet keeps your heart rate up, requires you to think creatively, and keeps your workout moving along efficiently. You're either exercising or walking it off. That keeps your awareness up and boredom down.

Vary your pace. Stationary running or cycling can become a semiconscious plod, anesthetized by television. Structuring tempo builds aerobic capacity, burns calories more efficiently, builds strength, and helps develop the ability to absorb force while in motion. Tempo changes do not have to be intense, only clearly drawn, whether you alternate 30-second efforts or do an "inverted pyramid" of descending durations of effort. Mentally, varying your tempo makes the time go by faster as well. With alternating durations of effort, you are pushing, recovering, or holding steady, and never simply tuning out.

Train movements, not muscles. The five basic movements to develop in any exercise session are limited to different forms of stepping, pushing, pulling, squatting, and rotating. There's no need to do one exercise for your biceps, another for your shoulders, and another for your chest. Two good pushing drills take care of them all. Instead of targeting the upper back and then the lower back, simply pull (in the form of pullups or incline pullups) and bridge (holding your torso stiff to build strength in your back). For the lower body, lunge, stepdown, and squat drills are all it takes, and body weight alone is usually more than enough load.

Train for the four elements: stopping, slowing, descending/ascending, and catching. Many gyms don't value the reduction of force—the catching of a ball, landing from a stepdown, or changing direction—because there's no easy way to measure it. Yet stopping, descending, and absorbing momentum are far more valuable for joint safety than any isolated strength-building exercise is. This means not only throwing a medicine ball but also catching each return throw or rebound. It means stepping downward on one leg, running downhill, developing footwork agility, and squatting or lunging with control.

Prepare to use the distant corners of your gym. Because gyms are not often set up for clients who move their bodies across space or in multiple directions, who toss weighted balls, or who need to do drills that require stopping and starting quickly, a more athletically based use of your health club will often require taking over its less popu-

lated areas. Empty basketball courts, aerobics classrooms, and other open areas are necessary in order to train dynamically indoors, so get used to feeling like a pioneer on the prairie.

While Gambetta's workout can be done in any commercial gym, some exercisers are looking for salvation outside the proverbial box. To build Revolution Defense and Fitness, a small commercial gym tucked away in a light industry business park in suburban Minneapolis, Damian Hirtz spent about as much on gear as the typical health club spends on its pec deck. Hirtz's low-tech fitness center is an affiliate of CrossFit and has a climbing rope, kettlebells, medicine balls, jump ropes, a set of heavy bags, a set of big plates, and a chinup station made from galvanized pipe he admits he bought in the plumbing aisle at Home Depot. That's about it. No machines, no mirrors, no benches.

It's not that he's cheap. It's just that it's hard to break the bank when you've intentionally turned your back on the vast majority of gear that adorns the floor of the typical gym. "Why do I want distractions?" says the 33-year-old father of two boys, ages 6 and 13. "My clients want a workout that's fast and efficient." One of those clients is Brian, a 36-year-old mechanic, who is currently banging out the 30 pullups required

Percentage more force produced doing squats with your feet flat on the floor instead of on an unstable surface

54

for today's "Dirty 30" workout, a timed set of 30 box jumps, walking lunges, kettlebell swings, medicine-ball wall throws, and other full-body exercises scrawled on a marker board. Hirtz allows Brian, and the other guys and one woman in attendance, to do the chinups with resistance bands to help them get over the bar. Or they get themselves up by swinging their torsos. Or they break up their work into smaller sets. Pulling is pulling.

All that's required is that they do today's workout together and mark their workout time when they're done. "You compete only against yourself," says Hirtz, "but you might work a little faster if you notice the guy next to you is working harder than you are." Joining us for today's effort are a 36-year-old bariatric surgeon named Chuck, a 33-year-old insurance underwriter named Mark, a 57-year-old musician named George, and a 36-year-old trainer named Gina. They share little in common other than no one looks overly fed or overly built. To a man (and one woman), they look lean and all-around strong. "Put them in any sport," says Hirtz, "and they can hang."

Build Big Power

Y ou'll use the same pair of dumbbells for each exercise in this routine. Choose a
weight that just barely allows you to do 12 biceps curls. If it's too light, you won't
build as much muscle, says Houston-based trainer Carter Hays, CSCS.

Too heavy and your form will break down first, your ligaments later. Proceed in circuit
fashion, moving from one exercise to the next without rest. At the end of the circuit, rest for
60 seconds. Repeat for a total of four rounds.

Dumbbell Front Squat with Arnold Press:

Hold a pair of
dumbbells in front of your chest with
your palms in. Bend at the hips and
knees to lower yourself until your
thighs are parallel to the floor. Stand
and press the weights overhead,
rotating your wrists so that your palms
face forward. Lower the dumbbells in
front of your chest so your palms face
you again. Do 12 reps.

Swiss-Ball Bent-Arm Pullover with Chest Press:

Lie with your
head and upper back on a Swiss ball
and raise your hips so your body forms
a straight line from your knees to your
shoulders. Hold the weights along the
sides of your chest with your palms
toward each other. Press the weights
up, then lower them halfway down.
Keeping the same bend in your elbows,
slowly lower the dumbbells behind
your head until they touch the ball.
Reverse until the weights are back over
your chest, press them up, and lower
them to the starting position. Do 12
reps.

Dumbbell Lunge with Biceps Curl:

Stand holding a pair of
dumbbells at arm's length at your sides.
Step forward with your left foot until
your right knee is an inch or two off
the floor and your left thigh is parallel
to the floor. Then do a biceps curl.
Push back up to the starting position
and repeat, this time stepping out with
your right foot. That's one rep. Once
you've completed 12 curls, place the
weights on the floor and continue
lunging for 12 more repetitions.

Double Your Strength

Ready to start building a stronger body? It won't take you long. Just three 15-minute weight workouts a week can double a novice weight lifter's strength, report scientists at the University of Kansas. What's more, unlike the average newbie, who quits a new weight-lifting program within a month, 96 percent of the study participants easily fit their quickie workouts into their lives during the 6 months of research. So follow their lead by using the "15-Minute Workouts" throughout this book. You'll increase strength, boost energy, and burn fat.

Schedule a Rest Week

You'll gain more strength by scaling back your lifting routine 1 week each month, report Canadian researchers. In the 3-month study, men who halved their training volume the final week of each month boosted their strength by 29 percent. Regularly planned rest periods are necessary for muscle healing and growth,

because they allow your muscles and nervous system to recover, says study author Robert Kell, PhD. He suggests that on the light-workout week, you cut your normal training volume for each exercise in half.

Count Down to Bulk Up

You know building muscle takes time. But how long? About 3 weeks, according to U.K. researchers. In a study, the scientists determined that visible muscle growth occurs after just 20 days of heavy weight training. In fact, the researchers found that by doing four sets of 7 reps of leg extensions 3 days a week, the lifters increased quadriceps muscle size by about 0.2 percent a day. Even though this growth isn't noticeable from day to day, the effect can be dramatic if you work all your major muscle groups 3 days a week, 52 weeks a year. In the past year, have you trained your entire body 156 times?

Fuel Up to Look Great

In a study, 17 men drank two protein shakes a day—either immediately before and after their workouts, or at least 5 hours outside of their training sessions. After 10 weeks, the researchers noticed a stark contrast: Men who sandwiched their workouts with protein built nearly twice as much muscle as those who didn't. "Your body uses nutrients to build muscle most effectively in the hour on either side of your workout," says Alan Hayes, PhD.

Boost Your Bench

How much did your bench press increase last year? Don't settle for satisfactory progress, even if you think your strength has peaked. In a study, Australian researchers found that even experienced lifters can boost their bench presses by 64 pounds in 4 years. Consider this a long-term goal for yourself. Break it down to a manageable 16 pounds a year and start chipping away with our strength-building workouts.

Get a Harder Core

Want a harder core? Then try a harder exercise. Canadian researchers determined that your abs work nearly twice as hard when you do a plank on a Swiss ball instead of on the floor. To perform a plank, get into pushup position but place your forearms on the floor or Swiss ball, then contract your abs and hold. One caveat: "Unless you can hold a plank for 30 seconds,

you shouldn't attempt the Swiss-ball version," says Micheal Clark, DPT, National Academy of Sports Medicine president. That's because trying the advanced exercise before you're ready could strain your back. Pass the test? Do three to five 10-second ball planks, resting on your knees for two beats between sets.

Know the Whey to Bulk Up

A blend of two types of protein builds more muscle than just one. In a study, researchers at Baylor University asked men to lift weights, then down either a whey-protein shake or a beverage containing both whey and casein protein. After 10 weeks, those who had the combo drink packed on about 5 pounds more muscle than those who had only whey. Call it a dual-action effect. Whey is absorbed quickly, so it feeds your muscles immediately; casein is more slowly digested, allowing it to

provide muscle-building nutrients for a longer period of time, says study author Chad Kerksick, PhD, a sports-nutrition researcher at the University of Oklahoma. We like PM Protein ($30, gnc.com) and Nitrean ($40, atlargenutrition.com).

Splurge on a Starbucks

Talk about a pick-me-up: A small study in the *Journal of Pain* found that 2 cups of coffee may cut postworkout muscle soreness. Researchers asked nine people who didn't usually drink caffeinated beverages or strength train to do 64 leg extensions. The subjects repeated the workout 1 and 2 days later, but this time took either a pill containing caffeine (equal to 2 cups of coffee) or a placebo. Caffeine takers reported

48 percent less pain the next day. Caffeine appears to block brain receptors for adenosine, the chemical that causes muscle soreness, says study author Victor Maridakis. Aching? Try 2 cups of coffee an hour before the gym.

For Strength, Take D

Wake Forest University researchers discovered that vitamin D may be the key to lasting strength, speed, and balance. In a study of 976 older people, those with the lowest blood levels of the vitamin were 10 percent weaker, slower, and wobblier than those with the highest levels. Vitamin D promotes calcium absorption, which is needed to build muscle, says study author Denise Houston, PhD. Unfortunately, milk—a top source—contains just 100 international units (IU) of vitamin D per 1-cup serving, and most other foods provide far less. Harvard University researchers say most people need 1,000 IU a day. So for an optimal dose, try Carlson's vitamin D ($13 for 250 1,000-IU soft gels, carlsonlabs.com).

Training Tips

How can I be more productive in the gym?

Time your rest intervals. By carefully monitoring rest periods between sets, you can accomplish in 30 minutes what used to take an hour. What's more, your levels of muscle-building hormones will soar throughout your workout. This increases size and attacks your body's fat stores. Try resting for 30 to 45 seconds between sets if your primary goal is endurance; 60 to 90 seconds for muscle growth; and 2 to 3 minutes for serious strength gains.

This guy at the gym won't shut up. How can I get him to leave me alone?

Did you try, you know, telling him? You don't have to be rude, just honest. "Let the person know that you would like to talk but you have to focus on your workout," says Michael Carrera, MSc, a trainer and coauthor of *Periodization Training for Sports*. If he keeps flapping his trap, slip on headphones (the international sign for "leave me alone") and wear weight-lifting gloves (the subconscious sign for "back off"). Sounds weird, but "when the palms are covered, our primal instincts kick in to tell us that the person could be holding a weapon," says Patti Wood, MA, a body-language expert. If nothing else, the gloves will give you a better grip when you strangle the guy.

Is a super-slow lift more effective than a normal one?

"Little or no science supports super-slow lifting as more effective than training at a normal tempo. Used occasionally, however, such variations can effectively add novelty to your workout program," says David Pearson, PhD, a professor of exercise physiology and director of the strength research lab at Ball State University.

How do I know when it's time to add weight?

Make sure you can perform all your repetitions with your current weight for two consecutive workouts. Example: When you reach the upper limit of your repetition range with, say, 200 pounds—12 reps, maybe, if you're lifting to pack on size— make sure you perform 12 reps with 200 pounds during your next workout before adding more. And always add weight gradually: about 5 percent for each new step.

How do I know when I'm doing an exercise correctly?

There are a few easy ways to tell whether you're doing an exercise the right way. First ask yourself: Are you feeling it in the right place? Does the exercise in question result in fatigue to the targeted muscle groups, or is the effort coming from somewhere else? Experiencing, say, neck pain during a set of crunches is a good indication that your form is off.

Then ask yourself: Can you control the weight? Relying on momentum to complete repetitions increases your risk of injury. Bouncing the barbell off your chest during a bench press is a prime example. You should be able to pause for a second or two in the most difficult position. For a bench press, pause when the bar is a few inches above your chest before pushing it back up.

Last, ask yourself: Are you using the full range of motion? Never sacrifice proper form for the sake of moving more weight. Doing an exercise properly means controlling the weight through the entire range of motion. Doing half reps on squats, for example, doesn't impress anyone; it simply means the weight is too heavy. Instead, lighten the load, and lower your body until your thighs are at least parallel to the floor. Then return to a standing position.

I'm skinny. What workouts are best for bulking me up?

"Instead of three sets of 8 to 12 reps per exercise, try two or three sets of 4 to 7 reps with heavier weights. This will boost strength and build more muscle when sets and reps go back up," says Steven T. Devor, PhD, a professor of exercise physiology at Ohio State University.

Is there a gym bag I can keep in my office that doesn't scream jock?

The best gym duffels have the same characteristics as the punching bags boxers pound: tough leather or nylon construction, durable stitching, and—the hard part—minimal logo action. Why don't more manufacturers make a simple black gym bag? We don't know, but carting those huge graphics and crazy colors into the office can undermine your carefully nurtured air of corporate gravitas. On the other hand, high-quality leather isn't the way to go either: You don't want to be nervous about dropping

your bag on the wet floor in the locker room.

Instead, look for dark monochromatic bags that can withstand some scuffing and have waterproof compartments inside. A really good combination is a nylon shell with leather handles; the different textures add sophistication and a nice richness. Prada makes a great gym bag that follows these design principles.

Another option, if you're after a more retro look, is to pick up a vintage canvas bag at an Army Navy store. It will have classic style and real character. Combine it with a waterproof insert or dry bag that can be found at any outdoors store and it's just as practical as a more expensive designer bag.

I heard that Sylvester Stallone got caught with human growth hormone. Can I get as big as him without it?

Trying to build Rocky-worthy 22-inch biceps without HGH is like Jeff Gordon trying to win the Daytona 500 in a go-kart. "It's highly unlikely that anyone will look like Stallone at his age, 60, without using HGH," says Pearson.

HGH supplementation allows weight lifters to exceed their genetic strength potential by forcing muscle fibers to grow beyond their normal limits, says Pearson. It also helps muscles recover faster between workouts, and the effects last longer than those stimulated by steroids. The result: more muscle in less time. But that doesn't mean you can't take advantage of your body's natural HGH production and turn heads at the beach. Use these tips to maximize your muscle growth.

Set some limits. In weight lifting, less is almost always more. "If you're doing more than 24 total sets per workout, or more than two exercises for each muscle, you're doing too much," says Pearson. "You're

also increasing your risk of overtraining, and when you overtrain, your muscles stop growing." Similarly, limit yourself to no more than four strength workouts a week, working your upper body and lower body on alternate days.

Hit the rower. "If you want to look buff, you have to keep your body fat low," says Pearson. "And you can't do that without aerobic conditioning." Nothing works better in this regard than rowing. It works just about every muscle in the body, and the more muscles you work, the more fat you burn. In fact, recent studies indicate that men burn fat as fuel up to 50 percent faster when they row than when they bike. Thirty minutes at least twice a week should do the trick.

Feed your muscles. As mentioned earlier, a study at Victoria University, in Australia, found that men who drank two protein shakes a day immediately before and after working out built nearly twice as much muscle as those who drank the same shakes at least 5 hours outside of training sessions. Look for supplements that contain both whey and casein protein.

Researchers at Baylor University, in Texas, discovered that men who downed this combo after working out packed on 50 percent more muscle after 10 weeks than men who consumed whey alone.

Is it okay to put my feet up on the bench while I bench-press?

Yes and no. If you have back problems, go ahead and put your feet up, says Joseph Warpeha, MA, CSCS, an exercise physiologist at the University of Minnesota. "As the weight on the bar gets heavier, the natural reaction is to arch the lower back excessively. This can cause pain in people with lower-back problems," he says. "Putting your feet up changes the lift's mechanics and eliminates that instinct."

But you won't be able to lift as much, because you'll be taking your lower-body stabilizers—hips, legs, feet—out of the equation. Instead, you'll be relying on your upper-body stabilizers to help raise the bar. "If your goal is to increase your bench-press strength or develop a bigger upper body, placing your feet on the bench may hinder your progress," Warpeha says.

But if your primary goal is gaining functional strength for athletics, changing the position of your feet definitely can help. Warpeha suggests taking it a step further by placing a Swiss ball a few inches below the base of the bench, extending your legs, and balancing your heels on the ball while lifting. It adds balance to the mix and engages your lower stabilizing muscles.

My right leg is a little stronger than my left. When I work my lower body, should I do as many reps as I can with each leg or the same number?

Sounds like you naturally favor your right leg, causing out-of-proportion strength. One bonus of free weights is that you can hoist more or less poundage on your weaker or stronger side, allowing you to balance your body. So work your left leg a bit harder than your right to increase strength on that side. Opt for a weight that lets you complete just 5 to 8 reps without cheating. Meanwhile, continue working your right leg with a lighter weight and do 10 to 12 reps. Your strength should start equalizing after about 8 weeks.

I tend to bounce when executing a squat. Any pointers for fixing my form?

Bouncing equals cheating: You're using momentum to do the work. It's also a good way to land on the disabled list, because you're more likely to screw up the form and let your knees jut out past your ankles, which is a surefire way to end up sidelined. Reduce the amount of weight you're lifting until you can do 12 reps with good form and no Tigger tendencies. To keep yourself grounded, focus on pushing your heels down into the floor as you come up.

Is 35 too old to be doing cleans and deadlifts?

"Most lifting injuries result from poor form or too much weight, not too many years. Have someone show you proper execution of both lifts, especially cleans," says Pearson.

How long can I go without lifting weights before my muscles disappear?

Contrary to popular belief, your muscles don't turn to mush as soon as you stop lifting. In fact, a recent study of recreational weight lifters found that 6 weeks of inactivity resulted in only a slight decrease in power (10 percent after 2 weeks) and virtually no drop-off in size or strength. You could go the whole summer without pumping iron—as long as you're keeping fit with activities such as swimming or tennis. These sports help retain muscle mass and offer the perfect physical and mental break from the tedium of

the gym. Come fall, you can return to the gym refreshed and ready to take your workouts to the next level.

People in the fitness industry call this phenomenon detraining. When you exercise regularly—be it aerobic or anaerobic—your body boosts the production of key enzymes and testosterone to help muscles grow and maintain themselves. When you stop training, there's no need for your body to invest precious resources in preserving muscle, and it gets the message after a couple of weeks. Fortunately, muscles have memory, so if you lift for a year and then go on a few-week hiatus, it will take only 6 weeks to regain what you've lost.

SPOT TRAIN

BY MYATT MURPHY
WORKOUTS BY MICHAEL MEJIA, CSCS

Build Bulging Biceps

Stop wasting time with the same outdated arm-curl routine you've been using for years. Try these three better—and faster—ways to build sleeve-busting muscle

First, here are three things you don't know about your biceps.

1. The visibility of your cephalic vein, which crosses your biceps, has nothing to do with how many curls you can perform. To make this vein pop, you need to drop your body fat below 15 percent. Don't be surprised if the vein is more pronounced on one arm than the other: Genetics also play a key role in determining its prominence.

2. Under a microscope, some muscle fibers look pinnated, or feather shaped. But the biceps's long parallel fibers give them the ability to bulge. This means that devoting just a little attention to your biceps, especially compared with other muscle groups, goes a long way toward making them grow.

3. The average guy's biceps are composed of about 1 pound of muscle. For both of your arms combined, that's just 3 percent of the amount of muscle mass in your entire body.

Remember that number: It's a good way to keep a perspective on how much you train your biceps compared with your other muscle groups.

Pick Your Plan

Here are three routines for the results you want.

THE CHINUP CHASER

Chinups work your biceps harder than curls do. Combining the two can be even more effective. Use this combo routine to gain strength, burn fat, and build bigger arms.

How it works: Perform three sets of the close-grip chinup (1) followed by three sets of the dumbbell single-arm isometric curl (6). Rest for 60 seconds after each set. Do as many chinups as possible in each set, and complete 10 to 12 reps in each set of curls. Perform this workout twice a week, resting for at least 2 days after each session.

THE SUPERFAST CIRCUIT

Working your biceps with a variety of exercises and repetition ranges is an effective way to stimulate maximum growth. This routine does just that, and it requires only 8 minutes, twice a week.

How it works: Do the towel inverted row (5), the rope cable hammer curl (4), and the dumbbell incline offset-grip curl (3) in a circuit, performing one set of each exercise before resting. Complete as many reps as you can of the first exercise, 5 to 7 reps of the second movement, and 8 to 10 of the last exercise. Rest for 60 seconds, then repeat

the circuit once or twice more. Perform this
routine 2 days a week, resting for at least 2
days after each session.

THE MULTITASKING WORKOUT

Your biceps brachii is the muscle known as
your biceps. Since your brachialis lies
beneath, developing it will push your biceps
higher. This workout trains both muscles by
modifying an exercise every man is familiar
with: the classic biceps curl.

How it works: Grab a dumbbell in each
hand, choosing the heaviest weight that
allows you to complete 8 to 10 repetitions of
the dumbbell biceps curl (2). For your first
set, perform the exercise as described, with
one exception: Use an overhand grip, your
palms facing behind you at first. Do as many
reps as you can, then rest for 60 seconds and
perform a second set of biceps curls with a
neutral grip (palms facing each other). Rest
again for 60 seconds and do the move once
more with an underhand grip, as shown.
Repeat once for a total of two rounds. Do
this workout twice a week.

1. CLOSE-GRIP CRUNCHES

*Note: **Stare straight
ahead at all times. It
will limit momentum.***

Grab a chinup bar with an underhand grip, your
hands spaced about 6 inches apart. Hang with
your arms straight. Keeping your face straight
ahead and your elbows pointed down, pull
yourself up until the bar is directly under your
chin. Then lower yourself to the starting
position.

2. DUMBBELL BICEPS CURL

Note: If your elbows move forward, you're cheating. Keep them pointing down.

Grab a dumbbell in each hand, using an underhand grip (palms facing forward). Let them hang at arm's length next to your sides. Without moving your upper arms, curl the weights up toward your shoulders, then slowly lower them.

3. DUMBBELL INCLINE OFFSET-GRIP CURL

Note: Grasp the weight so your hand is against the side of the plate, not in the center.

Set an incline bench at a 60-degree angle, then grab a dumbbell in each hand so your thumbs touch the plates (instead of holding the center of the handle). Lie on the bench holding the dumbbells at arm's length, palms facing each other. As you curl the weights, rotate your wrists so your palms face you at the top of the move. Reverse to the starting position.

4. ROPE CABLE HAMMER CURL

Note: **Don't allow your wrists to bend as you curl the weight.**

Attach a rope to a low-pulley cable and stand 1 to 2 feet in front of the weight stack. Grab an end of the rope in each hand with a neutral grip (palms facing each other). With your elbows tucked at your sides, slowly curl your fists up toward your shoulders, then return to the starting position.

5. TOWEL INVERTED ROW

Note: **Using towels challenges your grip, so it also builds your forearms.**

Lie under a Smith machine or squat rack with your legs straight and a bar set a few inches higher than arm's length. Loop two small towels over the bar, spaced shoulder-width apart. Grab each towel. Keeping your body straight, pull yourself toward the bar. Pause, then slowly lower yourself.

Hard Move, Harder Muscle

Ready for a challenge? Try this exercise at the end of your biceps workout. Do two or three sets of 12 to 15 repetitions, resting for 60 seconds after each set.

Single-Arm Cross Curl

Stand between the weight stacks of a cable crossover station and grab a high-pulley handle in each hand, with your palms up. Hold your arms out to the sides so they're parallel to the floor, but keep your elbows slightly bent. Without moving your left arm, curl your right hand toward your head. Flex your biceps. Then slowly allow your arm to straighten; control the weight throughout the exercise. Repeat the move with your other arm.

Note: Keep your upper arms parallel to the floor at all times.

6. DUMBBELL SINGLE-ARM ISOMETRIC CURL

Grab a dumbbell in each hand. Curl the weight in your left hand until your elbow is bent 90 degrees. Holding that position, curl the weight in your right hand toward your shoulder, then lower it. Complete your reps while maintaining a right angle with your left arm. Repeat on the other side.

Note: Keep one arm bent 90 degrees as you curl with your other arm.

BY MYATT MURPHY
WORKOUTS BY C.J. MURPHY, MFS

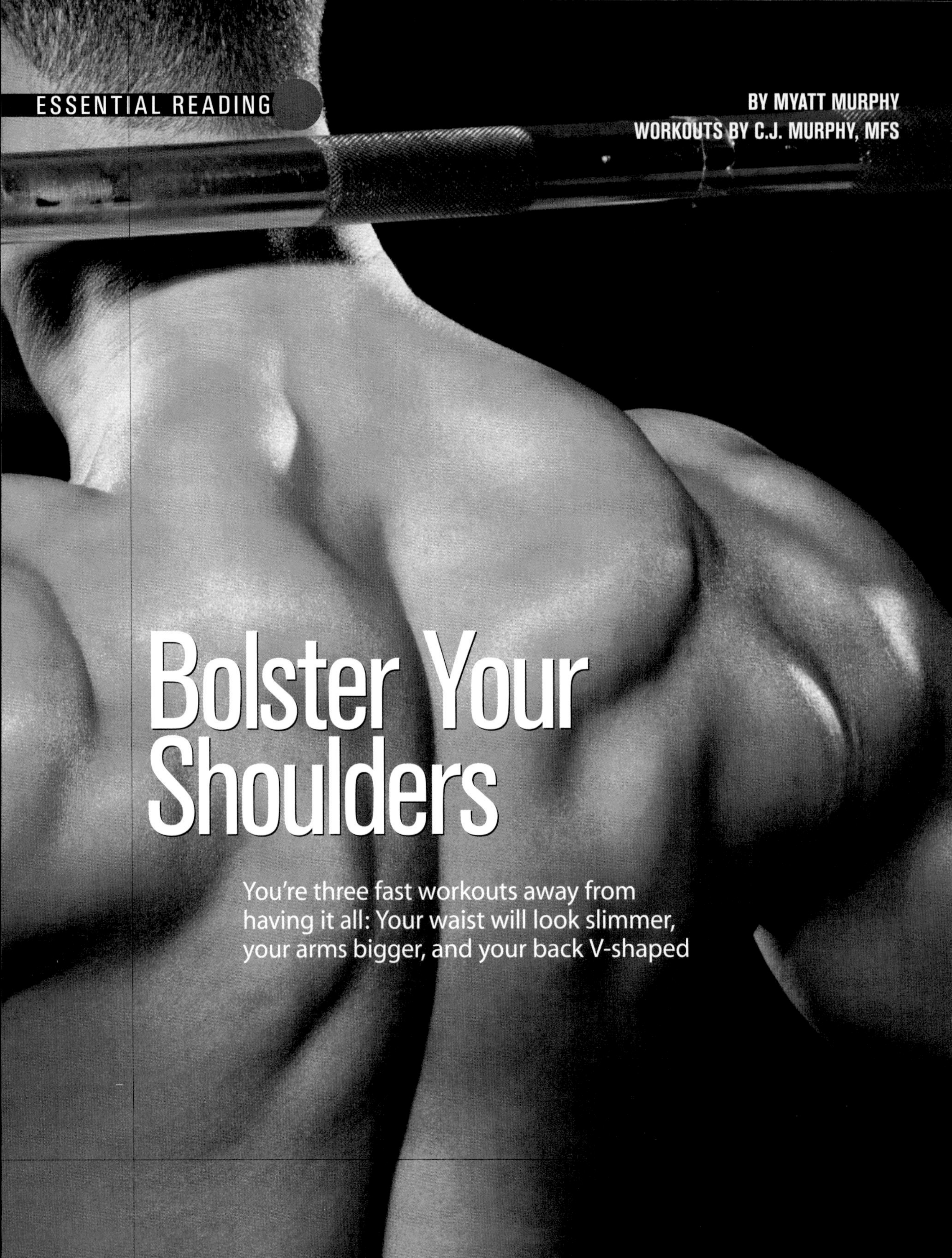

Bolster Your Shoulders

You're three fast workouts away from
having it all: Your waist will look slimmer,
your arms bigger, and your back V-shaped

We bet you didn't know this about your shoulders.

1. The last place your body deposits fat is in the shoulder, making it one of the easiest muscles to define. If your shoulders still don't pop after using the workouts here, take it as a sign that you need to focus more on fat loss.

2. You may feel tight now, but you were born with tremendous shoulder flexibility. Unlike the hip joint, which is anatomically similar to the shoulder, the shoulder socket is extremely shallow. This allows the arm to move freely in all directions. Do arm circles before your workout and stretch after your workout to maintain your range of motion.

3. The shoulder is the most unstable joint in your body. As a result, weight-room mishaps are commonplace. Protect yourself by refining your bench-press technique. Poor form causes more shoulder injuries than any move. To stave off trouble, keep your shoulder blades back and down as you raise and lower the weight.

Pick Your Plan

Here are three routines for the results you want.

THE BOLDER-SHOULDER SESSION

Your shoulders assist in many moves for your chest. So training them after your chest workout keeps your muscles under tension longer, a strategy shown to increase size. And it takes only one workout a week.

How it works: Do two sets of 10 repetitions of the dumbbell shoulder press (2) and dumbbell front raise (7). Then do two sets of 8 reps of the accelerated side raise (4). Finish with two sets of 8 reps of the cable reverse fly (6) and dumbbell Cuban press (8). Rest for 45 seconds between sets. Perform this workout once a week after your chest routine.

THE BIG-MUSCLE BREAKOUT

Use this routine to bust out of a rut. It shores up commonly weak areas, so you'll dodge shoulder pain and boost gains in all your upper-body lifts.

How it works: Twice a week, perform the dumbbell shoulder press (2), dumbbell front raise (7), cable reverse fly (6), and dumbbell Cuban press (8). Do two sets of 10 to 12 repetitions of each move, resting for 60 seconds between sets.

THE FULL-BODY STRENGTH CIRCUIT

This fast routine conditions your cardiovascular system and builds bigger muscle, so it's perfect for men who have time to train only two or three times a week.

How it works: As part of your total-body routine, perform one set of the push press (1), dumbbell shoulder press (2), or barbell high-incline bench press (3). Without resting, do a set of squats. Next, perform the accelerated side raise (4), cable single-arm side raise (5), or cable reverse fly (6) with lunges. That's a circuit. Do a total of three circuits, resting for 60 seconds between circuits. Complete 8 to 10 reps of each exercise and choose different moves each time you train.

1. PUSH PRESS

Note: Push your hips back and bend at the knees to lower your body slightly.

Stand holding a barbell with an overhand grip, and rest it on the front of your shoulders. Keep your elbows tucked in. Dip down about 6 inches, then drive yourself up with your legs as you push the weight overhead. Return to the starting position.

2. DUMBBELL SHOULDER PRESS

Note: Keep the weights level— don't allow them to tilt up or down.

Stand holding a dumbbell in each hand just above your shoulders with a neutral grip (palms facing each other). Press the weights straight up until your arms are fully extended, then slowly lower the weights to the starting position.

3. BARBELL HIGH-INCLINE BENCH PRESS

Note: Lower the bar to your chest just above your nipples.

Lie faceup on a bench set at an incline of 65 to 80 degrees. Hold a barbell over your chest with straight arms, your hands slightly more than shoulder-width apart. Slowly lower the bar to your chest. Press the weight back up to the starting position.

4. ACCELERATED SIDE RAISE

Note: Keep your arms straight throughout the exercise.

Stand holding a pair of light dumbbells at your sides. Raise the dumbbells out to your sides. When the weights are about a foot away from your body, increase your lifting speed. Pause when the weights reach ear level, then return to the starting position.

5. CABLE SINGLE-ARM SIDE RAISE

6. CABLE REVERSE FLY

Note: **Begin each repetition holding the handle at your hip, elbow slightly bent.**

Note: **Raise your arms until they're parallel to the floor.**

Stand between the weight stacks with your arms crossed in front of you, and grab a handle from each low pulley. Bend forward at the waist until your torso is almost parallel to the floor, arms beneath your shoulders. Pull your shoulder blades back, then raise your arms out to your sides. Lower and repeat.

Attach a handle to the low-pulley cable and stand with your left side to the weight stack. Reach across your body with your right hand to grab the handle. Raise your arm up and across your body until it's parallel to the floor, then return to the starting position.

7. DUMBBELL FRONT RAISE

8. DUMBBELL CUBAN PRESS

Note: Don't lean back. Stand tall and straight throughout the move.

Stand holding a pair of light dumbbells at arm's length with a neutral grip. Keeping your arms straight, slowly raise the weights in front of you until your arms are parallel to the floor. Pause, then slowly lower the weights.

Stand holding a pair of light dumbbells in front of your thighs with an overhand grip. Draw the weights up in front of your body, keeping the weights close to your torso and bending your elbows, until your upper arms are parallel to the floor. Without moving your upper arms or elbows, rotate your forearms until they point up, then press the weight overhead. Slowly reverse the path to the starting position.

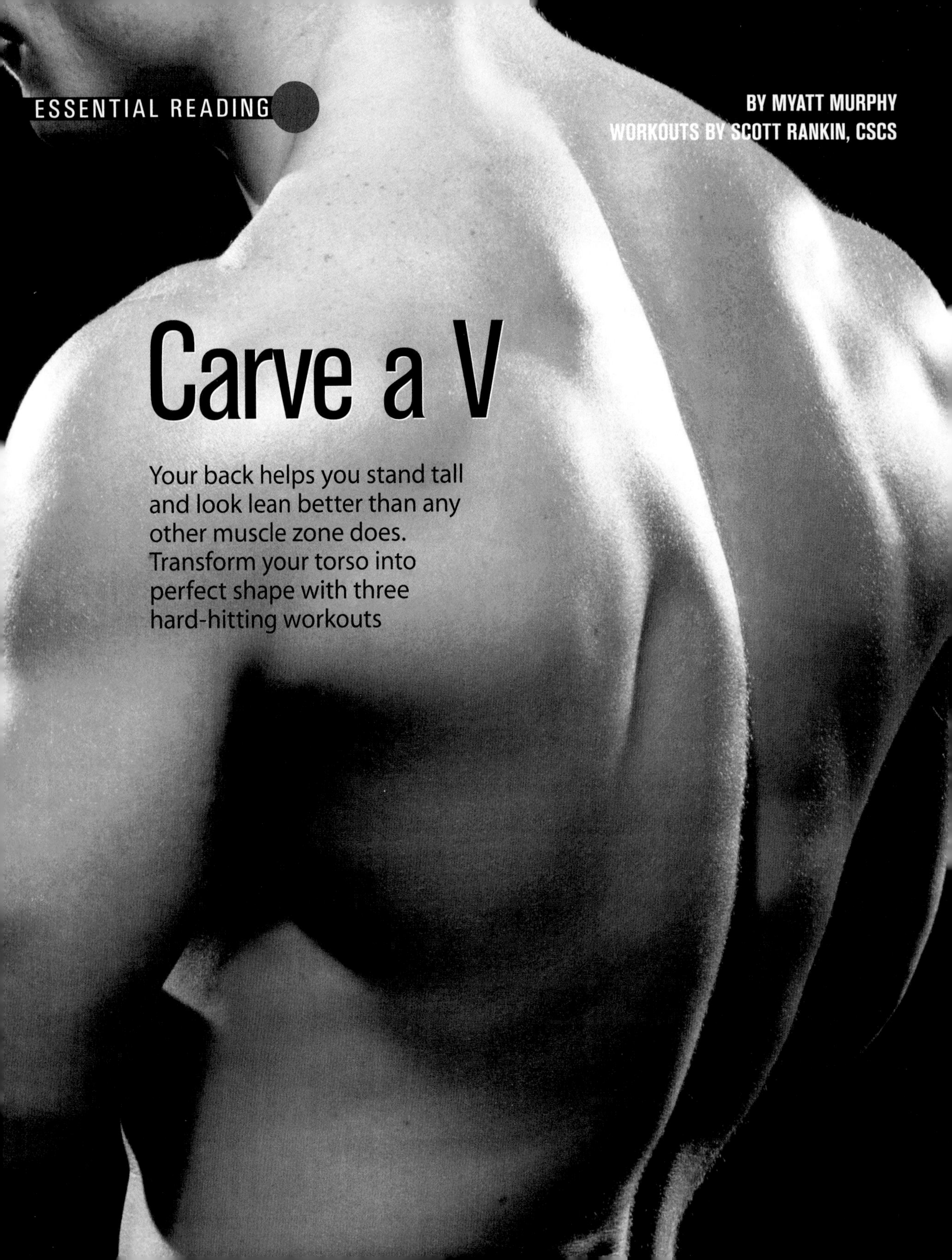

BY MYATT MURPHY
WORKOUTS BY SCOTT RANKIN, CSCS

Carve a V

Your back helps you stand tall
and look lean better than any
other muscle zone does.
Transform your torso into
perfect shape with three
hard-hitting workouts

MLB strength coaches rank the pullup as the most important exercise for your upper body. Here are three other things you don't know about your back.

1. Building your back can torch your belly fat. That's because the more muscle you train, the hotter your fat furnace burns. And there are no larger muscles than the latissimus dorsi, a.k.a. the lats. Master the pullup to bolster these muscles fast.

2. Your arms will lift more weight than the larger back muscles if you let them. For a better back workout, initiate rowing movements by squeezing your shoulder blades back. Then think about pulling the weight with your elbows, not your hands.

3. Anytime you train your back or chest, or even sit at your desk, your lats become stiff. Because these muscles attach to your spine and wrap around to your ribs, they're used in most upper-body activities. Stretch your lats every day to stay loose.

Pick Your Plan

Here are three workouts for custom results.

THE RECORD-BREAKING PULLUP CIRCUIT

Raise your personal best in pullups by 3 to 5 reps in 4 weeks, using a technique that emphasizes the lowering portion of the lift. It's a simple way to build the largest muscles of your back—your lats.

How it works: Do as many pullups (1) as you can. (If you can't complete a single rep, go to the next step.) Without resting, use a bench to hop up to the bar, and then lower yourself to a count of 10. That's one rep. Do 3 reps total, then perform the seated close-grip row (7) for 12 reps. Rest for 60 to 90 seconds, then repeat the circuit twice. Try this 3 days a week, resting for at least a day between sessions.

THE TALL-AND-MIGHTY COMBO

Shoring up your lower-back muscles, rear shoulders, and middle trapezius will instantly improve your posture. These two moves can do the trick.

How it works: At the start or end of your workout, perform the Swiss-ball back extension (6) and cable scapular retraction (5). Do two sets of 10 to 15 reps for each move, resting for 60 seconds between sets. Complete this routine one to three times a week.

THE BIG-MUSCLE FLEX PLAN

Mix and match your moves every time you use this routine, for new challenges and fresh workouts. This variety means you'll be more likely to stick to your training program.

How it works: Start with either the dumbbell single-arm row (2) or the barbell bent-over row (3). Do three sets of 12 reps, resting for 30 to 60 seconds between sets. Then do either the seated wide-grip row (4) or the seated close-grip row (7). Again, do three sets of 12, resting for 30 to 60 seconds between sets. Finish with a "drop set" of lat pulldowns (8)—that is, complete 10 reps with the most weight you can handle. Without resting, reduce the weight and do 10 more, then reduce it again for another 10. Do this routine twice a week.

1. PULLUP

Note: Pull yourself up until your chin is over the bar.

Grab the bar with an overhand grip (palms forward), your hands slightly more than shoulder-width apart. Hang with your arms fully extended. Pull yourself up over the bar, and then slowly lower yourself to the starting position.

2. DUMBBELL SINGLE-ARM ROW

Note: Pull the weight up so your elbow passes your torso.

Holding a dumbbell in your right hand, place your left hand and left knee on a bench. Hold the weight with your arm straight. Use your upper-back muscles to pull the dumbbell up and back toward your hip. Pause, then slowly lower the weight.

3. BARBELL BENT-OVER ROW

Note: **Maintain a slight bend in your knees throughout the movement.**

Stand holding a barbell with an overhand grip, your hands slightly more than shoulder-width apart. Push your hips back and bend forward until your torso is almost parallel to the floor. Draw the bar toward your rib cage. Pause, then lower the bar.

4. SEATED WIDE-GRIP ROW

Note: **Keep your back straight as you pull the bar to your abs.**

Sit on a bench or the floor and bend forward to grab the lat-pulldown bar from a low-pulley cable. Using a wide overhand grip, pull the bar toward your midsection. Resist the weight as you extend your arms back out in front of you.

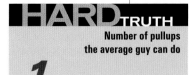

HARD TRUTH

Number of pullups the average guy can do

1

5. CABLE SCAPULAR RETRACTION

Note: This is a slight movement. The bar should move back only a few inches.

Attach a bar to a low-pulley cable. Sit on a bench or the floor and grab the bar with an overhand, shoulder-width grip. Without bending your elbows, pull your shoulder blades back as far as you can and squeeze them together. Return to the starting position.

6. SWISS-BALL BACK EXTENSION

Note: Your torso should be in line with your lower body at the top of the move.

Lie facedown on a Swiss ball and push your feet against a wall or hook them under a bench. Your chest should be off the ball. Cross your arms and bend forward at the waist until your midsection covers the ball. Then raise your torso up off the ball.

HARD TRUTH

Percentage of fat you would need to lose to instantly double the number of pullups you can do

10

7. SEATED CLOSE-GRIP ROW

*Note: **Staring straight ahead will help you keep your back straight.***

Attach a V-handle to a low-pulley cable and sit on a bench or the floor. Grab the handle and hold it with your palms facing each other. Pull the handle toward your midsection, and then slowly straighten your arms back out in front of you.

8. LAT PULLDOWN

*Note: **Keep your elbows pointed down as you pull the bar toward you.***

Sit at a lat-pulldown station and grab the bar with an overhand grip, hands slightly more than shoulder-width apart. Keeping your head and back straight, pull your shoulder blades down, and then pull the bar to your chest. Let the bar rise.

BY MYATT MURPHY
WORKOUTS BY CRAIG FRIEDMAN, MS, ATC, CSCS

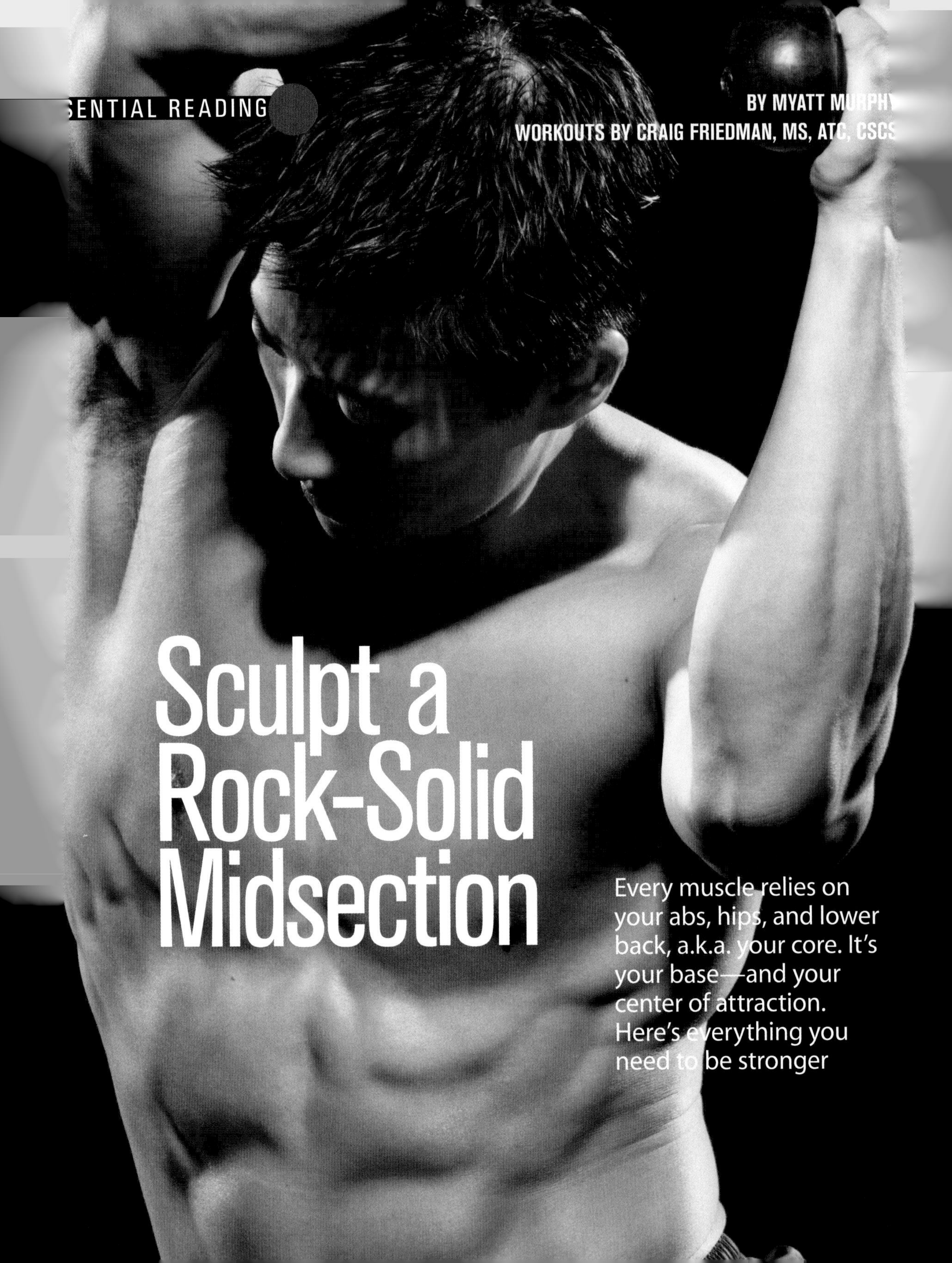

Sculpt a Rock-Solid Midsection

Every muscle relies on your abs, hips, and lower back, a.k.a. your core. It's your base—and your center of attraction. Here's everything you need to be stronger

Men who do core training report 30 percent less back pain. Here's some more about your core.

1. You can strengthen your core without moving a muscle. Whereas most muscles propel you, your core resists movement—for instance, to protect your spine when you twist your torso. So don't be surprised by how hard it is to stay still in this workout. You're conditioning your core to do its job more effectively.

2. Slouching sabotages your six-pack. Training your core helps correct poor posture. But an hour a week of core work can't compensate for the 50 hours spent slumped over your keyboard. The fix: Stay tall through your hips and keep your head up and shoulder blades back and down all day long.

3. Core muscles contract first in every exercise. All the energy you exert originates in your torso, before being transferred to your arms and legs. So a weak core reduces the amount of force you're able to apply to a barbell. When you hit a plateau in presses, squats, or any other strength move, ask yourself if you're training your core as hard as you can.

Pick Your Plan

Here are three routines for the results you want.

THE FAST-MUSCLE SEQUENCE

Beginning your workout with core exercises reinforces proper posture. That means you'll use better technique to lift more weight in every exercise, which translates to bigger muscles all over. The best part: It takes just 3 minutes.

How it works: Perform the side bridge (1), followed by the plank with diagonal arm lift (2). Hold the side bridge for 15 to 45 seconds on each side, then do 4 to 12 repetitions of the plank with diagonal arm lift. Do this routine at the start of every weight-training session.

THE PAINPROOF CIRCUIT

Have a creaky back? Then this is the workout for you. It improves the endurance of your core muscles, which removes excess strain from your back and distributes weight more evenly throughout your body.

How it works: Do the glute-bridge march (6), plank with diagonal arm lift (2), cable kneeling chop (5), and side bridge (1) in a circuit. That is, perform one exercise after another without rest. Complete 6 to 12 repetitions of the glute-bridge march, 4 to 12 reps of the plank with diagonal arm lift,

and 6 to 10 reps of the cable kneeling chop, and hold the side bridge for 15 to 45 seconds on each side. Rest for 60 seconds, then repeat the circuit once or twice. Perform this routine 2 or 3 days a week at the end of your workout.

THE PEAK-PERFORMANCE WORKOUT

When your core starts to give out, so does your game—no matter which sport you play. But use this six-exercise circuit and you'll move faster, with more power and greater ease. All told, you'll perform better in any sport—and in the weight room.

How it works: Do the plank with diagonal arm lift (2), glute-bridge march (6), Swiss-ball knee tuck (4), cable kneeling chop (5), side bridge (1), and single-leg lowering (3) in a circuit. That is, do one exercise after another without rest. Complete 4 to 12 repetitions of the plank with diagonal arm lift, 6 to 12 reps of the glute-bridge march, 6 to 12 reps of the Swiss-ball knee tuck, and 6 to 10 reps of the cable kneeling chop. Hold the side bridge for 15 to 45 seconds and perform 6 to 12 reps of the single-leg lowering. Rest for 60 seconds, then repeat the circuit. Try this at the end of your training, 2 or 3 days a week.

Hard Move, Harder Muscle

Squats train your midsection harder than many ab or lower-back moves. Single-leg exercises pose an even greater core challenge. Try this at the end of your workout.

Cable Single-Leg Squat to Row

Grab a mid-pulley handle with your right hand, with your arm straight and your palm facing left. Bend your left leg slightly and straighten your right leg behind you so it's just off the floor. This is the starting position. Row the handle toward your side as you straighten your torso and draw your right knee toward your chest. Do two or three sets of 10 to 12 reps with each leg.

Note: Pull the handle to your side, so your elbow passes your torso.

1. SIDE BRIDGE

Note: *Contract your abs and butt muscles forcefully to keep your body straight.*

Lie on your side with your forearm on the floor under your shoulder to prop you up, and your feet stacked. Contract your core and press your forearm against the floor to raise your hips until your body is straight from ankles to shoulders. Hold for 15 to 45 seconds, then repeat on the other side.

2. PLANK WITH DIAGONAL ARM LIFT

Note: *Your elbows should be bent 90 degrees and directly under your shoulders.*

Assume a modified pushup position with your feet shoulder-width apart, forearms on the floor. Keeping your torso steady, raise your right arm forward and to the right, so that it points to 2 o'clock. Hold for 2 seconds, then lower and repeat with your left arm, raising it to 10 o'clock. That's one rep.

HARD TRUTH

Percentage decrease in the size of abdominal-fat cells after 3 weeks of exercise

18

3. SINGLE-LEG LOWERING

4. SWISS-BALL KNEE TUCK

Note: Don't point your toes; keep your foot flexed toward you. Lead with your heel.

Note: Lift your hips as you bring your knees toward you so your shins rise off the ball.

Lie on your back with your legs extended straight up. Keeping your legs straight, lower your left leg until your foot is 2 to 3 inches off the floor. Return to the starting position, then repeat with your right leg; that's one repetition. Think about pushing the bottom of your heel away from your hip as you lower your leg.

Assume the pushup position with your shins resting on a Swiss ball, hands slightly more than shoulder-width apart. Keeping your abs tight, draw your knees toward your chest until your toes are on top of the ball. Slowly straighten your legs so the ball rolls back to the starting position.

5. CABLE KNEELING CHOP

Note: *Keep your torso upright as you extend your arms away from your body.*

At a high-pulley cable, grab an end of rope with each hand. Go down on your right knee, with your left knee pointing toward the weight stack; this is the starting position. Rotate your torso away from the stack as you pull your hands to your chest, then down and away from you. Reverse to the starting position. After your reps, change legs and rotate in the other direction.

6. GLUTE-BRIDGE MARCH

Note: *Don't allow your hips to sag at any time during the movement.*

Lie with your knees bent and your arms and heels on the floor. Push down through your heels and squeeze your glutes to raise your body into a straight line from knees to shoulders. Next, bring a knee toward your chest. Reverse the move, then repeat with your other leg. That's one rep.

HARDTRUTH
Percentage higher your risk of heart disease when you have a big belly

60

BY JOE DOWDELL, CSCS

Reengineer Your Body

This workout helped two
NBA stick figures bulk up
big-time. Use it to pack on
muscle like a pro today

Kickstart your best year in the gym with this total-body weight workout. Stick to it for a month, and you'll lay a foundation for impressive fitness gains.

Perform this workout 3 days a week with at least a day of rest between sessions. Alternate exercises with the same number (1A and 1B, for example) until you complete all of the sets in that pairing. Only then should you move on to the next pairing. See below for details.

Weeks 1 and 2: Perform three sets of 8 to 10 repetitions of every exercise except the hang clean (1A). For that, do three sets of 6 to 8 reps. Rest for 60 seconds between all sets except the hang-clean ones, after which you should rest for 90 seconds. Rest for 60 seconds between exercise pairings, as well.

Aim for a lifting tempo of 2 seconds up and 2 seconds down for exercises for the dumbbell curl to overhead press (3B), half-kneeling cable lift with rope (4A), and Swiss-ball plate crunch (4B). For 1A, explode up and then go back down in 2 seconds. For each of the others, take 1 second to go up and 3 seconds to go down.

Weeks 3 and 4: Perform four sets of 6 to 8 repetitions of every exercise except the hang clean (1A), the dumbbell curl (3B), and the plate crunch (4B). For 1A, do four sets of 4 to 6 reps; for 3B and 4B, do four sets of 8 to 10 reps each. Use the same rest-period protocol you used in weeks 1 and 2.

Your lifting tempo should be 2 seconds up and 2 seconds down for exercise 3B. For 1A, 4A, and 4B, explode up and go down in 2 seconds. For the others, it's 1 second up, 3 seconds down.

1A: BARBELL HANG CLEAN

Note: **Catch the bar in the crooks of your fingers.**

Grab a bar with a shoulder-width grip and dip your knees, as if you're about to jump. Quickly pull the bar up and rise onto your toes. As the bar approaches chest height, bend your knees, swing your elbows forward, and catch it at your shoulders.

1B: DUMBBELL ALTERNATING BENCH PRESS

Note: **Keep your shoulder blades pulled back into the bench.**

Lie flat on a bench holding dumbbells over your chest. Keeping one arm straight, lower the opposing weight to your shoulder and push it back up. Repeat with the other arm and continue alternating until you've completed all your reps.

2A: BARBELL SQUAT

Note: **Lower your body until your thighs are at least parallel to the floor.**

Stand holding a barbell across the back of your shoulders with an overhand grip, your hands and feet shoulder-width apart. Keeping your back naturally arched, bend at the hips and knees to lower your body. Push back to a standing position.

HARD TRUTH

Percentage less likely you are to stay lean when you skip workouts because you don't have enough time

76

2B: NEUTRAL-GRIP PULLUP

Note: Don't swing. Try to keep your body straight at all times.

Grab the parallel bars of a pullup-bar handle so your hands face each other. Hang with your arms straight. Pull yourself up as high as you can, aiming to clear the bar with your chin. Then slowly lower yourself back to the starting position, at a full hang.

3A: DUMBBELL ROMANIAN DEADLIFT

Note: Lower the weights as far as you can while maintaining the arch in your lower back.

Stand holding a dumbbell in each hand in front of your thighs. Maintaining the natural arch in your spine and keeping the weights close to your body, push your hips back and lower the weights. Squeeze your glutes and return to the starting position.

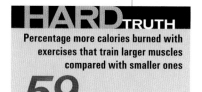

HARD TRUTH

Percentage more calories burned with exercises that train larger muscles compared with smaller ones

59

3B: DUMBBELL CURL TO OVERHEAD PRESS

Note: **Avoid using momentum to curl the weight up. Stand tall.**

Stand holding dumbbells down at your sides with your palms forward. Curl the weights up to your shoulders. Next, rotate your wrists as you press the dumbbells overhead so your palms face forward at the top. Reverse the move back to the starting position.

4A: HALF-KNEELING CABLE LIFT WITH ROPE

Note: **Keep a slight bend in your elbows throughout the move.**

Attach a rope handle to a low-pulley cable; assume a half-kneeling position perpendicular to the weight stack. Rotate your torso toward the stack and grab the rope with both hands. Explosively rotate away, raising your arms. Return to the starting position.

HARD TRUTH

Number of times more calories burned by muscle tissue than by fat tissue, even when you're not doing anything

10

Cure Your Skinny Legs

Bolster your weak spots—and beef up your chicken legs—with this lower-body workout, courtesy of Mike Robertson, MS, CSCS, a strength coach in Indianapolis. Perform this routine twice a week in place of your usual lower-body lifts for 3 weeks.

Double-Leg Vertical Jump

Assume an athletic stance. Dip down at the hips and knees, then jump up and reach as high as you can. Land softly with your hips and knees bent. Do two sets of 5 reps.

Single-Leg Vertical Jump

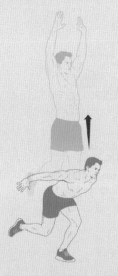

Perform as you would the double-leg vertical jump, but leap off one foot and land softly on the same foot. Do two sets of 3 reps with each leg.

Single-Leg Broad Jump

Stand on one leg with your knees slightly bent. Dip your knees and jump forward as far as you can. Land softly on the same foot. Do two sets of 3 reps with each leg.

Dumbbell Lunge

From a standing position, stride forward with one leg until your thigh is parallel to the floor. Then push back up and repeat with your other leg. Do three or four sets of 8 to 10 reps per leg.

4B: SWISS-BALL PLATE CRUNCH

Lie on a Swiss ball so your back curves over it. Hold a weight plate at your chest. Curl your body up and slightly forward, lifting your shoulder blades off the ball. Pause at the top and then slowly lower yourself back to the starting position.

Note: Keep your head and neck in line with your spine.

HARD TRUTH

Percentage of muscle mass lost through chronically performing 12-ounce arm curls, a.k.a. boozing

30

BY MYATT MURPHY
WORKOUTS BY CRAIG FRIEDMAN, MS, ATC, CSCS

Strip Away Fat

These workouts strip away fat in just 10 minutes and build big muscles with or without a gym. You'll look leaner—and stronger—in a few weeks

ere are three things you don't know about fat loss.

1. Squats may burn up to three times more calories than previously thought, according to a study in the *Journal of Strength and Conditioning Research*. They're also great for packing on muscle. Every workout in our plan features this classic move.

2. Aim high. Men who set higher expectations lose more weight, report researchers at the University of Minnesota. Stick to these routines and you can expect to shed 4 to 5 pounds in your first 2 weeks, and 1 to 2 pounds a week in the months that follow.

3. The calories you burn in a 30-minute jog may not matter as much as you think. More important is your calorie loss when you're not exercising. Intense weight training elevates your metabolism for 36 hours, so you lose weight all day and build bigger muscles.

Pick Your Plan

Here's how to fine-tune this workout for faster results and bigger muscles.

THE HIGH-DEF MUSCLE SEQUENCE

By training your major muscles in every session, you'll ignite a surge of fat-burning hormones, for crystal-clear muscle definition from head to toe.

How it works: Perform three sets of 6 repetitions of the dumbbell clean and press (3). Then do the barbell squat (1), followed immediately by the dumbbell single-arm row

(5). This pair of moves is a superset; complete three rounds of 8 reps of each—that is, three supersets. Next, do three supersets of the deadlift (2) and burpee (6). Do 8 reps of the deadlift and 30 seconds of the burpee in each superset. Rest for 45 seconds between sets. Try this 3 days a week, resting for a day between sessions.

THE HARD-BODY EXPRESS WORKOUT

Pick this plan when you have no time. You'll maintain muscle and maximize fat loss—in about 30 minutes a week.

How it works: Perform the deadlift (2), dumbbell clean and press (3), dumbbell squat (4), and farmer's walk (7) in a circuit, moving swiftly from one move to the next. Do 8 reps of the first and third exercises and 5 reps of the second exercise. Do the farmer's walk for 30 seconds. Complete two to four circuits, resting for 60 seconds between circuits. Perform this routine 2 or 3 days a week, with at least a day between sessions.

THE AT-HOME FAT BLASTER

No gym? Try this weight-free workout. It keeps your heart rate elevated and your fat-burning furnace stoked.

How it works: Start with 15 reps of bodyweight squats. Instead of holding weights, extend your arms overhead. Then, without resting, do 30 seconds of the burpee (6) and 10 reps of the single-leg Romanian deadlift (8) with each leg. That's a circuit. Do two to four circuits, resting for 60 seconds between circuits. Do this 3 days a week.

1. BARBELL SQUAT

Note: **Lower yourself until your thighs are at least parallel to the floor.**

Stand holding a barbell across the back of your shoulders with an overhand grip, your hands wider than shoulder-width apart. Keeping your back naturally arched, bend at the hips and knees to lower your body. Push back up to a standing position.

2. DEADLIFT

Note: **Start with the bar against your shins, with your hands just outside your lower legs.**

Stand with a barbell on the floor in front of you, with the bar over your toes. Bend your knees and grasp the bar with an overhand grip. Keeping your back straight, stand up. Keep the bar close to your body as you lift it. Slowly lower the bar.

HARD TRUTH

Fewer pounds of pressure on your knees when you lose 10 pounds of belly fat

40

3. DUMBBELL CLEAN AND PRESS

Note: Swing your elbows forward so your upper arms are parallel to the floor.

From the starting position, dip your hips and explode upward, forcefully pulling the weights up. As the weights near your chest, dip under and "catch" them on top of your shoulders. Stand, press the weights overhead, then reverse the move.

4. DUMBBELL SQUAT

Note: Hold the weights so your palms face each other.

Stand with your feet shoulder-width apart and hold a pair of dumbbells at your sides. Keeping your back naturally arched, bend at the hips and knees to lower yourself until your thighs are parallel to the floor. Push back up to a standing position.

5. DUMBBELL SINGLE-ARM ROW

Note: Pull the weight up so your elbow passes your torso.

Holding a dumbbell in your right hand, place your left hand and left knee on a bench. Hold the weight with your arm straight. Use your upper-back muscles to pull the dumbbell up and back toward your hip. Pause, then slowly lower the weight. Complete the reps with your right arm, then repeat with your left arm.

PAINkiller

I've been having a lot of knee pain lately and hamstring pulls. What gives?

If your lower-body muscles aren't balanced—and that's the case for most men—you're a likely candidate for knee pain and hamstring pulls. But avoiding leg injuries may be as simple as training your hamstrings harder. University of Nevada researchers found that athletes who performed two sets of hamstring exercises for every quadriceps movement balanced their leg strength in 6 weeks. Want to injury-proof your wheels? Try this workout. For 6 weeks, do twice as many sets of these exercises as you do lunges, leg presses, and squats.

Romanian Deadlift

Hold a dumbbell in each hand in front of your thighs. Keeping your lower back naturally arched, push your butt back and bend forward at your hips until the weights are at midshin level. Pause, then return to the starting position.

Swiss-Ball Hamstring Curl

Place your calves on a Swiss ball and raise your hips so that your body forms a straight line. Pull the ball toward your butt, using your lower legs and heels. Pause, then roll the ball back.

Good Morning

Rest a barbell on your upper back. Keeping your lower back naturally arched, push your butt back and lower your torso until it's parallel to the floor. Pause, then return to the starting position.

6. BURPEE

Stand with your feet shoulder-width apart. Bend at the hips and knees to lower your body as far as you can, then place your hands on the floor and straighten your legs behind you. Perform a pushup, then draw your knees back toward your chest until your feet are beneath you, and stand up.

PAINkiller

My shoulders sound like Rice Krispies. What does it mean?

If they've been snap-crackle-popping your whole life, you probably don't need to worry. "But if it just started, limits mobility, or causes even a little pain, then see a doctor," says Nick DiNubile, MD, an orthopedic surgeon specializing in sports medicine and the author of *FrameWork: Your 7-Step Program for Healthy Muscles, Bones, and Joints.* The noises can be a sign of damage to the rotator-cuff muscles or biceps tendons, or a labrum tear.

Another cause: crepitus, resulting when two inflamed tendons or bursae (sacs of fluid that pad friction points) rub together during movement, according to Bill Hartman, PT, CSCS, a physical therapist in Indianapolis. It's a common ailment as we age. Again, see a doc if you have pain or swelling.

7. FARMER'S WALK

Note: Don't lean forward or backward. Stand tall and straight throughout the move.

Stand holding a pair of heavy dumbbells at your sides at arm's length. Keeping your body upright, walk for the amount of time specified in your workout. If you're short on space, walk in a circle or figure eight.

8. SINGLE-LEG ROMANIAN DEADLIFT

Note: Keep your knee slightly bent throughout the exercise.

Stand on your left foot with your right foot raised behind you and your arms hanging in front of you. Keeping a natural arch in your spine, push your hips back as you lower your hands and upper body. Squeeze your glutes and press your heel into the floor to return to an upright position. Complete your reps on one leg before repeating on the other leg.

BY ROBERT DOS REMEDIOS, CSCS

Train Like an Athlete

Use this high-powered workout to carve the lean and muscular body you've always wanted

ome of the world's best-conditioned men use this workout, but it was designed with you in mind. As a collegiate strength and conditioning coach, I work with guys of average strength and size every day. My job is to turn them into elite performers.

My workouts have helped hundreds of average athletes become Division I scholarship players and even NFL gamebreakers. But by developing explosive speed, strength, and power, these men attain something more—the chiseled look of a high-performance athlete. Use this plan to redefine your body and raise your game. The training is short, intense, and if you put in the effort, highly effective.

4-Week Plan for Amazing Strength and Power

With this program, you'll feel stronger with every session.

Perform this workout three times a week with at least a day of rest between sessions. Do each exercise in the order shown. Complete three or four sets of each exercise except for the final movement (plank with weight transfer), which you perform just once for 30 to 60 seconds. Use this schedule for reps and rest.

WEEK 1

Perform 5 repetitions of the clean pull (1) and rest for 90 to 120 seconds between sets.

Do 10 reps of exercises 2 through 7, resting for 60 seconds between sets. Perform the plank with weight transfer (8) once for 30 to 60 seconds.

WEEK 2

Perform 3 reps of the clean pull (1) and rest for 90 to 120 seconds between sets.

Do 5 reps of exercises 2 through 7, resting for 90 seconds between sets.

Do the plank with weight transfer (8) once for 30 to 60 seconds.

WEEK 3

Perform 5 reps of the clean pull (1) and rest for 90 to 120 seconds between sets.

Do 8 reps of exercises 2 through 7, resting for 60 seconds between sets. Perform the plank with weight transfer (8) once for 30 to 60 seconds.

WEEK 4

Perform 2 reps of the clean pull (1) and rest for 90 to 120 seconds between sets.

Do 3 reps of exercises 2 through 7, resting for 90 seconds between sets. Do the plank with weight transfer (8) once for 30 to 60 seconds.

1. CLEAN PULL

Note: Keep your arms straight as you shrug your shoulders.

Load a barbell and roll it to your shins. Squat down and grab the bar overhand (palms facing you). In one explosive motion, pull the bar off the floor, straighten your legs, rise onto your toes, and shrug your shoulders. Then lower the bar to the floor.

2. FRONT STEPUP

Note: Keep your elbows high and your upper arms parallel to the floor.

Stand in front of a bench holding a barbell across the front of your shoulders. Place your right foot on the bench and push your body up until you're standing on the bench. Complete your reps on one leg before switching to the other leg and repeating.

3. SPLIT GOOD MORNING

Note: Bend forward as far as possible without rounding your back.

Stand holding a barbell across the back of your shoulders. Place one heel on two weight plates just in front of you. With that leg straight and your back leg slightly bent, bend forward. Return to the starting position. Do all your reps before switching sides.

4. PUSH JERK

Note: Hold the bar with an overhand grip (palms forward).

Stand holding a barbell in front of your shoulders. Dip slightly and then in one motion straighten your legs and push the weight overhead. When your arms are almost fully extended, widen your base and bend your knees. Return to the starting position.

5. MIXED-GRIP PULLUP

6. REVERSE-GRIP BENCH PRESS

Note: **Pull your elbows toward your body as you lower the bar.**

Lie flat on a bench. Grab the barbell using an underhand grip (palms up) and hold it over your chest with straight arms. Pull your shoulder blades back and down. Lower the bar to the center of your chest, then push the bar back up.

Note: **Space your hands about shoulder-width apart.**

Grab a pullup bar with a mixed grip (one palm facing toward you, the other facing away). Hang with your arms straight and brace your abs. Pull yourself up until your chin is over the bar, then slowly lower yourself. Reverse your grips on the next set.

7. ONE-ARM HORIZONTAL PULLUP

Note: Reach your free arm up toward the ceiling, as if punching up.

Lie under a secure waist-high bar with your heels on the floor and grab the bar with one arm extended over the center of your body. Pull up toward the bar, lower yourself, and repeat with the other arm. Too hard? Bend your knees or use two hands.

PEAK
performance

Jumpstart Your Workout

Are you ready to engage nearly all your muscles in just one move? Then begin your workout with the jump shrug. You'll build strength and muscle and also improve your agility and vertical leap.

Jump Shrug

With your knees bent and back straight, hold a barbell just below your knees with an overhand, shoulder-width grip. Keeping your back flat and arms straight, simultaneously thrust your hips forward, shrug your shoulders, and jump straight up. Land on the balls of your feet and repeat. Do three sets of 3 to 5 reps. Take 10 seconds to reset your feet between reps.

8. PLANK WITH WEIGHT TRANSFER

Assume the plank position with a light weight to the outside of your right elbow. Pick up the weight with your right hand and pass it to your left hand. Place the weight to your left. Move the weight back to the other side. Continue for 30 to 60 seconds.

Note: Brace your abs to keep your torso from rotating as you lift the weight.

Add Explosive Power to Your Arsenal

Build muscle and increase stamina in one fast-paced routine. Three days a week, perform this athletic sequence, courtesy of *Men's Health* Muscle Guy Mike Mejia, MS, CSCS.

Perform these moves in order, resting only as long as it takes to set up between exercises. Then break for 30 seconds and repeat the circuit once or twice. Rest a day between sessions, but stay active outside the gym.

Stair Shuttle: Stand at the bottom of a staircase. Place one foot on the first step, with your opposite arm slightly bent in front of you and your other arm behind your torso and slightly bent, as if you're ready to sprint up the staircase. Begin switching your feet and arms so you're sprinting in place. Go as fast as you can for 30 seconds.

position. That's one repetition. Do 2 or 3 reps in each direction.

Agility Run: Place three cones or small objects 5 yards apart in a straight line. The first marker is your starting

Crab-Walk Pushup: Assume the classic pushup position. Perform a pushup, then squeeze your abs forcefully and slide your left leg and left arm out to the side as far as possible. Do another pushup, then bring your arm and leg over so you're back in the starting

point. Sprint to the nearest cone and back. Then sprint to the farthest cone and back. That's one repetition. Rest for 10 seconds and repeat for 5 reps. Mix it up to include backpedals, side shuffles, and skips.

Interrupted Pullups: With an overhand grip, place your hands slightly more than shoulder-width apart on a bar. Pull your chin over the bar, then lower slowly. Perform two or three pullups, then rest for 10 seconds. Continue this sequence until you can no longer complete two pullups.

Go Solo

Stop using a spotter to squeeze out more repetitions: It's a waste of time and effort. A new study in the *Journal of Strength and Conditioning Research* reports that lifters who bolstered their rep counts using a second set of hands gained no more strength or size than their solo-lifting counterparts. But in debunking this common weight-room belief, study author Eric Drinkwater,

PhD, discovered something else: You're able to increase total reps if you do fewer reps per set. So if you're struggling to lift two sets of 12 reps, switch it up and tackle eight sets of 3 reps instead. You won't need that spotter's nudge—just his presence, in case your grip slips.

Mix It Up

Make boosting your bench press a guessing game—for your muscles. Varying your reps and resistance every workout can double your strength gains compared with a more conventional approach in which you mix it up every few weeks, report researchers at Arizona State University. "More-frequent changes appear to better stimulate the neuromuscular system, which is largely responsible for strength gains," says Mark Peterson, CSCS. Do three sets of 10 reps of each exercise on Monday, two sets of 15 on Wednesday, and four sets of 5 on Friday. Adjust the amount of weight you lift each day, so your muscles are always challenged.

Add a Wobble to Your Workout

The most unlikely workout aid? Bed pillows—they can make your legs stronger. When men attempted single-leg squats while standing on a cushy surface, their hip and leg muscles worked up to 13 percent harder, report Mayo Clinic researchers. It's a tricky maneuver, however, because you can easily lose your balance. If you can do three sets of 10 single-leg wobble-free squats while standing on a hard floor, bring on the pillow.

Flip Your Grip

At the National Strength and Conditioning Association's annual conference, scientists reported that men who performed the deadlift with an alternating grip—one hand grasping the bar overhand, the other underhand—could complete two more reps than when they used a traditional grip. As a result, the lifters hoisted an average of 713 more pounds each set. The alternating grip helps prevent the bar from slipping out of your hands, which allows you to lift more weight.

Jump Out of the Gym

Your legs get you airborne, but it's your arms that take you higher. German researchers report that your arm swing may play a bigger role in vertical elevation than quickly dipping your hips and knees before takeoff, a.k.a. the countermovement. In the study, men who jumped from a standstill, reaching to the sky as they went up, were able to leap 16 percent higher than men who performed the countermovement but kept their hands on their hips. However, doing the countermovement with the added arm pump proved most effective. This led researchers to speculate that building big biceps can propel you higher.

Build Bigger Arms

Looking for a new way to challenge your guns? Scientists in New Zealand discovered that Swiss-ball pushups train your arms 30 percent harder than regular pushups do. "The Swiss ball forces your triceps to stabilize your elbow and shoulder joints, which results in the recruitment of more muscle fibers," says lead investigator Paul Marshall, MS. In the study, men performed the movement just like a regular pushup, only with their hands on a Swiss ball. Bend your arms until your chest touches the ball, then push yourself back up.

Build an Eternal Six-Pack

The natural aging process may have a soft spot for hard abs. Finnish researchers have discovered that your core muscles atrophy significantly slower than your arms and legs do. Make the effort to carve your six-pack now, and it may stay strong for life.

Better Your Bench

The secret to a bigger bench press: Push with your legs. Canadian researchers found that raising your feet off the floor while benching shifts as much as 30 percent of the load off your upper body and onto an overmatched core, significantly weakening your lift. So grip the ground with your toes, says Greg Anderson, PhD, an elite trainer in Seattle and one of the study's authors. Doing so causes your thighs and glutes to contract—creating energy that'll help drive up the barbell—while ensuring that the proper muscles (chest, arms, and shoulders) are targeted. Trying to "bend" the bar with your hands will also help you through a hard lift.

Stretch to Protect

Just hearing the words "groin pull" is enough to make you wince. Stretching can help you avoid the real-life wrath of this injury. While studying football players, Australian researchers discovered that every man who suffered a groin injury also had tight hips. Protect your groin by increasing flexibility in your hip adductors, or inner thighs, says Mike Robertson, MS, CSCS, a strength coach in Indianapolis. Lie on your left side with your legs stacked, contract your glutes, and raise your right leg as high as you can. Hold, lower, and repeat. If your lift falls short of 60 degrees, perform side lunges to loosen up. Do 10 repetitions per leg.

Outlift an Olympian

Sculpt your body with a world-class maneuver. An exercise known as the jump shrug is easier and more effective than the Olympic-style lifts used in competition. The proof: University of Wisconsin researchers found that men generated 18 percent more power during the jump shrug than during a power clean, which is the gold standard of Olympic lifts. You simply pull the bar straight up during a jump shrug, so you're able to generate more power than in the very technical clean, says Glenn Wright, PhD.

Take the Fast Track to Muscle

Bored by your leg workout? Lace up your running shoes. Wind-sprint workouts boost lower-body strength, report Croatian researchers. In a new study, men who replaced their weekly weight workouts with three high-intensity cardio sessions increased their leg strength by 10 percent in just 10 weeks. Try their iron-free approach to bolster your base. At a football field or track, sprint for 10 yards, rest for 1 minute, and repeat twice. That's one set. Do a total of four. Rest for 3 minutes between sets and at least a day between sessions. Every 2 weeks, increase your sprint distance by 10 yards.

Hit the Showers

Hit the rinse cycle after your workout. Alternating between hot and cold in the shower will lessen postexercise muscle soreness, say researchers at Massey University, in New Zealand. After a training session, men who rinsed under both temperature extremes experienced muscle recovery 30 percent faster than a control group did.

Mixing up the water temp increases blood-flow to the muscles, says study author Hugh Morton, PhD. Aim for 10 minutes under the showerhead, switching between hot and cold at 2-minute intervals. "Make the temperature difference as dramatic as possible for the quickest recovery," Morton says.

Lift More, Instantly

Do you have chicken legs? Beef them up with a simple tweak to your exercise regimen. Pull your toes toward your shins during a lying leg curl and you'll be able to lift an extra 19 pounds, according to a new University of West Florida study. Known as dorsiflexion, this foot position allows the largest muscles in your calves (the gastrocnemii) to assist your hamstrings and glutes with the lift, say the study authors. But as you lower the weight for the negative portion of the movement, use the opposite approach: Extend your ankles so your toes point away from your shins. This forces your thigh muscles to work harder.

Sidestep Knee Pain

Eating papaya today can save your knees in the future, say Australian scientists who studied the diets and knees of nearly 300 adults for 10 years. MRI scans proved that the people who ate the most vitamin C–rich fruits experienced significantly less knee wear and tear, slashing their risk of osteoarthritis. Every one-serving increase in fruit intake per day decreases your risk of developing the disease.

Antioxidants help prevent cartilage damage, while vitamin C strengthens bone, says Flavia Cicuttini, PhD, one of the study's authors. Especially if you're a runner, be sure to add papayas, oranges, and apricots—all high in vitamin C—to your diet.

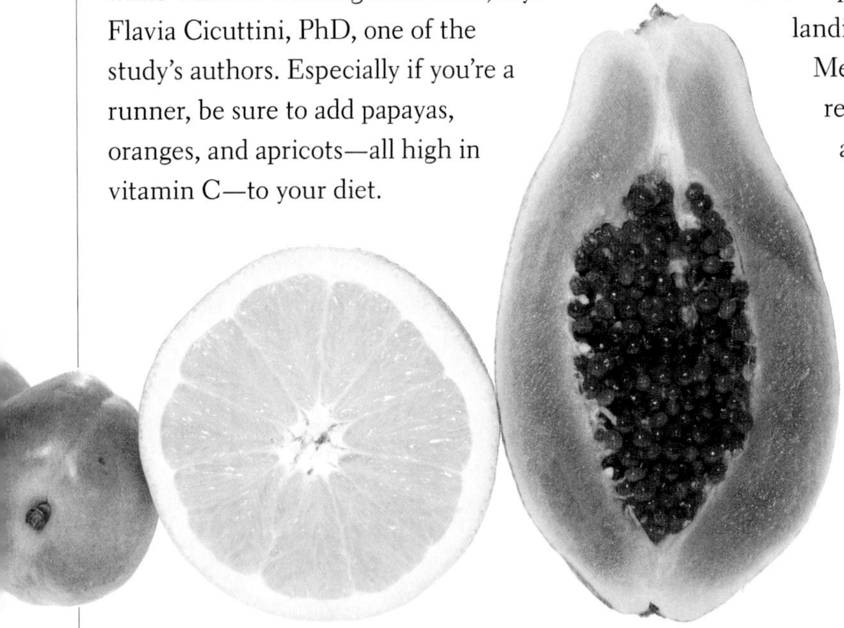

Don't Play Favorites

Want the perfect body? Then stop choosing sides. Lifters often train one leg harder than the other, report researchers at Ball State University. Call it favoritism by default. When one leg is stronger than the other, weight is distributed unevenly, limiting growth and increasing injury risk, says study coauthor Mike Robertson, MS, CSCS, a strength coach in Indianapolis.

Don't assume you're in balance: Take this test. Hop forward on one leg five times, landing on both feet on your final hop. Measure the distance you covered and repeat on your other leg. "More than a 10 percent difference in distance means you have a strength imbalance," says Robertson.

Training Tips

I can do eight biceps curls with my left arm and 10 with my right. How can I balance my strength?

Which arm do you start with? If you begin with your right, there will always be a bit of crossover neural fatigue (think slower firing nerves) in your left, making it feel weaker off the bat. So switch up your start arm. If that doesn't work, do as many reps as you can with each arm, but then do an extra set with your left.

Alternatively, and slightly more counterintuitively, keep the same routine for the stronger arm, but increase the weight and do fewer reps—4 to 6—with the weaker arm. Doing so will accelerate its muscle growth and balance out your arm strength in a few weeks.

Should I bench-press with my elbows pulled in close to my body or flared out?

Guys flare their elbows because it isolates the chest better, but it also limits the amount they can bench-press and puts them at risk of injury. Flaring narrows the distance between your upper-arm bone and your shoulder blade, which can cause nasty shoulder problems. At the same time, the technique increases the distance the bar must travel, cutting back on the total amount of weight you can lift. So unless you're trying to lose a benching competition, or hurt yourself, keep your wings tucked.

My right shoulder is lower than my left. Can I fix the difference with exercise?

If you have pain, weakness, or restricted motion in your shoulder that doesn't improve with rest, see a doctor. It could be a muscle tear or nerve problem.

No symptoms? Start training your shoulders and upper-back muscles with exercises that work one arm at a time. For instance, ditch the traditional lat pulldown for the single-arm lat pulldown using a pulley handle. And add the "pushup plus" to your routine: Assume the classic pushup position, bend your elbows to lower your body to the floor, and then push back up. At the top of the move, push a little farther so that your shoulders push forward and your upper back arches. Then return to the starting position. Do three sets of 10 to 15 repetitions.

"This trains a muscle on the inner portion of your shoulder blade called the serratus anterior, which helps keep your shoulder blades properly aligned," says Steve Petersen, MD, codirector of the shoulder-surgery division at Johns Hopkins School of Medicine.

Swiss-ball leg curls make my hamstrings cramp up. What else can I do to work my legs?

If you're having cramping during Swiss-ball leg curls, it's a sign that your hamstrings are both weak and tight, says *Men's Health* Muscle Guy Mike Mejia. Rather than trying to avoid the issue, let's address it head-on. The Swiss-ball leg curl is one of the best exercises you can do for your hamstrings and glutes. But first we need to condition the backs of your thighs with easier drills to build the strength and flexibility you'll require to nail this move cramp-free. Do two or three sets of 8 to 12 reps of the moves listed in the chart below.

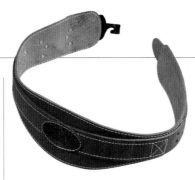

Should I wear a weight belt when I do squats?

Studies indicate that a belt can be a blessing and a curse. Yale University researchers found that men who wear belts while squatting show improved lower-back stability. But those same scientists warn that regular use of a belt can make your body so reliant on it that your core muscles become less supportive, making you more susceptible to back injuries when you train without one.

So forgo the belt and focus on both your form (e.g., placing the bar across your shoulders and keeping your back straight as you squat) and strengthening your core. Strong trunk muscles act like a built-in weight belt.

Do I need to keep my elbows tight against my sides when doing biceps curls?

Yes—if you really want to zero in on your biceps. When your elbows flap freely, you recruit your chest, shoulders, and back to help do the job. Because your biceps are relatively small muscles, they fatigue easily. So try to work them on days you don't target your chest and back because most torso exercises also engage your biceps.

How can I build bigger calves but take less time?

Your best bet is to steal a page from legendary trainer Vince Gironda, who first popularized this protocol for another guy who struggled with calf development: Arnold. Start with a weight that's roughly 30 to 40 percent of what you'd normally use for calf raises. Perform 10 sets of 10 repetitions. Here's the key: Rest for only 15

WEEK	EXERCISE	NUMBER OF TIMES PER WEEK
1	Leg curl	2
2	Leg curl	1
2	Romanian deadlift	1
3	Leg curl	2
3	Romanian deadlift	2
4	Swiss-ball leg curl	2
4	Romanian deadlift	2

seconds between sets. Because calf-muscle-fiber makeup differs from that of bigger muscles, your calves recover too fast with the old three-sets-of-10 approach. This routine will challenge your lower legs, and it will take less than 10 minutes to complete, so you can do it every day.

I can't squat any more weight. How can I get out of this rut?

Your roadblock may have little to do with your legs. "If your lower back is weak, it'll limit the weight you can squat," says C.J. Murphy, MFS, head instructor at Total Performance Sports, in Everett, Massachusetts.

Test your strength: Perform three sets of 20 reps of the Hatfield back raise. Can't do it? Your lower back is weak—as it is for most men—and it'll limit your performance in the squat and other exercises. Add the Hatfield back raise once a week after your squat routine.

Do I need to strengthen my rump to fortify my core?

Yes, and all jokes aside, it's the most important part of your core. The squat often receives the bulk of "butt-building" publicity, but if your glutes are indeed a weak link, you may be unknowingly altering your squats to use your quadriceps more. That's why we often recommend exercises like the one below before moving on to compound lifts, such as squats.

SINGLE-LEG SUPINE BRIDGE

Lie on your back with your right knee bent 90 degrees and your right foot flat on the floor. Folding your arms across your chest and lifting your left leg off the floor, bend your left hip and knee 90 degrees so your left knee is pointing to the ceiling. Brace your core and push your right foot into

until the middle of your back is off the ground. Hold this position for 3 seconds, then lower your hips and return to the starting position. Perform 10 reps with each leg.

I hate doing lunges because they're so hard. Will any other exercise work my lower body as well?

Any exercise that's hard is usually worth doing. Lunges are useful because they work large muscle groups in your legs and improve your balance. Check your form with a trainer to see whether you can make them more comfortable. If you're leaning too far forward, you might be straining your knees. The only other exercise in the same league for strengthening the lower body is the squat. Pick your poison.

PART FIVE

RUN FAST

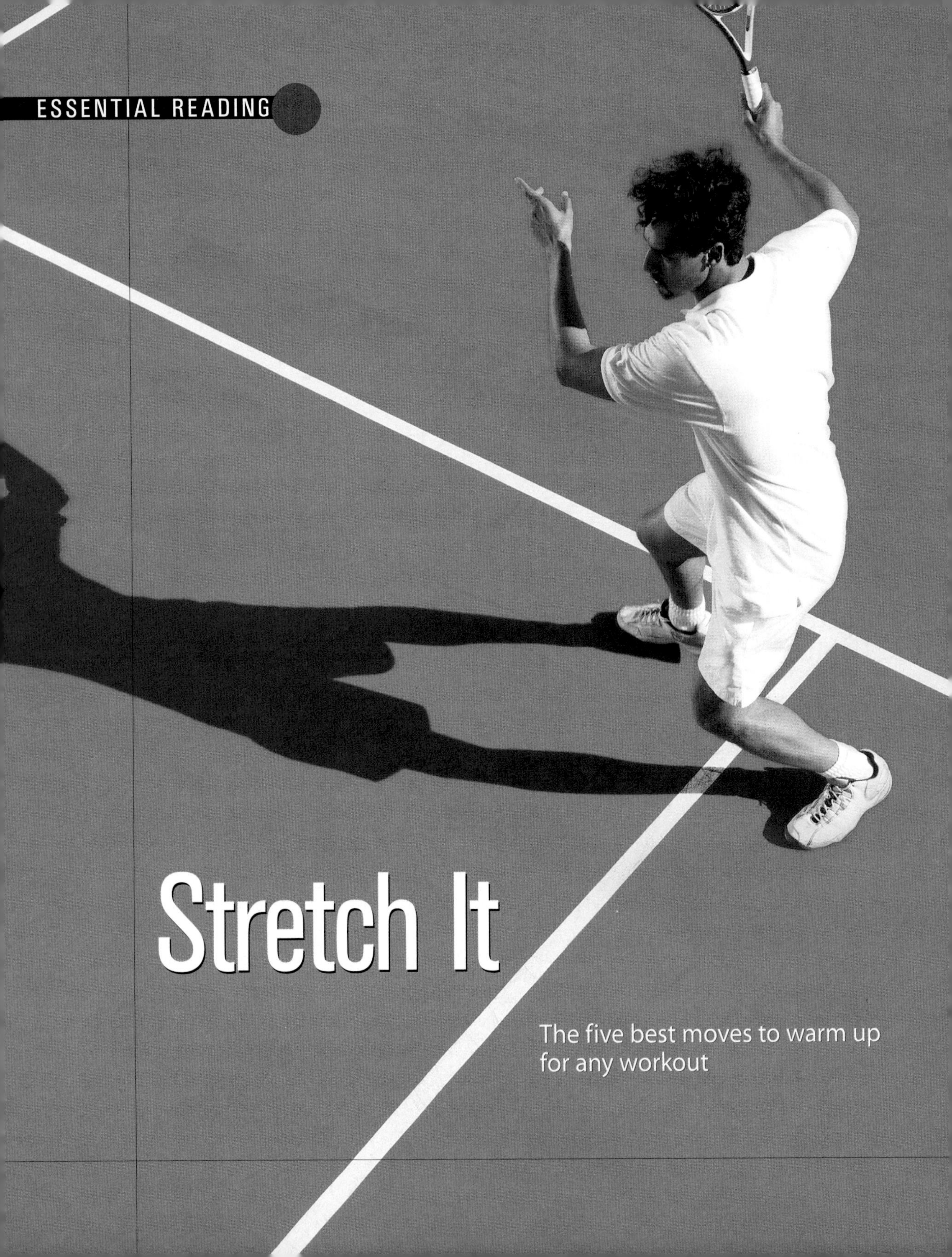

Stretch It

The five best moves to warm up
for any workout

There's something to be said for static stretching—the touch-your-toes-and-hold-for-30-seconds routine we all learned in gym class. It does a tremendous job of lengthening one's muscles, locking in strength, and reinforcing flexibility. "But it's best when done after a workout, to calm the nervous system or as part of corrective protocol," says Mark Verstegen, MS, CSCS, founder and president of Athletes' Performance, in Tempe, Arizona. "Doing static stretches before you exercise is like putting your muscles in a sleeper hold. You're turning off their circuit breakers right before you need them to fire."

Warm up with the following movement-based stretches instead. By actively moving muscles in and out of stretched positions (instead of stretching and holding), you will boost your heart rate, increase your blood flow, and get your nervous system firing. In short, "these stretches prepare your body for exercise, regardless of what type it is," says Verstegen. "They'll also increase your speed and power by 20 percent." Not bad for a 10-minute investment.

90/90 STRETCH

This exercise will stretch your torso and back muscles, which are especially important for rotational sports such as golf and tennis. Lie on your left side with your legs bent at a 90-degree angle. Place a rolled-up towel between your knees and extend your arms straight out from your chest. Then, keeping your knees together and your hips still, rotate your chest and right arm backward, trying to touch your shoulder blades to the ground. Exhale and hold for 2 seconds, then return to the starting position. Do 10 reps on each side.

HIP CROSSOVER

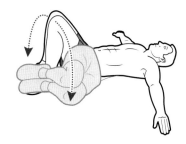

Lie faceup with your knees bent, your feet on the floor, and your arms extended out to your sides. Rotate your bent legs to the left until your left knee touches the floor, then rotate to the right. Do 10 reps on each side. You should feel a lengthening and stretching of the torso. This exercise is designed to build mobility and strength in your torso by disassociating the hips and shoulders.

HAND WALK

Stand with your legs straight and your hands flat on the floor. Draw in your belly button and walk out a few paces with your hands. Then, keeping your legs straight and your hands in place, take a few steps forward with your feet (flex your ankles, not your knees). Continue this caterpillar-like movement for 1 minute. This stretches the hamstrings, lower back, glutes, and calves. It's a great exercise prior to just about any sport.

FORWARD LUNGE, FOREARM TO INSTEP

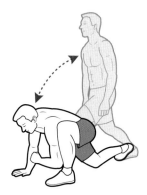

Take a large step forward with your left leg, as if doing a lunge. Place your right hand on the floor, even with your left foot, and move your left elbow down toward your left instep while keeping your right knee off the ground. Move your left hand outside your left foot and push your hips up to the sky. Finally, step forward into the next lunge with your right foot. Do 10 lunges per leg. You'll feel a stretch in your groin, your back-leg hip flexor, and your front-leg glute and hamstring.

PILLAR MARCHING

You should feel this total-body stretch everywhere. It's perfect for preparing for the demands of running. Begin with your back straight and your arms by your sides. March forward, alternately lifting each knee to waist height while pumping your arms like a drum major. March forward 20 steps for one set. Rest for 1 minute; repeat the cycle twice.

Master the Side Bridge to Build Better Abs

Don't underestimate the tame-looking side bridge. "Men think a good abdominal exercise has to make your abs burn," says Michael Boyle, MA, ATC, a strength coach. Here's the truth: Side bridges improve the stability of all the muscles surrounding your spine and stomach. In fact, Canadian researchers found that men who can perform the side bridge effectively are less likely to encounter back trouble.

Add this routine to your workout to bolster your core and help carve a six-pack.

Hold the moves for the times specified below, then switch sides.

Kneeling Side Bridge

Lie on your side with your forearm on the floor and your elbow under your shoulder, your knees bent 90 degrees. Contract your glutes and keep your abs stiff throughout. Raise your hips until your torso is straight from shoulders to knees.

Side Bridge

Lie on your side with your forearm on the floor under your shoulder, and your feet stacked together. Contract your glutes and abs. Push your hips off the floor, creating a straight line from ankle to shoulder and keeping your head in line with your spine.

Elevated Side Bridge

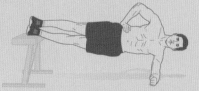

Use the same setup as for the side bridge, but stack your feet on a bench. Don't allow your hips to sag.

The workout: Do this routine two or three times a week.

WEEK	EXERCISE	SETS	TIME
1	Kneeling side bridge	2	30 sec
2	Kneeling side bridge	2	60 sec
3	Side bridge	2–3	45 sec
4	Side bridge	2–3	60 sec
5	Elevated side bridge	2–3	45 sec

Here are some benefits of this plan.

Less pain: Improving lower-back muscle endurance helps you stay upright and avoid strains.

V taper: The side bridge develops your obliques, the muscles that run along your torso.

More abs: Bridges challenge your deep abdominal stabilizers: the transverse abdominis and quadratus lumborum.

Run for Life

Want to feel younger, move smoother, and play safer? Try upping the tempo with a little speed conditioning

BY JONATHAN LITTMAN

"Two laps around," says Bill Collins, a slender man wearing skintight blue sweats. On the deserted upper deck of Texas Southern University's basketball arena, I join a huddle of runners hanging on Collins's every word. "Five times," he says, smiling, as we split into two groups and line up. "Five minutes' rest between."

Four of us crowd shoulder to shoulder on a thin strip of walkway separating the stadium's seats from a concrete wall: a brawny 30-something firefighter; a blond, pixieish 15-year-old soccer player; a 71-year-old Aussie; and yours truly, only recently getting serious about a fitness regimen. Fifteen extra pounds have lodged around my middle since my thirties, and age 50 is only two years away.

"Set…go!" Collins barks, and we're off. Our footsteps echo through the empty arena. The two-lap sprint is roughly a third of a mile. Our makeshift track is narrow, and the first corner looks unnervingly tight for four charging runners. One misstep and I will skid into the wall like a Roller Derby skater. The blond kid bolts ahead, and I tuck in behind on the turn. The Aussie grandpa elbows me out of the pack at the next corner. Stronger than I expected, I floor it on the second lap, but the fireman chugs by, and I'm dead last.

Gulping down breaths, I look up to see Collins running with another group. His feet spring off the floor. He sprints with the high, floating motion of a deer, his stride effortless. But when he swoops past the finish, you can feel the power in those legs. A shade under 6 feet tall, curly hair flecked with gray, his warm, light-brown face smooth and unlined, Collins looks a decade younger than his age. Sprinting is his passion and profession. At 56, he is a former world record holder in the 400-meter relay, and he continues to compete at the highest levels of masters competitions (for athletes 40 and older, contested in 5-year divisions). He owns 20 masters world records and has trained more than 2,000 Olympic, professional, and elite athletes, but unlike most competitors at his level, the affable Collins will share his secrets with you.

We all sprinted as kids. In my teens, I won 50-yard dashes, my quickness earning me a starter's position on the soccer team at the University of California at Berkeley. By my mid-twenties, I had more or less quit running, having made the shift to sports more generous to the aging athlete—cross-country skiing, swimming, in-line skating, and the occasional jog. Every time I asked my legs for more power, my body screamed no. When I hit 40, I ran out onto the soccer field to play with my teenage daughters. After less than an hour, my back ached and my hamstrings hardened like concrete.

Collins says it doesn't have to be that way. He insists that men can regain the quickness of youth with proper training and a little patience. So I decided to road test his speed-conditioning program, which he says is a safer and more effective fitness regimen than jogging long distances. "Forget what you think you know about how to run and

the importance of distance," says Collins, who teaches his trainees gradually to start striding like sprinters, driving forward with the knees up and shoulders pumping. The goal is to land more on the forefoot when running shorter distances—near the ball of the foot, which limits the amount of time the foot makes contact with the ground.

This is a new and somewhat controversial approach for recreational runners, but it seems to be gaining traction. A recent study buttressed Collins's view that intensive bursts of sprint-style exercise may actually be superior to long sessions. Researchers at McMaster University, in Canada, divided volunteer cyclists into two groups (studies use stationary cycles or treadmills for a controlled environment). One group pedaled five times a week at a moderate pace for 40 to 60 minutes; the other did 3 days a week of four to six quick bursts of 30-second sprints with ample rest in between. The sprinters demonstrated positive changes in skeletal muscle and endurance capacity equal to those who cruised for hours. Martin Gibala, PhD, an associate professor of kinesiology at McMaster, put it this way: "Short bouts of very intense exercise improved muscle health and performance comparable to several weeks of traditional endurance training."

For Kendon White, the burly fireman who just sprinted past me, the speed-conditioning program has helped him drop his resting pulse by 10 beats a minute and his waist size from 33 inches to 30, but that wasn't the extent of the benefits. "Training with Bill has given me the ability to do my job better," he says, "knowing that my body is not going to fail me. We just went through tests, a district-wide drill: I pulled a hose and carried it up three- and four-floor flights, carried dummies out of buildings heated to 200 to 300 degrees. I did the whole drill without any fatigue."

Mark Hastings, a 52-year-old Allstate man who has trained with Collins for two and a half years, has knocked 40 points off his total cholesterol levels and lost 15 pounds, and he now plays softball with his 30-year-old son without fear of injury. "The health benefits have been a blessing," he says, but he's having fun, too. Four months after joining Collins, Hastings competed in his first track meet, and today he runs nearly as fast as he did as a boy. Playing on his son's softball team with guys in their twenties has been an eye-opener—for his teammates. "Last week, I won the game with a home run," says Hastings, laughing. "We were down by two and had two runners on, and I hit an in-the-park home run. These young guys were going, 'Mr. Hastings, your form is so perfect. Did your coach teach you that?'"

Under Collins's tutelage, Hastings has honed his technique and improved the size and efficiency of the muscles critical to sprinting. Specificity is the key, says Collins: His program targets the muscles used for speed. We all have two kinds of muscle fibers—white fiber, commonly known as fast-twitch or type II fiber; and red fiber, or slow-twitch or type I fiber. As we age, we gradually lose the muscles that help us sprint

and jump (fast-twitch). By 40, a man's maximum velocity has likely dropped 7 percent.

The good news is that most sports—tennis, basketball, soccer—rarely demand top speed, which doesn't kick in until you've covered roughly 40 meters. In another recent study, Finnish researchers analyzed masters sprinters of all ages as they ran the first 10 meters of a sprint. Forty- to 49-year-old sprinters averaged just less than 5 meters per second during the initial sprint. Men a decade older were slower by less than a third of a meter, and those ages 60 to 69 were only a tenth of a meter slower than 50-year-olds. Translation? A sprint-trained 60-year-old tennis player can cover the court as well as an opponent 10 years his junior, because he has optimized the speed muscles. The Finns found that maturing men (unlike women) are able to make large increases in fast-twitch muscle and significant gains in strength, muscle size, and function.

This is why Hastings dusts practically every youngster on his softball team. His edge is that he regularly runs fast. "Once you start sprinting with your knees raised and your arms and shoulders pumping," says Collins, "you're effectively using 80 percent of your muscles—your calves, quads, upper torso, chest, shoulders, arms, and upper back."

HARD TRUTH

Percentage of runners who suffer from allergy symptoms while running

55

Hastings packed on muscle during the first 6 months of training, then lost 15 pounds in the second 6 months. That's because sprinting develops lean muscle mass. "Put a sprinter and long-distance runner side by side," says Collins. "What do you see? The sprinter is toned," he says, "because sprinting develops active muscles. It's not like in the gym where guys with bellies hanging over their belt buckles lift hundreds of pounds," adds Collins, who, by the way, bench-presses double his weight of 150 pounds.

But be forewarned. "If you do speedwork before doing proper preconditioning, you're at greater risk for muscular-tendinous injuries," says David Berkoff, MD, assistant professor of sports and emergency medicine at Duke University's sports medicine division. "Hamstring and quadriceps injuries often occur as a result of speedwork. As people get older, we start seeing Achilles tendon ruptures." With new athletes, says Dr. Berkoff, "you have to walk before you run. Building core strength keeps things biomechanically efficient. Once your body is conditioned, you can add small doses of sprints or higher-intensity work."

Yes, it's clear that running faster is risky. But running slowly won't help you play active sports, and I've strained enough muscles playing soccer and tennis that I'm ready to try something new. (Collins customizes workouts for sports such as basketball, tennis, and football.) There's something definitely exciting about the promise of running fast again, upright and strong, not

bent into the familiar death trot you see every day on local running trails. I called Collins late last November and began training with his program at home. This is what it looks like.

Phase I: Build Your Engine

Collins doesn't train beginners like he trains college sprinters. He teaches a full-body approach to running. "Even though you've been a couch potato for 12 years, your mind thinks you're still a great athlete," says Collins. "Basketball, flag football, and tennis all require quick movements. But those fast-twitch fibers—and ligaments—have been dormant. They're like brittle rubber bands. They're destined for injury."

The foundation begins with core strength, performing full-range situps, which he says develop the hip flexors better than crunches do. ("If you do them properly," he says, "they strengthen the complete core, from the back through the groin, quads, and all the abdominal areas.")

Weeks 1 and 2: Begin the core program with 50 full-range situps and 10 to 15 pushups a day, along with light stretching: "hamstring stretches, calf raises, and back raises (lie on your back and lift your upper body 4 inches off the mat, using your elbows)," says Collins. No running or jogging.

Collins: "I want you to do a minimum of 50 situps a day, full range. If you're out of shape, I want you to do 10, then rest, then 10, until you get your 50 in." Core work builds the structural support necessary to

The (Very, Very) Fast Way to Get Fit

These drills, courtesy of Bill Collins, shore up your core and bolster your lower body using movements that mimic perfect sprinting technique. They'll help you run faster and more efficiently, with less chance of breaking down.

Drive-Ups

Stand facing an aerobic step or bench, with your weight on the balls of your feet. (As you improve, you can increase the height of the step, but start with one that's about 6 inches high.) Place the ball of your left foot on the step, keeping your back straight, glutes and abs tight, eyes forward, and arms bent at your sides in a runner's position. Push off from the ball of your right foot, lifting your right knee and driving the right leg up until that foot is even with your left knee. As you bring your right leg up, your left arm pushes forward as your right arm pulls back, in a runner's motion. Hold for a moment, then return your right leg to the starting position. Make sure you stay on the balls of your feet or the move won't be effective. Do 25 on each leg, working up to 75.

The benefit: Conditions the lower back, abs, and hips to remain stable in the running motion. Also strengthens the fronts of the thighs, the glutes, and the calves.

Stepups

Stand facing an aerobic step or plyometric box, with your feet about shoulder-width apart. Keeping your abs and glutes tight, back straight, and eyes forward, step up onto the box with your right foot, then bring your left foot up onto the box as well. Then step down with your right foot, followed by your left; repeat. This is a very rhythmic movement, almost like marching. Your arms should be pumping in a runner's motion as you step up and down. Be sure to stay on the balls of your feet to get the most out of the exercise. Do 25 repetitions leading with your right leg, and 25 reps leading with your left. Progress to 75 reps on each side.

The benefit: Improves rhythm, balance, and coordination while building all the muscles of your lower body. Also teaches you to contract your glutes forcefully to generate more power in every stride.

Ball Squats

Hold a 6-pound medicine ball and stand with your feet shoulder-width apart, weight on the balls of your feet, back straight, abs and glutes tight, and eyes forward. Hold the ball straight out in front of you, squat down so that your knees bend at a 90-degree angle, and then stand up straight. The key to doing this exercise safely and effectively is to start with a lighter weight and squat down as far as you comfortably can, working your way toward that 90-degree angle at the knee. Start with sets of 15 to 20, and work up to doing three sets for a total of 45 to 60 reps.

The benefit: This exercise really improves your balance while it works your quads, glutes, abs, and arms.

Speed Lunges

This is Collins's creation, developed while studying speed applications in Germany. Stand with your feet shoulder-width apart, back straight, abs and glutes tight, and eyes forward. Lift your right leg and lunge it forward about 24 inches in front of you; land on the ball of your right foot. As you do this, your left arm pushes forward as your right arm pulls back, beginning the runner's motion. Staying on the balls of your feet, lower your left knee toward the floor until your left thigh is perpendicular to the ground. Rise up, pushing from the ball of your left foot, and lunge your left leg forward while pumping your arms; land on the ball of your left foot about 24 inches in front of you. Continue lunging forward for 10 yards, turn around, and lunge back to your starting point. Repeat, trying to cover more distance each time.

The benefit: Improves balance and mobility in your hips. Trains your thighs, glutes, and calves.

run high off your hips and drive your knees—a gazelle-like forward motion that can reduce the physical toll of running. Full-range situps, Collins insists, minimize the odds of back or groin strains when you run. The idea is to gain postural strength before you start running.

Weeks 3 and 4: Begin jogging and walking no more than 1 mile a day, and limit it to 2 days a week. Increase situps to 60 a day and pushups to 20 to 25 a day.

Collins: "Jog 400 meters, walk a little bit, jog a bit. We'll slowly work you up to that mile. If you start going any further, you might start to have problems. This way, you'll see what's going on with your knees, calf muscles, and hamstrings." A conservative preliminary routine, insists Collins, helps avoid the overuse injuries that plague distance runners.

Weeks 4 to 16: Begin 1-mile runs on Mondays and Fridays. Tuesdays and Thursdays, add light weights with high reps to your core program. Here's what Collins suggests: bench press, 40 to 75 pounds, two or three sets of 20 to 25 reps; overheads, 10 to 30 pounds, two sets of 25 to 40 reps; pushouts, 10 to 30 pounds, two sets of 10 to 15 reps; side-to-sides, 10 to 25 pounds, two sets of 4 to 8 reps. (Go to BestLifeOnline.com/speed for a description of this weight workout.) On Wednesdays, run stairs or stadium steps. Gradually increase Monday's distance to 2 or 3 miles, and Friday's to 2 miles.

Collins: "In the build phase, Mondays are dedicated to slow running, incrementally building distances to a maximum of 3 miles. Rest a day, and then on Wednesdays, run five sets of stair steps—60 meters of stadium steps if you have them, but it could be the stairs in an office building or even a 25- to 35-degree hill. On Fridays, increase your distance to 2 miles, but run at a slightly faster pace than Monday's. The weekend is an all-important rest period."

Phase II: Speed by Degrees

In this intermediate phase of the program, the distances gradually decrease and the pace picks up.

Weeks 16 to 20: Begin running 300- to 400-meter intervals, but no more than 2 miles total.

Collins: "Swap Wednesday's steps for faster-paced runs. Begin with 300- or 400-meter intervals, interspersed with 2 minutes of recovery. With shorter distances, concentrate on your technique [see "The (Very, Very) Fast Way to Get Fit" on page 253]. Find a pace that allows you to complete eight to ten 400s, or ten to twelve 300s."

Weeks 20 to 24: Mix in 1 or 2 days of faster running, depending on your conditioning level and flexibility. Begin to pick up the pace, running intervals of 250 to 350 meters, but not totaling more than 2,000 meters.

Collins: "Find a high school or college track, or pace out the distances on running trails or in parks. On Mondays, start with five 350-meter intervals or eight 250s, with 2 minutes' rest between each." Tuesdays and Thursdays are weights and core. On

Phase III: High Velocity

Five months of training have put you in the position to open the throttle. By now, your situp totals have grown to 700 to 1,000 a week. Weight load and reps have increased, too.

Week 24 and on: Collins teaches dozens of variations on the sprint workout. Here are three of his favorites, which he calls the Gold Standard, the Speed Ladder, and the Hundred Repeat Downs.

Collins: "Hundred-meter repeats are the Gold Standard for building speed, an anchor workout you can do once every week or two. Start by running 100 meters. Your rest is your 10- to 15-meter walk back to the finish line, which is now your start line. Go again and start slowly. Try to finish each 100 meters in 20 to 25 seconds. Run five 100-meter distances in a row. Go easy on the first couple or you might strain something. Rest a few minutes between the four or five sets."

"The Speed Ladder helps build acceleration. Start by running 20 meters four times. Your rest is longer as you walk back to the start line. Then run 40 meters four times, again resting by walking back to the start line, 60 meters four times, 80 meters four times—up to 100 meters four times, all with a full walk back to the start for recovery. Other than the walks, there is no complete rest.

"After a month of these drills, you can move on to the physically and mentally challenging Hundred Repeat Downs, which are sets of five 100-meter dashes with a

Wednesdays, run eight 150-meter intervals with a 50-meter recovery walk. "On Fridays, mix it up: 450-, 350-, 250-, and back to 350-meter runs," says Collins, with 3 to 4 minutes' rest. Varying distances and speeds will help you keep improving.

Don't jog or talk between intervals: Keep your concentration. "It helps to think about sprint training as a type of Olympic lifting," says Chris Carmichael, personal fitness coach to Lance Armstrong and head of a national training empire for recreational athletes as well as premier cyclists, runners, and triathletes. "After you do a set of clean-and-jerks, what do you do? You walk around the weight room shaking out your legs and arms. Walking around the track after a sprint set is the same approach to building power."

twist. The goal here is to reduce each new effort by 1 second. My slower group starts at 25 seconds and works down to 21. Start even slower if you're not fit. Five sets of these equal 2,500 meters."

"Drive it! Drive it! Drive it!" Collins cheers as I chug up the stairs. "Good arms! Good arms! Don't forget those arms, Jonathan. You've got to drive your arms."

I'm here at the Texas Southern University gym, joining Collins and a group of guys smack in the middle of phase II. This is a stadium night—meaning stadium steps— critical for developing the explosive type of

power Collins wants us to get. But equally important, it's a chance to work on our fundamentals. If you can't fly to Houston or train remotely (Collins analyzes video over the Internet and sends training modules, then he evaluates results via e-mail), you'd do well to have someone knowledgeable analyze your form before you undertake a speed-conditioning workout.

Many runners, myself included, tend to stride leading with the calves, which can strain hamstring muscles. Collins teaches running from the hips, which takes some getting used to. "Most of what we lose [over the years] is the range of motion in the hip," says Nancy Hamilton, PhD, professor of physical education and biometrics at the University of Northern Iowa, who has researched biomechanics and masters sprinters. "We start running from the knee. The hip is the largest and strongest joint in the body. It has a great range of motion. You can do a lot more with your hip than with your knee, if you can remember how to use it."

Tonight we're testing our form on the stadium steps. "Kendon! Don't sit back!" Collins shouts at the heavily muscled fireman pounding up the stairs. "You have to have a forward projection."

Here comes Hastings, chewing a wad of gum, 20 years Kendon's senior.

"Good, Mark!" Collins cheers, as Hastings powers up, strong, upright, and efficient.

Collins turns and explains, "Mark isn't exerting any more energy than the rest of them, but he's doing it right."

I laugh. "Old guys have to do it right!"

On Tuesday, I join Collins and the crew in the cramped, windowless Texas Southern weight room. We pump iron and work our way through a set of plyometrics—fast, explosive movements designed to develop muscular power. We start with "drive-ups," leaping from the ball of one foot up onto a wooden box. Collins demonstrates the right form, looking like a cross between a Marine sergeant and a salsa teacher as he takes us through a series of progressively taller boxes.

In the morning, I hobble over to the track at Rice University, where the group pounds up and down a ramp under the stadium, half a mile of intensive plyometrics that I wisely watch. On the track, Collins has us step over hurdles, a dynamic warmup forcing us to drive up our knees. Finally, he says, "Let's try a little speed." Eight 250-meter sprints, separated by a walk after each. Collins puts me with the Aussie, Bob Cozens, another aging male champ, and the women. The old boys smoke me, as does Collins's charming wife, Stephanie, who can still pop a quarter mile in nearly a minute.

Little by little, though, the speed returns to my legs. In the last two heats, I'm only a couple of seconds behind these astonishing sprint-trained 70-year-old men, and with some grit in my final push, I hang with Stephanie down the stretch.

Okay, so I'm still a long way from all-out sprinting, my form still stinks ("Stop reaching! Drive those arms!"), and an hour after the workout, I'll be humbled by a painful calf cramp. But at this moment, I can't

PAIN killer

I have jumper's knee. Do I need to go under the knife?

Tell your doc: Drop the scalpel. Squats can cure jumper's knee faster than surgery can. Doctors at the Norwegian School of Sport Sciences treated 40 cases of jumper's knee, a type of tendon inflammation, with either surgery or a 12-week exercise regimen and found that those who trained were 20 percent more likely to fully heal. "Exercise stimulates collagen, a building block of the tendon," says lead author Roald Bahr, MD, PhD. See a doctor to rule out an ACL sprain before you try the study's regimen: three sets of 15 squats on a 25-degree decline board, twice a day.

believe my 200-meter pace was nearly 10 seconds faster than 2 weeks before. I haven't run this fast since I was 25!

As I pack up, Collins reminds me that the workouts are tough and my buddies will think I'm nuts. I'll have to resist the urge to go too fast too soon. On the plane, I begin calculating. After only 2 months of Collins's program, my resting pulse has dropped to 60 beats a minute, my waist slimmed an inch to 33, and my chest broadened. In a couple of weeks, I'll be up to 100 situps a day. By spring, I'll be ready for a little more speed-work. I'll muscle my fifty 45-pound bench presses up to 100 at 70 pounds. Cut back on my beloved wine, and I'll shed 10 pounds. I've checked last year's times for the regional masters championships. If I can get these legs turning nearly as fast as they did in high school, I'll crack the top two in the 400 or 800 meters.

How hard can that be?

Shake It Up

Build your own triathlon with these three-part, boredom-busting cardio routines

BY MATT FITZGERALD

The sport of triathlon was born when swimmers, runners, and cyclists grew tired of doing just one sport. By combining three events into one, the runners built swimmers' shoulders, the swimmers pumped up cyclists' legs, and the cyclists looked even leaner.

We've created a series of "fitness triathlons" that will help keep your workout fresh while building strength and endurance throughout your body.

The Multisport Tri

This workout provides all the benefits of a real triathlon, but because you're not actually competing, you'll do the swim last, when it's convenient. No pool? Use a rowing machine instead.

How to do it: Pedal a bike at a steady, comfortable pace—an effort level of 5 or 6 on a scale of 1 to 10—for 10 minutes. Hop down and run outside or on a treadmill for 10 minutes at an effort level of 5 or 6. Finally, head to the pool or rowing machine and do another 10 minutes at the same intensity.

Mix it up: Short on time? Cut the final leg in half and increase your intensity to 8.

The User-Friendly Tri

You can complete this routine in one section of your gym and still challenge your cardiovascular system in new ways.

How to do it: Choose any three cardio machines, such as an elliptical trainer, a treadmill, and a stationary bike. On the first machine, do 10 minutes at an effort level of 5 or 6. Move on to the next machine and complete 10 minutes at an effort level of 9 or 10. Finally, do 10 minutes on your last machine at an effort level of 5 or 6.

Mix it up: Change the order of the machines each time you train, so the hardest (middle) segment always provides a new challenge.

The Speed-and-Power Tri

This builds speed, power, and lower-body strength.

How to do it: Choose any three cardio machines that allow you to adjust the resistance or gradient, such as a treadmill, bike, or stairclimber. Warm up for 2 minutes at an effort level of 5. Step up your effort to maximum for 30 seconds by increasing the machine's resistance level or incline while maintaining the same cadence. Return to the warmup effort level. That's one interval. Do three intervals, then move on to the

PAINkiller

How can I banish lower-back pain?

Pro cyclists make their living with their legs, but when the road turns rough, the lower back pays the bills. "As soon as your back starts fatiguing in a race, you lose efficiency, and you can't take advantage of the power in your legs," says George Hincapie, the reigning USPRO road-racing champ.

Take a page from Hincapie's spine-fortification plan with this simple exercise.

Bird-Dogs
On all fours, with your knees directly below your hips and your hands directly below your shoulders, raise your right arm and your left leg and hold them parallel to the floor for 2 seconds. Lower them and alternate arms and legs. Start with three sets of 10 to 15 repetitions.

next two machines and do three intervals on each.

Mix it up: Instead of raising the incline or resistance during your 30-second bouts, pick up the cadence of your maximum effort.

The More-Muscle Tri

This workout mixes strength training with aerobic work for greater strength and less fat.

How to do it: Jump rope for 30 seconds, rest for 30 seconds, and repeat five times. Then perform a total-body workout consisting of basic body-weight moves, such as squats, pushups, stepups, chinups, and crunches. Do one set of each, without resting. Finish with a 10-minute jog at a medium pace.

Mix it up: Swap the calisthenics for a dumbbell circuit.

Rule the Race

Break your personal record with
these fresh training techniques

You say you "just want to finish," but truth be told, you want to kick your own ass. We consulted studies published in the *Journal of Strength and Conditioning Research* in the past 12 months to find the smartest strategies for sending your performance soaring. Pick your distance and follow our advice. We guarantee you'll leave your former self, and a pack of others, in the dust.

Your Race: 5-K

Game plan: Gun it

Run your first mile of the race at least 6 percent faster than your typical pace. In a study of collegiate distance runners, those who jacked up their pace for the first mile finished 32 seconds faster than when they started at their average mile pace.

Do this: Determine your max heart rate (220 minus your age), then figure out 65 to 75 percent of that. That's what your heart rate should be at your average pace. Add 6 percent (or more) to that pace time and you've got your first-mile pace.

Your Race: 10-K

Game plan: Plyometrics

If you've always been partial to 5-Ks but want to step up your training to rock a 10-K, add a bit of jumping to your weekly workouts. This can increase your running efficiency (how quickly oxygen flows to your muscles) by nearly 5 percent, making the extra miles a cinch.

Do this: Split-squat jump. Start in a lunge position and jump up and forward, pushing

Good Get: The Hamstretch

No, it isn't a beach chair the fat guy from *Lost* sat in one too many times. This funky-looking contraption actually helps you stretch your hard-to-target hamstrings without stressing your back. Simply place your leg in the sling while lying faceup and pull the handle toward you until you feel a stretch. Hold for 10 seconds. Switch legs. It weighs just 2 pounds and splits in two for easy stowing ($40, hamstretch.com).

off your front leg. Land in a lunge and repeat continuously for 10 yards. Rest for 45 seconds. Do 3 reps and work up to 6. Complete the drill 3 nonconsecutive days a week.

Your Race: Half-Marathon or Longer

Game plan: Sprint uphill and downhill

Running hills preps you for the inevitable slopes you'll encounter over 13.1 miles, and the downhill portions teach your brain to execute a faster stride rate—how frequently your feet hit the ground. In a 2006 study, runners who trained this way improved their speed on flat terrain by up to 3.5 percent.

HARD TRUTH

Percentage of runners who suffer from allergy symptoms while running who see an allergist

21

Midnight Madness

Hide and Seek Treasure in the Heart of the City

The race not your place? Try geocaching, a high-tech urban scavenger hunt that goes on around the clock.

The Rules

Participants hide containers, known as "caches," all around the globe. Then they post coordinates (latitude and longitude) at geocaching.com. Anyone can find a cache using a GPS device. Our pick: Trimble Geocache Navigator, tracking software that's downloadable to GPS-enabled cell phones, gives you access to 200,000 caches in the United States ($7 per month via Sprint or Nextel phones, geocachenavigator.com).

The Cache

With more than 600,000 active caches hidden in 220-plus countries, you can hunt one down anytime and almost anywhere. About 85 percent are hidden and found in the United States by geocaching fans of all ages.

The Reward

Each container holds a logbook and a "treasure"—not a pile of gold, but maybe a $20 bill, a book, or a figurine. The container itself can be anything from Tupperware to a mannequin leg. After discovering the cache, sign the logbook, take the treasure, and leave a new one (or the old one if you wish). Whatever you do, don't put chocolate in there. Anything that can rot or lure animals is verboten. Later, go back online to brag about your find and pick your next adventure. Maybe Belize?

Do this: Find a gentle slope (equivalent to a 3-degree incline on the treadmill) that's about 20 yards from top to bottom. Sprint up, then down. Rest for 30 seconds. Repeat eight to 12 times, 3 nonconsecutive days a week. *Form note:* Don't try to fight gravity; let it carry you down the hill to prevent sore quads.

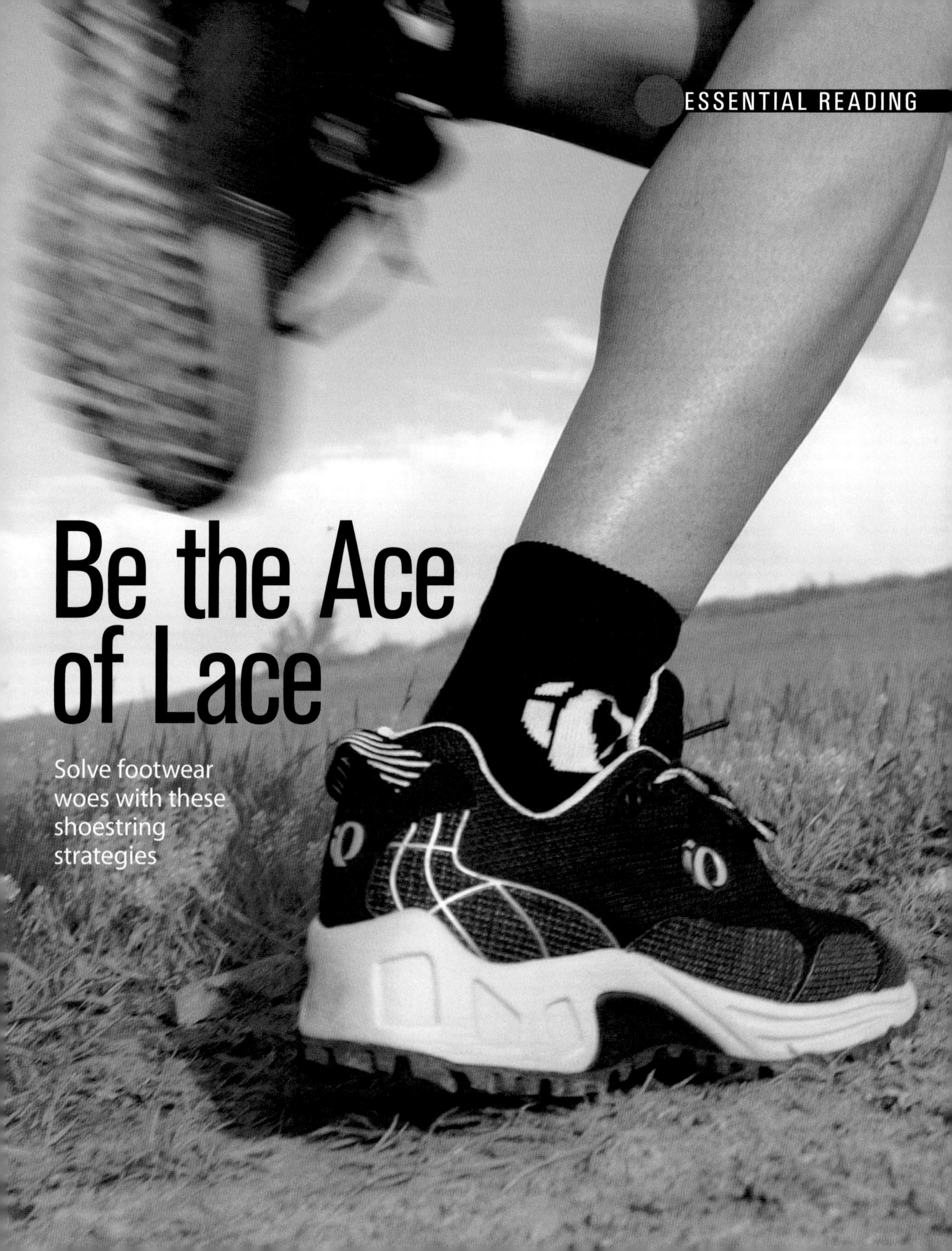

Be the Ace of Lace

Solve footwear
woes with these
shoestring
strategies

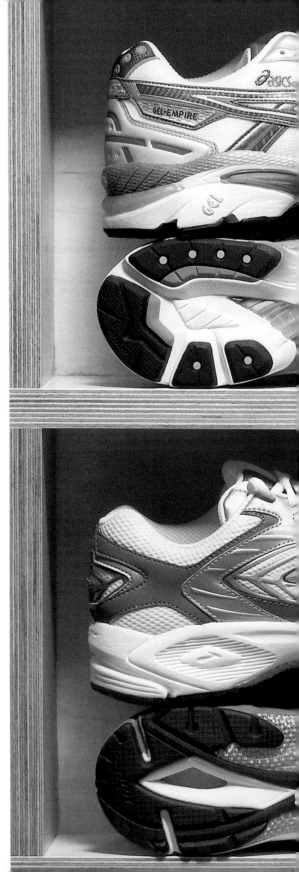

F our hundred million. That's the number of ways a shoe with seven pairs of eyelets can be laced, according to Australian mathematician Burkard Polster. Okay, so 99 percent of those options are as nutso as Polster is, but the ones here could save your feet—or at least save you the humiliation of exposing your mangled dogs in the locker room. Find your foot issue and re-lace accordingly.

Problem: My Shoes Feel Tight Near the Toes

Solution: Dual laces. "The shoe should be snug only in the back two-thirds," says Paul Langer, DPM, author of *Great Feet for Life*. "You should have wiggle room for your toes." To let the ball of your foot breathe, start one lace two eyelets from the toes, lace it up firmly toward your ankle, and tie a bow. Then start a shorter one in those second-to-last eyelets and lace it gently all the way to your toes. Tie it up and you're done.

Problem: My Shoes Are Always Coming Untied

Solution: I/M Active FlexHold shoelaces. These smart strings feature ActiveHold technology, essentially a rubberized tread that runs through the entire lace. The rubber keeps your shoes knotted during vigorous workouts, and elastic woven throughout the lace flexes with your foot to minimize blisters where too-tight laces can cause the shoe to rub against your skin ($6, studioim.com).

Problem: I Have High Arches

Solution: The skip pattern. If you have high arches or a bony bump on the top of your foot, this method will alleviate some of the pressure on your instep. Starting at the toes, lace the traditional way through the first three or four pairs of eyelets. Then, instead of crossing over, lace through the next pair on the same side. Crisscross up the rest of the way and tie them normally at the top.

Problem: My Laces Are Too Tight or Too Loose

Solution: The North Face Arnuva 50 Boa. This funky footboat never needs to be tied—just twist the knob on the back of the heel and a cable system tightens the shoe with each click, evenly distributing fit. It's streamlined enough for the treadmill but sturdy enough for light hiking ($125, thenorthface.com).

Problem: My Heels Don't Stay Put

Solution: The heel-lock lacing technique. Lace up normally, but after the second-to-last eyelet, don't cross over. Instead, thread the lace through the top hole on the same side to make a loop. Do this on each side. Now cross over and thread the laces through the loops. Cinch back and forth to get the loops to lie flat, then pull tight and tie a bow.

BY STEVE MAZZUCCHI

Use Your Bean

In 2007, scientists in South Africa discovered something peculiar about fatigue: It doesn't begin in the muscles. Indeed, that burning you feel in your quads near the end of a 10-K or in your pecs during a final bench press originates farther north, say the scientists, whose finish-line biopsies of exhausted marathoners showed plenty of glycogen (the body's main fuel) and ATP (a chemical that stores energy) in the runners' muscles. Their conclusion: Fatigue sets in not when muscles run out of gas, but when the brain tells them to conserve energy.

"This is likely a survival mechanism," says Timothy Noakes, MD, the study's lead author and a professor of exercise and sports science at the University of Cape Town. Early man was an endurance athlete, after all, and his body needed a reserve of go-juice in case a saber-toothed tiger attacked or a woolly mammoth got ornery. Sure, the stakes are lower today, but our innate energy reserves remain, and if you can tap into them, you'll gain an edge in everything from pickup games to cardio sessions. Here's how.

Program Your Pace

A study in the *British Journal of Sports Medicine* found that the brain has a governor that regulates pace based on distance and expected effort.

"That's why unfamiliar routes seem harder," says Alan St. Clair Gibson, PhD, chair of sports sciences at Northumbria University, in England. "If your brain doesn't know how much energy you'll need for a workout, it errs on the side of caution." Use interval training (e.g., alternating between 2 minutes of hard running and 2 minutes of jogging) to overcome this brain block. Just 20 minutes a week can teach your brain that running faster won't harm your body.

Sweat with a Smile

Projecting a positive attitude can restructure your brain to enter a state of bliss while exercising, allowing you to work out harder, says Chris Bergland, Triple Ironman champion and author of *The Athlete's Way.*

Researchers at Wake Forest University agree, noting that feelings of pain result from both immediate and expected experiences. Fight fatigue with affirmations. "Repeating 'I'm strong and swift' will rewire your brain to believe it," says Bergland.

Zen Out

That burning sensation in your muscles is due to the buildup of lactic acid. "And tense muscles accumulate it faster than relaxed ones," says Dan Czech, PhD, graduate director of Georgia Southern University's sports psychology program.

When you run, are you moving your legs freely or pushing them? If it's the latter, imagine the tension draining from your muscles and your legs moving with ease. "After a few minutes, you'll feel more energized," says Czech.

Envision Success

"Physiologically, the brain doesn't distinguish between imagined and real experiences," says Steven Rosenberg, PhD, team

Lunges hurt my knees. Is there an alternative?

Before you give up on lunges altogether, evaluate your technique. Many men lean forward at the waist during lunges, which puts added pressure on their knees, says Houston-based trainer Carter Hays, CSCS. "Too much energy is going forward, rather than straight down."

To avoid leaning, imagine a 2-foot box marked in four equal squares on the gym floor. Position your feet in squares diagonally across from each other, keep your knees flexed over your toes, and look ahead as you complete the lunge. Picture a pole running from the middle of the box up through your torso.

Still in pain? Try stepups; they're easier on the knees, says Mike Robertson, CSCS, a strength coach in Indianapolis.

Step Ups
Stand in front of a bench or step. Place one foot on the bench, then drive through your heel and step up. Step down slowly to the starting position. Do three sets of 6 to 12 reps with each leg, three times a week.

psychotherapist for the Philadelphia Flyers. Taking 5 minutes to visualize running 7 miles with energy to spare, therefore, will reinforce the same neural patterns as actually doing so, giving you a mental leg up before you hit the road.

"Alternatively," says Rosenberg, "if you're trying to squeeze out a few more curls, picture the action—arms extending, weight lowering, biceps contracting, weight rising—and then do it."

Bolster Your Core to Speed Up

Squeezing in a fast workout usually means little or no time for your core. But with this challenging regimen, you'll train your torso with every exercise, for a stronger six-pack and a sturdier spine.

Complete these four exercises without rest. Once you've done all the movements, rest for 45 seconds; repeat twice. Perform three times a week.

Pullup with Leg Raise: Grab a pullup bar with an overhand grip, hands slightly more than shoulder-width apart. Cross your ankles and bend your knees until your feet are behind you. Pull your chest to the bar. Using your abs and hip flexors, pull your knees up and in toward your chest. Lower yourself. Do 4 to 6 reps.

Lateral Raise with Rotation: Stand holding a pair of dumbbells at your sides. With your arms slightly bent at the elbows, raise the weights up until your arms are parallel to the floor. Rotate your torso as far as possible to one side. Rotate back to the center, and lower your arms. Repeat on the opposite side. That's one rep. Do 6.

Lunging Crunch: With your back to a high-pulley cable, hold the rope handle at your chest so that the ends drape over your shoulders. Lunge forward. As your front foot hits the floor, do a standing crunch. Sink down until your back knee is just off the floor. Brace your abs as you stand up. Do 10 reps with each leg.

Chest Press with Crunch: With your feet on the floor and your back on a Swiss ball, hold a pair of dumbbells at your shoulders. Press the weights up. Once your arms are straight, lift your shoulder blades off the ball, pushing the weights higher. Pause, then lower your shoulder blades and the weights. Do 10 reps.

Strike It Rich

Here's proof that we don't always do as we're told: Seventy-five percent of runners land on their heels, even though it's known that striking the ground with the midfoot is faster, states a Japanese study. The researchers, who analyzed gait patterns of competitors in an elite half-marathon, also discovered that heel-strikers didn't fare as well overall as midfoot runners, whose ground-contact time was 17 milliseconds less than that of the heel-strikers.

Landing on your midfoot causes your ankle and heel to flex, turning you into a human shock absorber. To fix your form, run quietly, so your footfalls aren't loud, and you'll unconsciously switch to a midfoot strike.

Lie Down

How's this for backward advice: Flop down on the ground after a race. Lying on your back speeds recovery, according to a study in the *Journal of Applied Physiology*. Researchers asked nearly exhausted racers to either lie on their backs or sit upright. The stretched-out group's heart rates slowed 25 percent faster than those of the sitters, and they produced twice the amount of sweat, helping their bodies cool.

When a person sits, his blood pools in muscles, causing a drop in blood pressure, says Glen Kenny, PhD, a professor of human kinetics at the University of Ottawa. "But when the body senses this, it triggers a reactive increase in heart rate and blood pressure, and a decreased sweat rate." Lying down helps bloodflow to the heart, preventing this response.

Tread Lightly

Staying distracted while running helps you exercise for 20 percent longer, according to Belgian researchers. That's why Life Fitness is now manufacturing a treadmill that syncs with your iPod's music and video libraries. An LCD screen on its console allows for watching your latest downloads.

Work the Slopes

Need a speed boost? Doing uphill and downhill sprinting in the same workout increases your flatland speed. Researchers at the University of Athens put athletes through a 6-week training program over sloping and flat ground—they ran uphill, downhill, over flat ground, or an uphill-downhill combination. The combo runners

increased their sprint speed by 3.5 percent; others didn't improve.

The transition between the two slopes improved the sprinters' neuromuscular systems, increasing their stride rate, according to study author Giorgos Paradisis, PhD. Run like the fast group: twelve 40-meter sprints on a 3-degree slope, three times a week.

Leave the Gloves at Home

Wearing gloves can kill your morning jog, say Stanford University researchers. They found that cool hands enabled runners to go up to twice as long as they normally would. The reason: Your palms contain special blood vessels that act as vents, allowing your body to shed heat while running.

"Exercise capacity decreases as muscle temperature increases, and wearing gloves accelerates this effect," says study author Craig Heller, PhD. Don gloves if your hands hurt from the cold. But ditch them 10 minutes into your run, which is how long it'll take for your palms to heat up.

Tri Hydrating

Drink water soon after finishing a triathlon's swim. The earlier you hydrate during the cycling leg of a triathlon, the faster your closing run will be, according to a University of North Carolina study. Researchers had seven triathletes complete two Olympic-distance triathlons over 2 weeks. During the cycling stage, racers downed 24 ounces of water either between miles 5 and 20 or

6 and 25. Those polishing off their water by mile 20 averaged 1 minute, 19 seconds faster in the run.

If you drink right before the run, the water won't be absorbed fast enough to provide optimal benefit, say the study authors. It takes 20 minutes for 8 ounces of water to hydrate your body.

Rock Out

Athletes have known for years that listening to music improves their performance. (Check the lists at right to see how some superstars load their iPods before competition.) The latest science behind the music/athletics connection comes from England's Brunel University. Researchers had 36 fit men run 400-meter time trials while listening to medium- or up-tempo tunes, or without music.

Results show that the pacing effect of listening to fast music enhances runners' anaerobic endurance, according to Costas Karageorghis, PhD, the study author. The "synchronous effect"—matching stride to the beat—can work for distance runners, too.

STEVE NASH
"I Just Wanna Love U," Jay-Z
"The Seed," the Roots
"Pictures of You," the Cure
"Emotional Rescue," the Rolling Stones
"Rebel Rebel," David Bowie

LANCE ARMSTRONG
"Times Like These," Foo Fighters
"King without a Crown," Matisyahu
"Smile Like You Mean It," the Killers
"Touch the Sky," Kanye West
"Dani California," Red Hot Chili Peppers

TOM BRADY
"Speed of Sound," Coldplay
"Get By," Talib Kweli
"The Light," Common
"Smells Like Teen Spirit," Nirvana
"Public Service Announcement," Jay-Z

FREDDY ADU
"Motivation," T.I.
"On Fire," Lloyd Banks
"My Style," Black Eyed Peas
"Diamonds from Sierra Leone," Kanye West
"The Point of No Return," Immortal Technique

DONTRELLE WILLIS
"More than a Feeling," Boston
"Lose Yourself," Eminem
"Let Me Ride," Dr. Dre
"Get Back," Ludacris
"I'm a Hustla," Cassidy

Fight Your Arch Enemy

Do your dogs start barking when you finish a pavement-pounding run? You could be one of the 2 million Americans with plantar fasciitis—tears in the tissue that runs along the sole of your foot, causing pain in your heel and arch. But a new exercise can relieve foot pain and speed healing, according to a study in the *Journal of Bone & Joint Surgery*.

Researchers had 82 patients do either the traditional Achilles tendon stretch or the new move, called the plantar fascia stretch, three times daily for 8 weeks. Those who did the new move had much less pain, because, it turns out, this stretch targets the plantar fascia more directly. To do it, cross the ankle of your sore foot over your opposite knee while sitting. Pull your toes back toward your shin until you feel a stretch in the arch. Hold for 10 seconds, release, and repeat 10 times. Do three sets a day.

Save Your Skin

We thought the main pitfall of marathoning was gnarly feet, until we heard that distance runners have an increased risk for skin cancer, according to a study in the journal *Archives of Dermatology*. Researchers compared the skin of 210 marathoners and 210 nonrunners and found the runners had more spots and damage typical of basal and squamous cell skin cancers (the most common kinds) and atypical moles, which can signal deadly melanoma.

But sun exposure may not be the only culprit: Research shows that more than 90 minutes of high-intensity exercise impairs immunity, which may make your skin more vulnerable. This research is no excuse to skip your workout, says study author Christina M. Ambros-Rudolph, MD. "Just wear water-resistant sunscreen—at least SPF 15—and clothing that covers your shoulders, upper arms, and head."

Try a Water Workout

The cross-country and track teams at Oregon's Linfield College have a less than 1 percent stress-fracture rate among their athletes. Their secret: underwater running. In the *Journal of Strength and Conditioning Research*, team coach Garry Kilgore, PhD, recommends bounding through the water, elongating your stride. "You'll experience force against your muscles, which is great for overcoming weaknesses."

Strategize

Triathlons require planning as much as they do fitness. Here's how you can shed minutes from your time without training harder.

Boost your stroke by 5 percent: You'll encounter 26 percent less resistance and drag through the water's current if you wear a unitard-like bathing suit, say Australian researchers. Try Speedo's FS PRO Bodyskin ($340, speedousa.com).

Cut your ride by 7 percent: Triathletes who swam at 90 percent of their maximum ability and drafted off competitors completed the cycling stage of a triathlon faster than those who sprinted, according to a Chinese study.

Strengthen your stride by 30 percent: Varying cycling intensity—5-minute intervals, alternating between 80 percent and 100 percent effort—will increase your leg power during the run by lowering your muscles' lactate levels, report French researchers.

Start Fast to Finish Fast

In your next road race, go out quickly at the start and you'll beat the guys who save energy for a late kick. The *Journal of Strength and Conditioning Research* published a study of 11 collegiate distance runners who ran three 5-K trials at different paces in the first mile: their average mile pace, 3 percent faster than average, or 6 percent faster. The fastest early pace resulted in finish times that were 32

seconds quicker than the finish times of the average-pace starts. Slower starters ran faster final miles, but they never made up for time lost at the start.

Take advantage of your adrenaline surge at the start of a 5-K. It'll pay off in a faster time.

Go Plyo

Still pshawing plyometrics? Consider this: Researchers at the Australian Institute of Sport had 15 expert distance runners add three 30-minute sessions of plyometrics to their workouts each week. In just 9 weeks, they boosted their running efficiency by almost 5 percent—meaning they ran 5 percent farther using the same amount of energy. Add the drills that follow to your workout twice a week, and they could make your next 10-K feel like a 9.5-K.

SIDE-TO-SIDE ANKLE HOP

With feet together, hop side to side (about 2 to 3 feet each way). Use only your ankles and calves. Do two sets of 15 explosive hops.

STANDING LONG JUMP

Dip into a quarter squat position. Push your arms back, then extend your lower body as you jump out and up. Do five sets of six jumps.

DOUBLE-LEG HOP

Step forward with your right leg. Then bring your left leg forward and jump as the left foot joins the right. Do five sets of six hops on each leg.

SINGLE-LEG SIDE JUMP

Balance on your left foot. Then jump wide to the right and land on your right foot. Reset, then jump back to the left. Do four sets of six jumps.

Go for Whole Grains

You've tried prerace carbo-loading, but it turns out that fiber may be the real secret to endurance, according to a study in the *International Journal of Sport Nutrition and Exercise Metabolism*. Researchers asked eight runners to eat low-fiber cornflakes and white toast with jam one morning and high-fiber All Bran and fruit another morning, then wait 3 hours and run until exhaustion.

After the high-fiber breakfast, the runners lasted 7 minutes longer and burned more fat. Fiber slows digestion, keeping energy levels steady. And when you're burning fat (not muscle), your brain thinks you have fuel to keep going, explains study author Clyde Williams, PhD. So pregym, snack on high-fiber dried apricots and pick whole-grain pasta before your next race.

Be Fast at Any Age

Sure, your cardio endurance peaks in your late twenties. But according to a study in the journal *Sports Medicine,* you shouldn't experience a considerable slowdown until age 70—that is, if you keep training. Take a look at how little your current pace should fall.

AGE GROUP	ELITE MARATHON MILE PACE	DROP-OFF
30–40	4:46 (minutes per mile)	n/a
50	4:55	3%
60	5:19	12%
70	6:02	26%
80	6:40	40%

Beat Your Best Time

You already know to taper before the big race. But are you tapering the right way? Canadian researchers recently discovered that cutting your total running time in half for 2 weeks prior to a competition will allow you to peak on race day.

You'll recover from the fatigue of training while maintaining your fitness level, says the lead study investigator, Laurent Bosquet, PhD. "Decreasing exercise intensity will cause detraining, but simply manipulating the workload will not." So if you're pounding out 40 miles a week and averaging 9 minutes a mile, cover 20 miles at the same pace.

Training Tips

I've started running again, and my knees are totally killing me. Help!

Take a few days off, or cut your mileage by 50 percent and then begin increasing your distance by 10 percent a week. Stretch your hamstrings several times a day, and ice your knees for 15 to 20 minutes after runs. If symptoms persist, see a doctor.

My muscles cramp often in endurance races. Any advice?

Cramping is caused by several factors, but if you're in good shape and warm up beforehand, your fitness level isn't the culprit. A loss of fluids and electrolytes is most likely the underlying cause of your knots. When you're properly hydrated, your muscles receive a steady flow of oxygen; when depleted, they spasm and stiffen. So it's important during long, strenuous workouts to replace water and electrolytes, such as potassium and sodium.

If you do find yourself cramping up midrace, stop immediately and stretch the muscle carefully so it can't worsen. Then apply this self-massage: Knead the muscle like dough. If you still have a knot that won't flex, apply firm, steady pressure on the spot using your fingers or the heel of your hand.

My lungs burn when I run outside in the winter. How can I exercise without pain?

Frigid winter air can shock temperature-sensitive nerves and dry out your airways, inflaming your lungs. "Similar to what happens when you put an ice cube against your teeth, the temperature change combined with the dry air sends signals to your brain," says Kenneth Rundell, PhD, a health-science professor at Marywood University, in Pennsylvania. How's that for a reason to stop running until spring?

Not so fast: You can beat the cold by tricking your body. Before you head outside, complete a vigorous, 10-minute warmup. The effort will temporarily deplete the immune-system chemicals that would otherwise react to the cold, dry air and produce the inflammation.

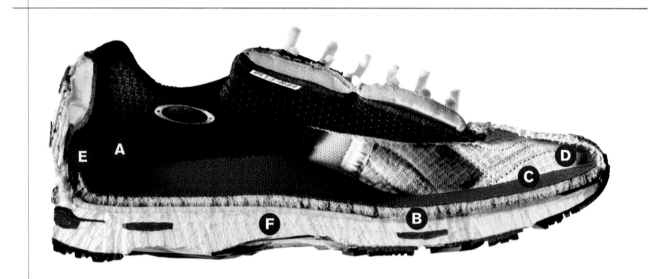

How can I fit myself for new running shoes?

First, are you sure you want a new pair? "If you're running injury-free, the worst thing you can do is buy a different shoe," says Robert Butler, PhD, a running-mechanics researcher at the University of Evansville.

Unless your body cautions otherwise, wait to replace your kicks until their breakdown point—about 350 outdoor miles or 450 treadmill miles (cardio machines are slightly easier on shoes).

Then, when selecting a new pair, look to your old soles for direction. If the bottom of your shoe has worn down between the second and third toes (the big toe is number one), your running mechanics are normal—stick with the type of shoe you have. Wear at the big toe shows that your foot pronates, or rolls inward on impact; a shoe with motion-control technology will help. If the fourth and fifth toes are worn, you underpronate—you run on the outside edges of your feet. Buy an extra-cushioned shoe. Here are some specifics to check for at the store.

A **Cushioning:** Look for a firm response in the heel, not a mushy or soggy feeling. Soft heel cushioning causes your foot to sink deep into the shoe, stressing your Achilles tendon.

B **Flex point:** The ball of your foot should align with the shoe's widest zone. This zone contains notches that allow the shoe to flex. If the ball of your foot falls behind this zone, it'll cause your arch to bend instead of your toes when running and you'll strain your arches.

C **Removable insole:** For a foolproof fit, take out the insole and step on it. You should have an index finger's width between your big toe and the insert's front end, says Douglas Richie, DPM, a former president of the American Academy of Podiatric Sports Medicine.

D Toe box: Wide is better. A narrow box can blacken toenails. Neither your pinkie nor your big toe should extend beyond the shoe's normal frame.

E Back heel: Blood flow increases and ligaments swell while you're running, which can add a half size to your foot. Slip your index finger between your heel bone and the shoe's rear wall. If there's no wiggle room, the shoe is too small.

F Arch support: The shoe's toe box should bend when pressed diagonally onto a hard surface. If the arch collapses first, it's an inferior shoe that'll strain your foot.

How can I find the best running shoes for me?

Start at home, barefoot, using the following "wet test" to determine foot type: Wet the sole of your foot, then step on and off a flattened brown grocery bag.

If you see half of your arch, you're a normal pronator and the world of running shoes is your oyster.

If you see your entire arch, you're an overpronator and your arches collapse inward as you run. Your best bet is to wear motion-control shoes, which employ devices such as dual-density midsoles and supportive posts; try Saucony's Grid Stabil 6 ($90, saucony.com).

Finally, if you see just a thin line on the outside of your arch, you're a supinator (i.e., your feet don't roll inward sufficiently when you run). Buy neutral-cushioned shoes such as Asics's Gel-Foundation 7 ($90, asics.com), which have soft midsoles and no stability devices, so they encourage your feet to roll inward as you run.

I often wait until I have joint pain to replace my running shoes. So bad, I know. What's a safer way to determine when they're shot?

Do your feet—and the rest of your body—a favor and never go that long without swapping out sneaks again. Check for visual signs of deterioration (cardio machines are slightly easier on shoes). Start shopping when you notice cracks on the bottom or sides of the sole, an imprint of your foot on the insole, or the toe area of your shoe separating from the sole.

Hit a specialty running store—call a local running club and ask which shop they recommend—and bring your trashed kicks. Looking at how your shoes broke down can help determine the best new pair for you based on your running style.

I'm a runner, and I want to build abs. Do I have any shot at a six-pack?

Running can either strengthen or weaken your abs, depending on your form. "If you keep your torso straight and your shoulders back, running and jogging can be extremely beneficial for reinforcing abdominal stability," says Craig Friedman, CSCS, a trainer at Athletes' Performance, in Tempe, Arizona.

If you slouch, you'll take your core out of the equation. Can't maintain the proper ab alignment? Make sure you're picking up your feet. "Lift your feet higher by sliding them up under your butt," Friedman says. "This will add more lift to your stride, helping you stay tall through the hips."

Will running on a treadmill hurt my back?

"Running or walking on a flat treadmill should not, by itself, cause back pain. But what could is using the incline too soon, too long, and too steeply," says David Pearson, PhD, a professor of exercise physiology and director of the strength research lab at Ball State University.

How can I make running on a treadmill as challenging and interesting as running outside?

If you're not panting by the end of your run, your body (and mind) may be bored with your routine.

Stoke your fat-burning furnace by shaking things up. Start by increasing your incline or speed on the treadmill, gradually taking it to the next level. Simulate outdoor winds by alternately increasing and decreasing intensity every 2 minutes. Modifying even a 20-minute run will increase your calorie burn—and that's always exciting. Also, walk backward on the treadmill to give your knees a break.

How can I halt my postmarathon weight gain?

Retrain your stomach and your brain to match your mileage drop. Dial back the starchy carbs by

one-third and instead eat nutrient-rich foods, such as blueberries and tomatoes. And switch to 15-minute interval workouts on the stationary bike in place of long runs. They're easier on your knees, and you'll burn more calories in less time.

Why is the 40-yard dash the standard NFL speed-measuring stick, and how can I run mine faster?

Most plays in the NFL last 3.5 to 5 seconds, and most players run 40 yards or less per play. That's why coaches use it as the ultimate speed test. They dissect the test into four sections, but the key for you is to condition your body for quick bursts of speed, lasting between 5 and 12 seconds. This will make you faster and stronger in explosive sports like basketball and tennis, and you'll begin carving that athletic look of an NFL running back. Here's how.

The 5-second workout: Run 5- to 12-second repeats on a track, treadmill, VersaClimber, or flight of stairs. Sprint for 5 to 12 seconds, then walk back to the starting position and repeat for a total of 6 to 8 repetitions. Do this drill twice a week to build explosive speed.

Why do so many runners drop dead of heart attacks, and how can I avoid becoming one of them?

It's not that so many runners drop dead of heart attacks. It's that there are a helluva lot of guys out there with time bombs in their chests, and each year a handful of them find just the right trigger to set them off. Their deaths, however, highlight one of the great paradoxes of running: "On one hand, studies prove that running reduces your risk of having a heart attack," says Paul Thompson, MD, director of preventative cardiology at Hartford Hospital, in Connecticut. "But there's a law of diminishing returns, that you can get too much of a good thing."

Most exercise-related heart attacks occur in high-endurance athletes such as marathoners, although the death of Broncos running back Damien Nash after a basketball game shows that even exhausting stop-and-go workouts can prove fatal to a bad heart.

"Exercise is a stress test," says Arthur Siegel, MD, director of internal medicine at Harvard's McLean Hospital, in Belmont, Massachusetts. "And the more

severe the test, the greater your chances of overdosing." In a study of 60 nonelite runners competing in the Boston Marathon, Dr. Siegel found that 40 percent of the athletes showed signs of transient heart injury following the race. "Their hearts looked stunned, as if they had been slapped," says Dr. Siegel, who has competed in marathons himself. The effect was temporary, adds Dr. Siegel, but it nevertheless illustrates the strain that intense exercise can have on the body.

In and of itself, this strain isn't enough to put a healthy pump at risk. "But if you're a middle-aged man with risk factors such as high blood pressure or diabetes, it can spark a cascade of events that leads to a heart attack," says

Dr. Siegel, adding that this often involves the rupture of unstable coronary plaque.

Reduce your risk by scheduling a checkup with your doctor before you begin a running regimen and request an EKG or a 64-slice CT scan, both of which can catch heart disease in its early stages. Also, take your pulse every morning after you wake up. "As you run, your resting pulse decreases," says Dr. Siegel. "If you find that yours is increasing, it's a sign that you're pushing your heart too hard."

PART SIX

HAVE FUN

BY DAVID SCHIPPER

Train Like the Pros

Use these training
secrets to get new
game—and a new
body

You've seen these guys on SportsCenter, catching TD passes, shooting three-pointers, and hitting homers. Their success secret: rigorous training. Use their cross-training tricks to elevate your favorite game, too.

The Baller

Tony Gonzalez
Age: 31
Tight end, Kansas City Chiefs
Part-time hoops junkie

Tony Gonzalez's greatest offensive performance came in the 1997 NCAA basketball tournament, not in an NFL game. A two-sport athlete at the University of California at Berkeley, Gonzalez came off the bench to score 23 points against Villanova, leading his team to an upset victory and into the Sweet 16. NBA scouts took note, impressed by Gonzalez's physicality and sound fundamentals. (He made 64 percent of his shots as a freshman.)

But Gonzalez, now a Kansas City Chief and future hall of fame tight end, knew better. "Except for Charles Barkley, you don't see successful 6'5", 275-pound NBA forwards," he says. "My future was in football."

Even so, Gonzalez's love of roundball proves invaluable to his gridiron game. "When I play basketball, I'm practicing the offensive skills I need in the NFL—especially footwork and agility—but without the impact on my body," he says. That's why Gonzalez continues to play serious hoops every off-season, from weekly pickup games

Gonzalez's B-Ball Assists

Employ the hip check. To dominate on the glass, place your backside or elbow firmly against your opponent's hip as soon as the ball hits the rim. You'll be able to rebound and score easy put-back points. "It's simple and fundamental, but effective," says Gonzalez. "I do the same thing in football to gain space from my defender."

Stay in motion. Break to the basket after every pass you throw. Don't get the ball? Immediately switch to an "L" cut. Here's how: Once you're under the goal, lock your defender behind you with a hip check (above). Then run to the free-throw line. As soon as your foot touches the line, break horizontally toward the closest wing, your body facing the ball. You'll be wide open to receive a pass. From there . . .

Practice to deceive. "A good head fake is the most important but least used move in pickup basketball," says Gonzalez. Try his most effective move: Pump the ball as if you're about to shoot. Then, as you bring the ball back down, throw a strong head fake to the left, and drive right. The first move gets your defender in the air, and the second gets him moving in the wrong direction, leaving you an open path to the hoop.

to games in semipro summer leagues. He's even had a stint with the Miami Heat.

"I'm a junkie for the game of basketball, especially the camaraderie and the physical challenge," says Gonzalez. "And after I've perfected one-on-one moves on a constricted court, there's no way a defender can guard me one-on-one on a football field."

The Fighter

Al Harrington

  Age: 27

  Forward, Golden State Warriors

  Part-time heavyweight

  Al Harrington's dad hit him hard at least once a week. "It was quality time shared by a father and son," says Harrington, whose pops was a boxer in the Army. "Both he and my stepfather brought me into the sport when I was young."

  You might say the Harringtons' family heirloom—pugilism—was passed on from generation to generation in their New Jersey garage. More Gleason's Gym than automobile storage, the garage had heavy bags hanging from above, headgear and gloves lining the walls, and a mock ring left clear of clutter. "My family had an advantage in life, because as boxers we carried ourselves stronger than other people," says Harrington, a forward for the upstart Golden State Warriors.

  Although boxing provided the young Harrington with a confident swagger, he dropped the gloves after making the NBA. Perhaps not coincidentally, his game took a beating, lacking a scoring punch. But he found his remedy in a return to the ring. "After those first couple of years, I decided to train as a professional boxer in the off-season," says Harrington, who enlisted Mike Tyson's ex-trainer to help him. His scoring and rebounding averages began to soar.

  "I'm now a bad man," says the Warrior, quoting Muhammad Ali. "The boxing skills—quicker hands, faster reactions, wider vision—are a huge benefit to my game, but the biggest advantage is knowing that nobody is training as hard as I am."

Harrington's Knockout Advice

Take a swing. You don't need equipment to train like a boxer. "Try throwing punches continually for just 3 minutes, the length of a round," says Harrington. You'll feel how intense boxing can be. Rest for 2 minutes, and repeat as many times as you can for a great fat-loss and conditioning workout.

Stay on your toes. "This is the key to moving your feet quicker in the ring and on the court," says Harrington. Whether you're shuffling side to side or waiting for your opponent to make a move, you're always in a prepared, athletic stance, no matter your sport.

Find your swagger. Boxing has given Harrington confidence. "It makes you stand a little taller," he says. But it's not because you're fighting; it's because of how physically intense the activity is. "Training hard and being in peak condition makes you confident that you can take whatever life throws at you," he says.

The Striker

Chad Johnson
Age: 29
Wide receiver, Cincinnati Bengals
Part-time soccer nut

Johnson's Soccer Secrets

Aim high and tight. In a study, Hong Kong researchers found that goalkeepers rarely stand in the center of the goal. They favor one side, hoping to bait the opposition into kicking toward the open side, which in turn enables them to anticipate the shot. Eliminate this advantage by aiming your shots at the corner above the goalkeeper's head. "Top corner shots can't be stopped. It's the best way to score a goal," Johnson says. A soccer ball's sweet spot: bottom right (if you're right-foot dominant). Strike it with the top of your big toe.

Keep your feet moving. Johnson uses a classic soccer drill to increase his speed on the football field. Here's how to do it: Place a soccer ball a foot in front of you. Jumping quickly, alternate touching your big toes on top of the ball, without kicking it forward. Do this for 40 seconds, rest for 60 seconds, and repeat twice more.

Give your workout a kick. Here's why you should buy a soccer ball: "The faster I can run while controlling the ball, the more agile I'll be while not kicking one," says Johnson. That's because soccer conditions your feet to switch smoothly between sprints and cuts. "It's all about making your lower body move in different ways," he says. For a great conditioning and sports workout, trade your 30-minute jog for 10 minutes of intermittent sprints while dribbling a soccer ball. Simply sprint with the ball for 20 seconds, rest for 60 seconds, and repeat seven times.

"I call it 'acting a fool,'" says Chad Johnson, describing his touchdown dances and flair for the dramatic. "And it all began when I was a 4-year-old soccer player."

Johnson, the Cincinnati Bengals' all-world wide receiver, was raised in a Miami household that lacked the funds for peewee football registration. So he played soccer instead. As an offensive-minded forward with speed to burn, he was a perfect fit for a sport that celebrates the individual.

"All I wanted to do was shake defenders," says Johnson. "It's the same mentality I have as a wide receiver, using skill, flash, and tricks to embarrass opponents."

When he entered high school, Johnson was forced to choose between soccer and football, because the seasons overlapped. He made the decision with his head, not his heart. "Soccer is the most challenging game I've ever played, but it couldn't have generated the income I earn today."

Still, you'll always find a checkered ball in Johnson's NFL locker. "I pull it out before games and during practices to improve my foot speed and transitional skills," he says. "My teammates respect it. They know I'm working to better myself and not just playing a game."

The Wave Rider

Ryan Zimmerman

> Age: 23
> Third baseman, Washington Nationals
> Part-time longboarder

At age 13, Ryan Zimmerman found a surfboard sticking out of a trash can. "So I grabbed it and taught myself to ride," he says. He hasn't stopped. "Surfing is all about relying on instincts," says the Washington Nationals' star third baseman. "My muscle memory takes over." Like it does when he plays the hot corner in the majors. Surfing also taught Zimmerman about bouncing back from failure. "When I fall, I stay calm and just get back up."

Zim's Surfer Zen

Find your happy place. Hitting the waves with his surfboard helps Zimmerman destress and refocus. "It's just so quiet and relaxing out in the water," he says. It's the same type of mental respite that helps any guy return to his day job with renewed vigor. But if the sea isn't your refuge, join a league. A study found that competitive team sports—such as softball, soccer, and flag football—relaxed men more than competitive individual sports did, because of the emotional support teammates provide. On the flip side, golfers had the highest anxiety levels. The reason: the scorecard, which serves as a constant performance evaluation and source of stress.

Go the Distance

The University of Florida men's basketball team
is hunting for a repeat national championship.
Here's how they train their bodies for full-court fitness

L et the fans worry about the 33-game regular-season schedule, the Southeastern Conference tournament, and March's season-ending win-or-go-home tourney. The University of Florida Gator hoops squad is just trying to survive its coach's morning drills.

"We practice harder than we play in games," says Lee Humphrey, UF's starting shooting guard, who in 2006 sank a school-record 113 three-pointers. Sure, Humphrey's comment is the same cliché you'll hear from any athlete. But when you consider the controlled chaos that is the Gator game plan—a hard-charging offense with hustle reminiscent of the great Celtics teams of the '80s—you realize just how intensely these players condition their bodies when nobody's watching.

"We press the ball on defense and run all out on offense, so we have to be in great shape," says Al Horford, a 6'10", 245-pound rebounding beast who disappointed NBA scouts by returning to school for a second championship. One glance at Horford and you know the Gators take strength training as seriously as cardiovascular conditioning.

Which is perhaps why Matt Herring, UF's strength-and-conditioning coordinator for basketball, is owed as much credit for the team's success as Humphrey, Horford, and Joakim Noah, their *Sports Illustrated* cover star. In the 40-minute contest that is college hoops, superior conditioning is often the difference between equally talented teams.

"I have them handling heavy loads in the weight room, so they can not only control their own bodies, but maintain their

movements when people hang on them," says Herring. "Nothing is outside their comfort zone."

He meets his players at 6 a.m. daily on their home hardwood in party-happy Gainesville. No smiles here, though; these training sessions are grueling. Says Herring, "Every team that reaches the NCAA tournament will have played a ton of games. We're all going to be broken down. It's a matter of who's beat up the least." So Herring's built a workout that makes players tougher and more resistant to injury. And for those of you not on scholarship? It'll make you look and feel like an athlete. That's because the by-product of the Gators' training plan is a lean, rock-solid frame capable of executing anything you ask of it.

The Gators retained their title in March 2007. They were confident because the NCAA doesn't crown the best team. It weeds out the weak, allowing the fit to rise.

Train Like a Gator

The Gators' workouts are planned around movements, not muscles. "We're training the body the way it actually functions," says Herring. "Our players must move forward, backward, sideways, and rotationally. They need to be reactive, dynamic, and explosive." That's why this plan develops strength and power—for jumping and sprinting—as well as the stability and flexibility needed to do both while twisting and turning. And because these exercises work your entire body at a demanding pace, you'll burn excess belly fat.

Perform each pair of exercises as a superset—doing one set of both movements before resting as little as possible. Complete a total of three sets of each exercise, then move on to the next superset.

SUPERSET 1

OVERHEAD LUNGE MATRIX

Hold a medicine ball over your head with both hands. Step forward (toward 12 o'clock) with your left leg, lowering yourself into a lunge. Rise and lunge toward 3 o'clock, then 6 o'clock. Switch legs and lunge toward 12, 9, and 6 o'clock. Face 12 o'clock between reps. Once around the clock equals a set.

MEDICINE-BALL THROW

Stand 6 feet from a wall, facing it, with your feet shoulder-width apart. Hold a medicine ball over your head with your arms extended. Without taking a step, lower the ball behind your head and throw it powerfully toward the wall, then catch it. Repeat three times, for a total of 4 repetitions.

SUPSERSET 2

DUMBBELL SQUAT WITH ROTATION PRESS

Stand holding two dumbbells at your sides at arm's length, your palms facing each other and your feet shoulder-width apart. Squat down, lowering your body until your thighs are at least parallel to the floor. As you push your body back to the starting position, curl the weights to your shoulders and press the right dumbbell overhead as you rotate your torso to the left. Return to the starting position and repeat the entire movement, this time pressing the left dumbbell overhead as you rotate to the right side. That's one repetition; do a total of 6 reps.

CABLE SINGLE-ARM ROTATIONAL ROW

Attach a single-arm handle to a low-pulley cable, grab the handle with your right hand, and stand facing the weights. Place your left foot 12 inches in front of your right. Your right arm and the cable should form a straight line. Simultaneously squat down and bend forward at your hips so that your right knee is bent 45 degrees and your torso forms a 45-degree angle with the floor. This is the starting position. Now pull the handle to the side of your rib cage as you stand and rotate to your right.

Pause, then return to the starting position. Do 4 reps. Repeat with your right leg forward, holding the handle with your left hand.

SUPERSET 3

DUMBBELL SNATCH SQUAT

OVERHEAD LATERAL LUNGE

Stand with your feet hip-width apart and hold a light weight plate in front of your hips with both hands. With your left leg, take a wide step directly to your left side, keeping your toes pointed forward. Simultaneously raise the weight overhead and lower your body by bending your right knee until your right thigh is parallel to the floor, then push back up and lower the weight. Repeat with your right leg. That's one repetition. Do 4 reps. (Too hard? Try it without raising the weight overhead.)

Grab a dumbbell with your right hand and let it hang at arm's length in front of you, your palm facing your body. With your feet shoulder-width apart, bend slightly at your waist and knees until the dumbbell hangs below your right knee. In one movement, jump up as you thrust the dumbbell overhead while keeping it close to your body (as if you're trying to touch the ceiling). As you land, immediately lower your body into a squat while keeping your arm raised. Push yourself to a standing position, then lower the dumbbell and repeat. Do 2 or 3 repetitions with each arm.

Cardio Tips from Four Up-Tempo Teams

Cardio Challenge 1: University of Florida Gators

The biggest difference between your pickup game and college ball: pace of play. Think you can hang? Try completing UF's sprint pyramid. Starting at the baseline (either goal), sprint 1 length of the court. Rest for twice the amount of time it took to complete that sprint. Then sprint 3 lengths of the court, followed by a rest of twice your sprint time. Continue increasing the sprints to 5, 7, and 8 lengths, adapting the rest interval appropriately after each. Then decrease, doing 6, 4, and 2 lengths. Still sprinting? Of course not. That's because whether your school's hoops team is a national champion or unranked, its members' fitness levels are elite status. Use this cardio challenge to measure up, and then train up.

Cardio Challenge 2: Bucknell University Bison

Their reputation as a powerhouse underdog precedes them—so there's no letting up. Jerry Shreck, the Bison's strength-and-conditioning coach, puts his team through 22s. Sprint from one baseline to the other and back. "Then repeat for a total of 4 court lengths, finishing in under 22 seconds," Shreck says. Take 44 seconds to recover. Start with four rounds and work your way up; the Bison do a total of 22 sprints.

Cardio Challenge 3: Air Force Academy Falcons

To increase their agility, the Falcons run the "arrow" drill. Sprint in a straight line for 5 yards (you're now standing on the arrow's tip), shuffle 5 yards at a 45-degree angle back and to the left, then shuffle up to the tip. Next, shuffle 5 yards at a 45-degree angle back and to the right, shuffle up to the tip, and backpedal 5 yards back to your original starting point. Rest for 90 seconds. Repeat three times.

Cardio Challenge 4: University of Connecticut Huskies

Thanks to Chris West, UConn's strength-and-conditioning coach, few teams keep up with this NCAA big dog. West's secret: the hourglass drill. Standing at the corner of a baseline, sprint across the court to the opposite baseline's far corner. Then face the court and laterally shuffle your feet along the baseline until you reach the opposite corner. Sprint back across to the other baseline's far corner. Again, shuffle down the baseline (facing the court) until you reach the corner. Complete the drill in under 24 seconds. Rest and repeat for a total of 10 minutes. UConn goes for 30 minutes.

Aim Higher

Amaré Stoudemire, the 6'10" center for the Phoenix Suns, has moved fast after microfracture knee surgery. He already has his sights set on a new challenge: elevating his vertical leap, from 38 inches to 42. "I dropped 2 inches because of the injury, and I want my 2 back," says Stoudemire. "And then I want to gain 2 more on top of that."

Ready to erase your pain and raise every facet of your fitness? Here are Stoudemire's secrets for snatching that extra inch or two—and then some.

Run with guys who can torch you. After rehab, Stoudemire first wanted to regain his speed. So instead of running with other big men, he lined up with the guards.

"You can run 4 miles a day, but it won't get you in basketball shape," he says. "You have to run drills."

To get your lungs back, try "sixes."

Run from baseline to baseline and back three times, for a total of 6 lengths of the basketball court. Rest for 30 seconds, then repeat the drill twice. Stoudemire aims to complete each six in under 31 seconds.

Boost your weight-room gains. Picture this and be inspired: "The most impressive thing I've seen Amaré do was 36-inch box jumps last year after he started getting his elevation back," says Erik Phillips, ATC, head strength-and-conditioning coach for the Phoenix Suns.

But before jumping onto plyometric boxes yourself, Phillips says it's critical to bolster lower-body stability with moves such as multiplanar hops. (See opposite page.)

Fix your pains with foam. Wherever Stoudemire goes, there goes his foam roll. "It keeps my muscles loose," he says. Aaron Nelson, ATC, head athletic trainer for the Suns, suggests this foam-roll move to help heal or prevent knee pain: Lie with the outside of your thigh on a foam roll and glide up and down from your knee to your hip. Pause for 30 seconds on any tender spots. Next, roll over your calves. Then stretch your calves, hips, and hip flexors.

The Comeback Workout

Save your joints and jump higher with this 5-minute routine.

Knee injuries aren't caused by weak legs alone. "It's not only how strong your quadriceps or hamstrings are," says Micheal A. Clark, DPT, sports therapist for the Suns and a chief architect of Stoudemire's comeback. "It's also about the control you have through your core."

When you jump, if your ankle's tight or your hips and abs are weak, your knee may cave in slightly, priming the joint for injury on landing. You can see this happen at the exact moment you land, prior to your next takeoff. It's called the "amortization phase," and it speaks volumes about your explosiveness and risk of knee pain.

A study presented in 2007 by the National Academy of Sports Medicine shows that if your knee caves in, knee stress increases. Inward movement lengthens the amortization phase, so it has a dampening effect on your spring. As a result, you can't sky as high.

Take this test to determine your risk of ankle, knee, and hip problems. Stand in front of a mirror, toes pointed straight ahead, and perform an overhead squat. (With your arms extended overhead, sit back at the hips and bend your knees to lower your body toward the floor.) "If your feet move or your knees cave, you're more susceptible to injury," says Clark. The workout below will help save you a lifetime of knee pain. In fact, Stoudemire does it before every game. "It will be my secret for having a long career," he says.

Single-Leg Balance Reach

Stand on one leg with that knee bent about 15 degrees. Squeeze your abs and glutes. Point the lifted foot's toes toward the floor and straighten that leg out to the side. Don't allow the arch to cave in on the foot you're standing on. Bring your foot back to the center without letting it touch the floor, and repeat. Do two sets of 12 to 15 reps on each leg.

Multiplanar Tube Walk

Loop resistance tubing around your ankles and slide it up your legs until it's above your knees. Stand with your knees slightly bent, hands on your hips. Keeping your abs tight, sidestep 12 to 15 times to your right, then back to your left. Repeat forward and backward.

Multiplanar Hop

Standing on one foot, jump forward and land softly on the other foot. Then reverse the move back to the starting position. Keep your chest up and your knee over your second and third toes, and don't let the arch of your foot cave when you land. Repeat out to the side, then go backward at a 45-degree angle. That's one repetition. Do 12 to 15 repetitions on each leg.

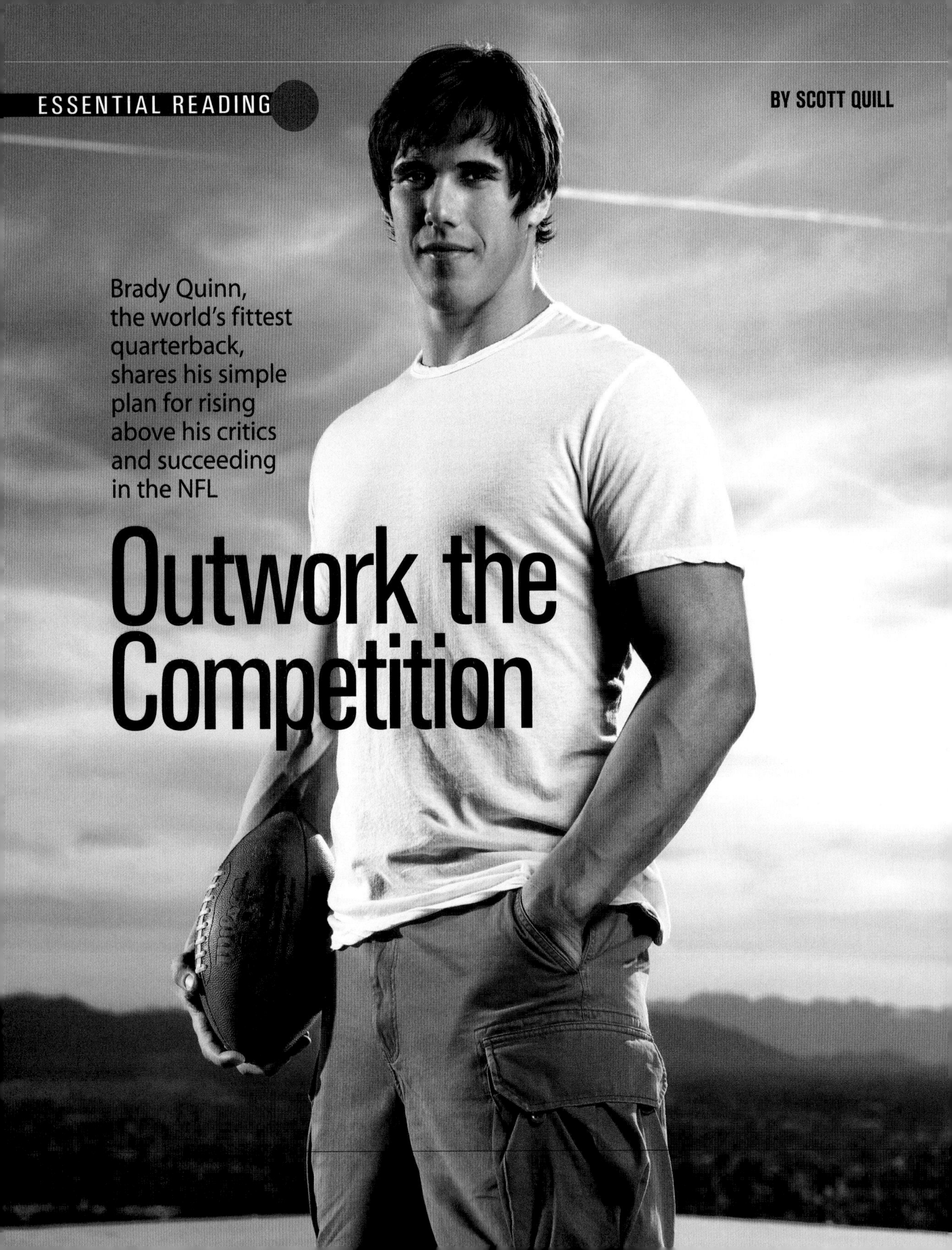

ESSENTIAL READING

BY SCOTT QUILL

Brady Quinn, the world's fittest quarterback, shares his simple plan for rising above his critics and succeeding in the NFL

Outwork the Competition

"**S**olid but not special."
That was the draft-day scouting report on Brady Quinn. And it seemed that every team was buying it. Once projected as the NFL's top selection, the Notre Dame quarterback slipped to number 22—where Cleveland nabbed him with their second pick in the first round.

But as I look at Quinn standing waist-deep in a pool during his *Men's Health* cover shoot, "solid but not special" is not the phrase that comes to mind. "Can't miss" seems far more appropriate. At 6'3", 236 pounds, and a remarkable 5 percent body fat, Quinn is a striking image of health. Armed with a football, he takes a deep breath and disappears into the sparkling blue chlorine bath. A moment later, the 22-year-old explodes out of the water, turns in midair, and fires a sopping-wet spiral into the Phoenix sun. Naturally, it hits me right between the numbers.

For the photographer, agents, and on-set guests, Quinn is kindly showcasing the powerful arm and physique that made him a Heisman Trophy favorite and the most prolific passer in Fighting Irish history. There's no doubt the guy looks like a superstar in every frame of our film. But what about on an NFL field?

Forget the GMs, scouts, and radio hosts. Quinn wants to answer that question himself: "I have a lot of confidence in my God-given ability. I think that ability, combined with my work ethic, will allow me to flourish in the NFL."

Body Chemistry

When it comes to his body, Brady Quinn is all business. That's why he uses a scientific approach whenever he tries a new supplement, even if it's just protein powder. "To find out if a supplement works, I make sure it's the only change I make to my diet and workout," says Quinn.

Employ the same system, using this scientific strategy from Chad Kerksick, PhD, a sports-nutrition researcher at the University of Oklahoma.

1. Record your weight, body-fat percentage, and circumference measurements (waist, chest, and biceps).

2. Take the supplement as directed for 4 weeks (unless, of course, you experience negative side effects), and keep a detailed workout log.

3. After 4 weeks, take your measurements again, and compare improvements in performance and recovery with those of the previous month. Was this product worth it or worthless? If the answer is the latter, abstain from all supplements for 2 weeks before your next product test.

After watching him on the field for 4 years, and in the gym for 2 days, call me a believer.

"I'm thinking dorsiflexion right now!" exclaims Quinn as he strolls around the weight room at Athletes' Performance (AP), in Tempe, Arizona. He takes a step back and raises his right foot off the floor to demonstrate. His toes are pointing up, toward his shin. Quinn's trainer, Luke Richesson, nods in approval.

Richesson encourages this odd behavior because he says it will make Quinn faster,

Ramp Up Your Playbook

Win the bragging-rights bowl big with these five trick football plays

When it comes to backyard battles, history isn't made by "get-open" routes but with defense-duping trick plays. We asked Boise State offensive coordinator Bryan Harsin, whose gadget plays helped his Broncos topple Oklahoma in the now-legendary Fiesta Bowl matchup, to develop the following five must-run routes. Read on and ramp up your team's playbook.

The Statue of Liberty, Boise-Style

This play won Boise State the Fiesta Bowl in OT. The QB drops back with both hands on the ball while the RB hovers in the backfield as if he's there to block. Meanwhile, the C and WRs draw the rest of the defense up the right side of the field. The trick: In one motion, the QB fakes a pass with his right hand and slips the RB the ball with his left. The RB then dashes downfield.

A perfect goal-line play.

The Hook and Ladder

The middle-right WR runs a slant to the left as the wide-left WR runs a 15-yard flag route. The QB throws to the wide-left WR. The trick: After catching the ball, he pitches it to the slanting middle-right WR, and it's off to the races as the left WR throws blocks.

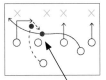

The catch and pitch occur at the same point on the field and should be one quick, seamless motion.

---

shaving at least a couple of tenths off his time in the 40. The idea is for Quinn to learn to keep his ankle cocked back—dorsiflexed—as his foot strikes the ground. This transforms his ankle into a sort of coiled spring, allowing him to propel his body forward with greater explosiveness when sprinting. "It may seem like a small detail, but dorsiflexion is one of the most effective ways an athlete can improve his running mechanics," says Richesson, a performance specialist at AP. His NFL client list includes DeAngelo Hall, the 2006 "NFL's Fastest Man."

Quinn keeps his feet dorsiflexed throughout his workout, even while he's doing pullups. The action has no connection to such an exercise, but Richesson's instructions are to practice it not just at the gym but also at every moment: at dinner, in the shower, and (if you're really dedicated, Brady) on the john.

Quinn's free fall from the top slot in the NFL draft is mostly attributed to what he hasn't done. Despite his long list of gridiron accomplishments, scouts and prognosticators began to downgrade Quinn in January, citing his lack of noteworthy performances

The Flea Flicker

The C snaps the ball and then starts running straight down-field. The QB hands off the ball to the RB. The trick: Before reaching the line of scrimmage, the RB pitches the ball back to the QB. The RB then picks up the rushing defender normally blocked by the C. This gives the QB time to aim and fire to the wide-open C.

With ball in hand, the RB should gun right at the defender, then flick.

The Cross Pick

The right WR runs a shallow cross as the three left WRs run right slants. The trick: As the right WR comes across, the middle-left WR stops, turns, and blocks the right WR's defender (like a basketball pick). The QB hits the open right WR. Touchdown.

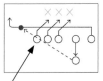

The middle-left WR should act like he didn't hear "hike," pausing one beat to better time the block.

The Hitch and Go

The far-wide WRs run short post patterns and the QB throws to either one. On the next down, let it slip that you're doing the same play. The WRs run the same posts. As each WR turns, the QB fakes and the defender—tasting an interception—will cut to the middle. The trick: When the defender bites (the "hitch"), the WRs run upfield (the "go") and await the QB's pass.

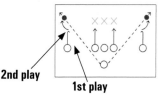

2nd play **1st play**

in big games, particularly the three bowl games that Notre Dame lost with Quinn under center.

More concerns were raised in February when Quinn opted out of the Senior Bowl, citing a nagging knee injury. Then he drew criticism for announcing ahead of time that he wouldn't participate in any individual workouts, including throwing drills, at the NFL Combine.

With his reputation in desperate need of some good publicity, Quinn realized he had to give the press something new to talk about. On day 2 of the NFL Combine, he

unexpectedly took part in the 225-pound bench-press test and shocked the football world by grinding out 24 repetitions—more than any quarterback in Combine history.

That's typical of Quinn's approach with his critics. "It showed that he's not going to shy away from competition," says Mark Schlereth, an analyst for ESPN's *NFL Live*. Yet despite his impressive showing, Quinn's stock continued to waver, largely because of the spanking his Fighting Irish took from

JaMarcus Russell and the LSU Tigers in the Sugar Bowl, Quinn's final collegiate game.

"That last vision is indelibly marked in everyone's head," says Schlereth. And that includes Quinn's. Before walking off the field, he took a mental picture of the scoreboard, which read 41–14 in favor of LSU. "I try to use it as motivation before any set I do when I lift weights," Quinn says. "I always work out better when I'm kind of pissed off."

If micromanagement of the angle of Brady Quinn's feet sounds nitpicky, the rest of his workout is downright obsessive-compulsive. As a standing rule, Richesson has told Quinn not to touch a dumbbell, barbell, or medicine ball until he straightens up. In this case, "straighten up" is meant in the literal sense. Quinn must first make sure his abs have been braced—imagine that you're about to be punched in the gut—and his shoulder blades have been pulled back and down. Next, he's to hold one hand 6 inches above his head as a cue to remind himself to stand as tall as he can. Quinn reviews this posture checklist before every set of every exercise he performs. Then, and only then, is he permitted to pick up a weight.

"This preexercise routine should probably be standard procedure at all gyms," says Matthew Rhea, PhD, the director of human movement at A.T. Still University, in Arizona. "Poor posture, which most guys have, is bad enough for your body without exacerbating it with the stress of added weight."

The effect of these small but critical postural adjustments, says Richesson, extends beyond the gym, which is, of course, the whole point. In a study, Australian researchers discovered that by training with this type of perfect posture, you develop nerve pathways between your brain and muscles that help your body move more efficiently and with better alignment on the playing field. And this, in turn, results in an athlete who's stronger, faster, and more resistant to injury.

Just as dorsiflexion has seeped into all aspects of Brady Quinn's life, so has the posture checklist. We're 5 hours into his cover shoot, and our leading man has been smiling and flexing on demand the entire time. Yet when he has a chance to sit, he tells me he's bracing his abs. "Guys always think they need to do so many abs exercises, but your abs should be activated in everything you do," says Quinn. "I've been working my abs all day."

"If Brady's not conscious of his core while he's driving or at the computer or eating, then 30 minutes in the gym won't do him any good," says Richesson. That may sound like an exaggeration, but Richesson says that your body adapts to the posture you most often assume. If you sit at a desk all day with your shoulders slumped and your neck protruding forward, then you'll inevitably have a posture that looks more like Neanderthal man than Superman. Want to be the best you can be on the playing field? Think about posture every waking minute.

That's why Quinn is "relaxing" poolside with his chest out, shoulders pulled back,

Arm Yourself

We ran a battery of tests on a dozen footballs—gauging accuracy, average distance, and durability—so you can go long this season. Here's your roster.

AFL Game Ball

Average distance: 34 yards
This durable leather ball is best for the annual backyard rumble.
$70, spalding.com

Black Max

Average distance: 44 yards
A *Men's Health* **favorite, the ball has** a weighted center that makes spirals a cinch.
$10, digginactive.com

Pro Spiral Street

Average distance: 37 yards
At three-fourths the size of an NFL ball, this colorful pill is easier to chuck and catch.
$25, nflshop.com

Nerf Weather Blitz

Average distance: 40 yards
Water won't turn this Nerf into a brick. Sling it during the mud bowl or at the beach.
$10, hasbro.com

Nerf Vortex Howler

Average distance: 48 yards
With its tomahawk tail, this waterproof whistling weirdo flew the farthest.
$10, hasbro.com

and core tight. Posture, like the Sugar Bowl loss, can't escape his mind now.

One convenient aspect of preparing for the brutality of professional football is that Quinn's daily routine hasn't had to change much. After all, he bought into the importance of weight training years ago.

In 10th grade, Quinn's shoulder began feeling sore after pitching and playing quarterback. So his dad, a former marine, showed him a few exercises, including external rotation. (See "Stand Tall.") External rotation is one of the most effective ways to strengthen your rotator cuff, perhaps the most valuable group of muscles and tendons for any guy who slings a ball for a living. Soon the pain disappeared, and he was throwing harder than ever.

"I really started to love lifting because I saw the results on the field," says Quinn. "I think my work ethic in the weight room has given me an advantage over a lot of guys."

While 28 of the first 64 picks in this year's NFL draft trained alongside Quinn at AP, according to Richesson, Quinn was always the first guy at the gym in the morning, and the last guy to leave. "His mentality in the weight room more closely resembles that of a linebacker than a quarterback," says Richesson. Case in point: That record-breaking performance he put in at the Combine beat out half of the linebackers who participated.

But the rest of Quinn's iron workout may be even more impressive than his bench press. When doing pullups, for instance, Quinn can pump out 5 repetitions with 70 pounds hanging around his waist. Combined

Stand Tall

One simple exercise may have saved Brady Quinn's throwing arm, and it could save your posture. It's called external rotation. To find out whether it can help you, take this test.

Stand as tall as you can, but relax your shoulders and arms. Now look at your hands. If they fall in front of your body instead of at your sides, you have a posture problem.

Here's why: The largest muscles of your chest and back—your pecs and lats, respectively—attach to the inside of your upper arms and, as a result, rotate them (and your palms) inward. Conversely, your rotator-cuff muscles—which start at your shoulder blades—attach to the outside of your upper arms, rotating them outward.

Ideally, the strength of your rotator cuff will counteract that of your pecs and lats, allowing your hands to fall naturally to your sides. "Unfortunately, due to weak rotator cuffs, most guys' upper arms are internally rotated," says Mike Robertson, MS, CSCS, a strength coach in Indianapolis. "That pulls the shoulders forward, causing a slumped posture."

To restore balance, do external rotations twice a week. Grab a dumbbell with your left hand and lie on your right side. Place your left elbow on your left hip, and bend your arm 90 degrees. Without changing the bend in your elbow, raise your forearm up and back as far as you can. Do 12 reps, switch sides and arms, and repeat. Rest for 60 seconds, then do one more set for each arm.

with his body weight, that's more than 300 pounds—and without cheating, of course. Like everything else he does in the weight room, Quinn performs every pullup with precision: He starts each repetition with his

PEAK
performance

Touch the Rim

You want hops? Master all four phases of jumping: countermovement, propulsion, flight, and landing. "Most men neglect countermovement—the initial downward phase," says Robert dos Remedios, CSCS, director of speed, strength, and conditioning at College of the Canyons, in Santa Clarita, California. Dip down, lean forward, and use your arms. And give yourself extra lift by performing these workouts.

WORKOUT 1

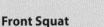

Dumbbell Jump Shrug

Stand holding a pair of dumbbells with an overhand grip (palms toward you) in front of your thighs. Dip slightly and shift your weight forward. Keeping your back flat and arms straight, simultaneously thrust your hips forward, shrug your shoulders, and jump straight up. Do four sets of 5 repetitions.

Front Squat

Stand holding a barbell across the front of your shoulders and bring your elbows forward so your upper arms are parallel to the floor. Initiate the move by pushing your hips back. Lower your body until your thighs are parallel to the floor. Quickly press back up to a standing position. Do 6 reps in the first set, then subtract 1 rep and add weight each set. Complete four sets total.

arms completely straight, and squeezes his shoulder blades together as he pulls his body up until his chin is above his knuckles.

And while most celebrity quarterbacks can't imagine doing squats with more than a couple of hundred pounds on their backs, Quinn squats nearly 500. More important, though, he excels at "front" squats, in which he typically uses a load of 315 pounds. In this exercise, Quinn holds the barbell in front of his body, resting it just above his collarbone—instead of across his upper back as in the classic version of the lift. "The bar placement keeps your torso more upright, and forces your core to work harder," says Richesson.

"Work harder" may well be Quinn's credo, and it's continually fueled by his naysayers. "I don't want to say there's a chip on my shoulder," says Quinn. "But thinking that way helps to get me where I need to be mentally when I'm training."

Countermovement Jump

Dip down by bending your hips and knees. Swing your arms back, then up as you jump as high as possible, reaching for a mark on the wall or backboard. Land softly with knees bent, shoulders slightly forward, and butt and hips back. Reset and repeat. Do four sets of 8 reps.

WORKOUT 2

Dumbbell Jump Squat

Stand holding a pair of light dumbbells at your sides. Lower your thighs so they are parallel to the floor, then bend forward slightly at the hips so your shoulders move in front of your feet. Push off the floor explosively to jump as high as possible. Land with your knees soft and sink down into your next squat. Do four sets of 5 reps.

Dumbbell Stepup

Holding heavy weights, lift one foot and place it on a bench, then push your body up until your weight-bearing leg is straight and your other foot hangs off the bench. Return to the starting position. Do 6 reps with each leg, then subtract 1 rep and add weight each set. Do four sets.

Tuck Jump

Stand with your feet shoulder-width apart and your knees slightly bent. Jump straight up as high as you can and bring your knees toward your chest. Land on the balls of your feet with your knees slightly bent and quickly go into your next jump. Do four sets of 8 reps.

Alternate between workouts 1 and 2 each time you train your lower body, for more power, greater ups, and softer landings.

Although scouts may question Quinn's ability to carry a team in big games, no one can question his heart. And that's a trait he shares with every great quarterback who has ever played in the NFL.

No, he wasn't the number one pick. But neither were Dan Marino (27), Joe Montana (82), or Tom Brady (199). Truth is, the only parts of Quinn's future that the draft has dictated are his ZIP code and signing bonus.

Back at AP, Quinn is resting between sets of barbell squats. "I think you're going to surprise people when they see you move," Richesson says to him.

"I don't like to tell people that," Quinn replies, smiling. "You always want to exceed expectations."

BY GRANT DAVIS

Find Your Center of Power

A veteran of 13 bone-crushing seasons in the NFL explains the importance of hip flexibility

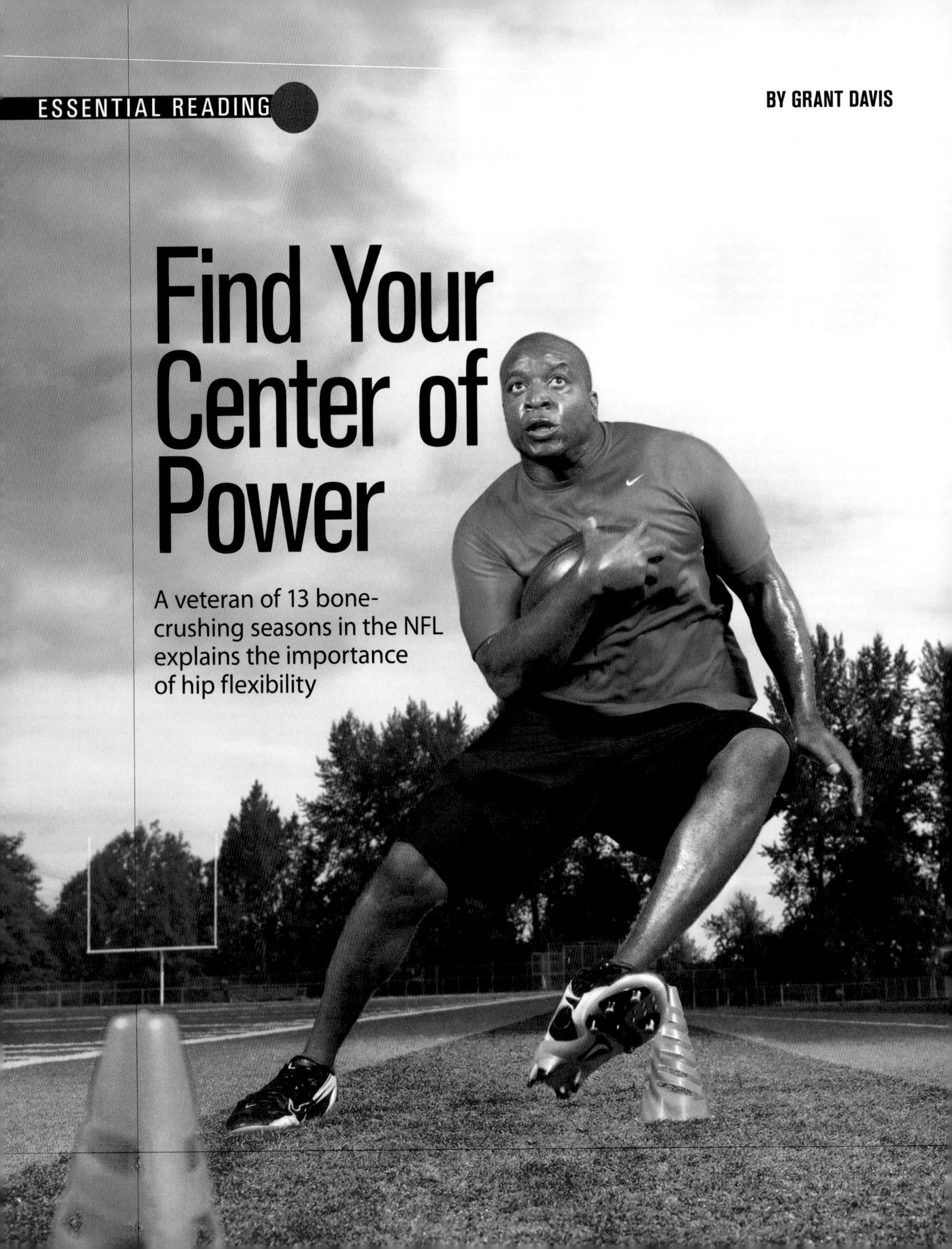

Mack Strong thought his career was over. As a fullback for the Seattle Seahawks, his job is to plow through linebackers who weigh 100 pounds more than he does, and he was doubting himself. It started 8 years ago, when his doctor found bone spurs (which occur naturally from age) on his right ankle. The doctor removed them, and Strong began physical therapy, but the pain in his ankle wouldn't go away. Strong lacked balance during weight-room sessions, and he couldn't run fluidly. With training camp weeks away, this was serious.

Strong took his struggles to the team's trainer, who explained that ankle problems can result from the hips being out of alignment. Strong's ankle problem showed he had been favoring his right side, and his knee and ankle didn't align properly with his pelvis. The trainer believed that if Strong made his hips more flexible, the pain in his ankle would go away, and he'd be able to access all the strength in his legs and drive through linebackers. So, to improve the limberness of his hips and the muscles that support them, Strong took up yoga and Pilates.

It wasn't easy. His first Bikram yoga class was so strenuous that he gave up after 30 minutes. Strong doesn't even know how many poses he tried before he stopped, but the amazing thing was that a day later he felt more stable and enjoyed greater mobility in his hips. Strong kept going back, and after a month, his ankle felt 100 percent, and he made it through the entire 90 minutes. On the field, Strong could warm up and recover faster than ever.

Pilates started as something Strong and his wife could do together; they would work through a series of torso-blasting, core-strengthening exercises on floor mats and a reformer machine. Now he's addicted to the ridiculous torso strength he's developed. Yoga keeps his hips flexible. Pilates makes them stable.

Strong has relied on a combination of the two to keep him game-ready ever since. The average NFL career lasts 3 years, but his has lasted more than four times longer thanks to his strong, limber hips. When Strong retires, he vows to do yoga and Pilates to help keep him agile and pain-free. Here are five of his favorite exercises for strong, flexible hips.

You Can Do It, Too

Use these exercises to increase the flexibility in your hips so you can run faster and prevent lower-body injuries.

INNER-THIGH RAISES

To strengthen your inner thighs (adductors), rig a low-cable pulley with an ankle cuff. Set the weight to 10 pounds, slip the cuff onto your left ankle, and grasp the machine with your left hand. Pull your left leg in front of and across your right leg as far as you can (don't tilt your hips), pause for a beat, and lower your foot. Do 10 repetitions on each leg for one set, and complete three sets. (You can also isolate the outer thigh by attaching the cuff to your outer ankle.)

WALKING DUMBBELL LUNGES

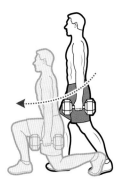

These will improve your balance and strengthen the muscles connected to your hips. Grab a 10- to 20-pound dumbbell in each hand. With the weights at your sides, take a large step forward with your right foot. Your right thigh and right calf should form a 90-degree angle, your left thigh should be perpendicular to the ground, and your back should be straight. Take 12 steps forward using the same lunge motion. Do the lunges walking backward until you reach your starting position. Repeat twice for a full set.

FROG STRETCH

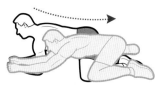

This stretch will relax the muscles on the insides of your thighs (your groin), which helps keep your legs limber. Begin by getting down on your hands and knees with your back parallel to the ground. Spread your knees as wide as you comfortably can while keeping your toes together. Lower onto your forearms. Keeping your back as straight as possible, slowly push your hips back and let your entire body sink toward the ground. While breathing deeply, hold this pose for 20 seconds. Slowly rise back onto your hands.

ONE-LEGGED PIGEON

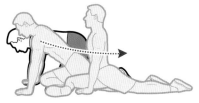

Use this exercise to loosen the muscles—glutes, hamstrings, and quads—around your hip sockets. Begin by getting down on your hands and knees. Bring your right knee forward to your right hand, and slide your right foot in front of your left knee (the outside of your right calf should lie on the floor). Slide your left leg back until the top of your left foot rests on the floor. Straighten your torso, using your hands to steady yourself. Sink your hips toward the floor while keeping your hips level. Hold for 20 seconds, and then repeat with your other leg.

THREE-PART BENCH STRETCH

During a run, ride, or game, use this routine to loosen your hamstrings, hip flexors, and quads. Raise your right heel onto a bench and lean forward to isolate your hamstring. Hold for 20 seconds, then release. Let the arch of your right foot lie flat on the bench. Stand straight and keep your right leg straight for 20 seconds. Lower your leg, turn away from the bench, and raise your foot behind you; the top of your right foot should rest on the bench. Stand straight for 20 seconds. Repeat with your left leg.

Increase Your Velocity

Train your obliques and you'll throw farther, swing quicker, and pitch harder. Follow this advice from Ben Potenziano, ATC, strength coach for the San Francisco Giants.

WARM UP

Rotational Movements

Stand with your arms straight out from your sides, so your body looks like the letter T. Step forward with your right foot and twist your upper body to the right. Return, then step forward with your left foot and turn left. Do 8 reps in each direction.

TRAIN YOUR

Cable Chops

Stand with your left side facing the weight stack of a high-pulley cable and grab the handle with both hands. Bend your knees and rotate your hips to the right as you pull the handle down and across your body toward

your right shin. Reverse the motion. Do 8 to 12 reps on each side.

PREPARE YOUR MUSCLES FOR POWER

Medicine-Ball Twist

Stand with your side facing a wall and hold a medicine ball at your opposite hip with both hands. Keeping your arms straight, rotate your upper torso toward the wall forcefully and release the ball. Catch and repeat. Do 4 or 5 reps on each side.

BY LIESA GOINS

Ride High

How snowboarding's founding
father toughens up for the slopes

When Jake Burton walks onto a ski slope, heads turn. Not because of who he is—iridium goggles and winter shells disguise the snowboarding legend—but rather because of his seniority. At 52, Burton is part of a small cadre of boarders known as "grays on trays." "Our sport is clearly youth driven," says Burton, alluding to the fact that 75 percent of boarders are 30 years his junior, "but you can also do it forever. The younger guys know they want to be riding at my age, so it's cool that I'm out there."

The mere fact that Burton is still carving turns after 38 years on the slopes is remarkable, both because of the sport's toll on his body (he has broken the same leg twice) and the demands of his business. As founder and chairman of Burton Snowboards, he commands a multimillion-dollar company that controls 40 percent of the $300 million snowboarding market. His days are crammed with meetings, interviews, and conference calls. Yet no matter how busy he gets—he's on the road 100 days a year—he finds time to exercise, alternating between strength and cardio workouts so that he's never in the gym for more than 45 minutes.

"Workouts are the hardest thing to fit in," he says, "but the strength feels so good that it feeds on itself." Here are three more ways Burton stays king of the mountain.

Work the stabilizing muscles. Snowboarding year-round keeps Burton's legs in shape. Though he still works them in the gym, he focuses on his upper body, using light weights and high reps to bolster the stabilizing

An Exercise in Stability

Stand firmly on two feet with these balance-boosting exercises.

Back Extension
Position yourself in a Roman chair and bend over at the waist, lowering your torso until it's nearly vertical. Return to the starting position. Do three sets of 15 reps.

Torso Swivel
Sit in a rotary torso machine, adjust the armrests 45 degrees to your right, and twist left as far as you can. Do 10 reps, then repeat on the opposite side. Do three sets.

Yoga Warrior Pose
Spread your legs and extend your arms out to your sides. Turn your right foot out 90 degrees; bend your knee until your thigh is parallel to the floor. Hold for 10 breaths. Repeat on your left side.

PEAK
performance

Streamline Your Stroke with These Four Simple Tips

Freestyle swimming makes for an ideal summer sweat session: The sport taxes your cardiovascular system while building your beach muscles. The hitch? You need good form.

We've pulled pointers from David Marsh, who won 12 NCAA championships as head swim coach at Auburn University and is now CEO of Mecklenburg Aquatics, in Charlotte, North Carolina. His tips will help you go from tadpole to torpedo in no time.

Take a Deep Breath

Instinct: You lift your neck to breathe, throwing your body out of alignment.

The Fix: Imagine your spine as a fixed axis moving forward through the water. Keep your head down and roll your shoulders forward with each reach. "As your arm extends and you roll to that side, turn your head to sneak a breath," says Marsh.

The Drill: The corkscrew

Swim three strokes of freestyle without breathing, then overro-

tate your torso until you're on your back. Take three backstrokes, and then roll back into freestyle. Alternate roll sides. Do 10 reps of 50 yards (10 x 50), with 10 seconds of rest after each 50.

Kick with Your Core

Instinct: You kick from the knees, disrupting your balance in the water and fatiguing your quadriceps muscles.

The Fix: Kick from the hips. Small, rhythmic flutters propel you more efficiently than large, flailing kicks, which disengage your powerful hips and upper thighs. Think of your legs as extensions of your core. Your knee should bend only slightly with each kick.

muscles that keep him balanced on the slopes. Key to his routine are back extensions, cable rows, and torso swivels, which together work every muscle from his hips to his shoulders. (See "An Exercise in Stability," on page 315.)

Stay flexible. Burton also credits his athletic longevity to Bikram yoga, which is done in a room heated to at least 105°F to facilitate the stretching of muscles. "It combines strength and flexibility," says Burton, "which are key to staying in shape for snowboarding." These qualities also help him

HARD TRUTH
Liters per hour the average man sweats during intense exercise

1.12

The Drill: Fin sprints

Wearing foot fins, push off the wall on your back, with your arms stretched above your head and your biceps pressed against your ears. Do a 10 x 50 set, completing each 50-yard swim and ensuing rest period in 1:30 intervals.

Pull Through

Instinct: You paddle with your hands instead of pulling yourself through the water using your forearms.

The Fix: Anchor your hand, wrist, and forearm as you drive forward into the water. Imagine wrapping your forearm over a Swiss ball and pulling yourself over it, says Marsh. Prevent your elbow from dropping inward, which weakens the anchor and your pull power.

The Drill: Closed-fist sets

Swim laps with your fists closed. A lack of grip forces you to anchor your forearms. Do a 4 x 50 set of only fist strokes; rest for 10 seconds after each 50. Then do a 6 x 50 set of full strokes in 1:30 intervals, focusing on pulling with your forearms.

Build a Better Workout

Instinct: You treat your swim workout like a casual jog, doing longer sets at a medium pace.

The Fix: Elite swimmers train by tackling "building sets," which begin slowly and end with all-out sprinting. They boost conditioning and help create fatigue-proof strokes. "Second place goes to the guy whose technique crumbles first," Marsh says.

The Drill: Count strokes

Try matching your number of strokes on the first, easy lap with the number in the final, sprint lap. Do a 5 x 100 set in 3:00 intervals. The first 25 yards: Swim long and easy. The second: Swim at 50 percent effort. The third: Swim at 75 percent effort. The final lap: Swim at 90 percent effort.

bounce back from spills and navigate tough terrain. "I'm able to twist and compress easier, and that helps me dig into turns and 360s."

Mix it up. Cardio is an integral part of Burton's routine, but you won't find him on a StairMaster. Instead, "I'll hike up a mountain and snowboard down," he says. Burton also likes to go for 1,500-meter swims, and if he has time, he'll challenge his sons—ages 10, 13, and 17—to some skateboarding on the family's half-pipe. "Skating is great cross-training," says Burton, "but it takes balls knowing that if you fall you're going to hit plywood. Snow is much more forgiving."

Spin
Your
Wheels

How Tate Donovan
shaped up by cycling

BY BOB COOPER

In many ways, Tate Donovan is just your average guy. Sure, the 43-year-old actor dated Jennifer Aniston (in her pre–Brad Pitt days), stars in shows like *The O.C.*, and played the lead in the biopic *Neal Cassady*. But like any businessman, he paid his dues climbing to the top, and now that he's there, his rewards are long hours and a job that alternates between actor and upcoming director.

"Directing, especially, takes a lot of endurance," says the New Jersey native. "You have to stay focused all the time, which is tough during a 14-hour workday."

Such a schedule also leaves little time to exercise, and until a few years ago, it showed. He carried a soft 180 pounds on his 6-foot frame—not fat, but not desirable, either, in a town like Hollywood. But that all changed in 2002, when he met celebrity trainer Riley McAlpine. "I happened to take her spin class," says Donovan. "Soon she was taking me for outdoor rides and encouraging me to swim and run."

Donovan greeted her invitations with enthusiasm, making workouts a nonnegotiable part of his day and quickly transitioning from an occasional runner to a triathlete in training. In fact, not 3 months passed before he won his first competition, the Malibu Triathlon, beating out longtime competitors David Duchovny and Jon Cryer. This September, Donovan will make a bid for his fourth win. Here's how the busiest biker in Hollywood keeps pedaling past the competition.

Look for windows of opportunity. "It's

A Rainy-Day Rider's Workout

Celebrity trainer Riley McAlpine offers four indoor workouts that will help make you faster.

Hill surges: To build leg strength and increase the force of your pedal stroke, warm up in an easy gear for 15 minutes, then set your bike's resistance to high and pedal at 60 rpm for 6 minutes. Rest and recover at 95 rpm for 3 minutes, and then repeat the process six times. Extend the recovery time to 15 minutes after the third and sixth power surges.

One-legged pedaling: After warming up, rest your right foot on a chair next to the bike and pedal at 80 to 90 rpm for 30 seconds with your left. Repeat six times, alternating legs, and then pedal evenly with both legs at an easy pace for 10 minutes. Repeat the entire set. This will train your neuromuscular system to eliminate dead spots in your stroke.

Commercial breaks: Position your bike in front of the television, warm up for 15 minutes, and then turn on your favorite show. Whenever it breaks for commercials, switch into a higher gear and start pedaling at 80 rpm. When your show comes back on, ease into a lower gear and pedal at a moderate pace. Repeat these intervals for the length of the program.

Endurance drills: To build your aerobic threshold, pop in an inspirational cycling movie (try the 1979 classic *Breaking Away*) and spin your wheels for 1 to 2 hours at an easy to moderate pace. Focus on making perfect circles with your pedal stroke by keeping your heels down.

tough to fit exercise into my day," says Donovan, "so I sneak off the set whenever I can." According to scientists at McMaster University, that's all it takes. In their study,

Assume the Position

Good posture is key to avoiding injury. Here's how to seat yourself.

Adjust your seat so that your leg is straight if you place your heel on the pedal at the bottom of its revolution. Doing so will give you a perfect bend in your knee when you clip in your toe. Next, arch your back (like a bridge) and bend your elbows slightly. Finally, push your shoulders forward so that your pecs help carry the weight of your upper body.

cyclists who performed 20-minute intervals (periods of exercise followed by periods of rest) achieved similar gains in performance as those who cycled for 90 minutes.

Pay a registration fee. Donovan always has a few races on his schedule, from the New York City Marathon to local triathlons. "Races are great motivational tools," he says. "They give you deadlines and a reason to stick to your workouts."

Schedule stretching sessions. In a typical week, Donovan bikes one day (70 miles), swims the next (1 hour), runs the third (8 miles), and then repeats the 3-day cycle. On the seventh day, he stretches. "I use yoga to stay flexible," he says. "Plus, after yoga, I feel totally blissed-out and ready for my next workout."

Strive for Balance

Your balance is your best ally for healthy ankles. In a study of more than 700 basketball and soccer players, those who performed the exercises below had 38 percent fewer ankle sprains than those who didn't do the exercises. Perform each move for 30 seconds on each leg, three to five times a week.

Single-Leg Balance

Hard: Stand on one leg for 30 seconds.
Harder: Try it with your eyes closed.

Single-Leg Dribble

Hard: Dribble a basketball while balancing on one leg.
Harder: On one leg, throw chest passes to a partner.

Unstable Balance

Hard: Stand on a balance board.
Harder: Rotate your hips from side to side while standing on the balance board.

Single-Leg Unstable Balance

Hard: Stand on a balance board on one leg.
Harder: Do it with your eyes closed.

Unstable Dribble

Hard: Stand on one leg on a balance board and dribble a basketball.
Harder: Using the same setup, pass the ball to a partner.

Chill Out

Finish your workout the right way and start your next session even stronger

ooling down after a sweaty gym stint falls low on the priority totem pole, right down there with flossing and organizing the junk drawer. But slowly returning your heart rate and blood pressure to normal is important because it reduces the risk of injury. It also makes you forget the pain of a good workout, increasing the chances you'll do it again, explains Fabio Comana, an exercise physiologist with the American Council on Exercise. Here's how to cool down smart and finish on a physical and emotional high.

After You Lift . . .

Do this: Pamper the muscles you've just worked by stretching for 5 minutes. Then, for 5 minutes, slide sore body parts over a foam roller. Finally, try a contrast shower—alternate between 3 minutes of hot water and 1 minute of cold. Why? Cold-water shots slow your metabolism and take down swelling to lessen the likelihood of soreness overload.

PAIN killer

How can I KO my knee pain?

One reason Mr. Miyagi was indestructible: Karate kicks decrease your risk of a knee injury, concluded a study in the *Journal of Strength and Conditioning Research*. Martial artists were found to have about 20 percent greater hamstring strength—a proven knee stabilizer—when compared with a fit control group. That's because karate athletes kick repeatedly during drills, initiating each kick from their hamstrings, say the study authors.

After You Run . . .

Do this: Finish up with light intervals, suggests Chris Bergland, Triple Ironman champion and author of *The Athlete's Way*. Run at a challenging pace for 20 to 25 seconds, then walk or jog for a minute or two. Repeat three to five times. Then stretch your calves, glutes, groin, hamstrings, hip flexors, and quads. This will help postrun carbs get into your muscle cells to replace lost glycogen.

After You Ride...

Do this: Spin easy for 10 to 20 minutes, says Amber Neben, two-time winner of the Tour de l'Aude, the biggest women's cycling stage race, which rolls in France. Then 86 muscle soreness with an ice massage: With a "popsicle" you've made by freezing water in a Dixie cup, rub the aching area for 10 minutes, take a break for 10 minutes, and rub again. Repeat for up to an hour.

After You Swim...

Do this: Dip underwater five or six times, and each time blow out all your air. Then swim one-tenth the distance of your workout, nice and easy. Although the impact-free nature of swimming feels relaxing, a cooldown is critical to slowing your heart rate and preventing muscle cramps and injuries, says Janet Evans, four-time Olympic gold medalist and author of *Janet Evans' Total Swimming.*

Carve More Muscle with Just One Machine

Avoid gym lines and head straight to the cable crossover station. With this fast, full-body routine, you'll train on every plane of movement. The result: "Bigger muscles and a more athletic body," says Robert dos Remedios, CSCS, director of speed, strength, and conditioning at College of the Canyons, in Santa Clarita, California.

Sculpt picture-perfect muscles with these four simple exercises. Perform three or four sets of 8 to 12 reps of each exercise, resting for 30 seconds after each set.

your feet, right leg forward. Bend at the knees and lower your body as you press the weight overhead and bend your torso to the right. Do all your reps to one side, then switch arm and leg positions and repeat.

Squat and Row: Attach a rope handle to a low-pulley cable and grab with both hands. Stand facing the weight stack, your elbows bent and your hands next to the sides of your torso. Lower your body by bending at your hips and knees as you allow your arms to straighten in front of you. When your thighs are parallel to the floor, reverse the movement back to the starting position.

Punch and Pull: Grab the handle of a low-pulley cable with your left hand, and the handle of the opposite high-pulley cable with your right. Face the low pulley and stagger your feet, left foot forward. Hold your right hand next to your shoulder, keeping your left arm straight. Pull your left hand back as you

punch your right hand forward. Do all your reps, then switch arm and leg positions and repeat.

Split Squat and Press: With the weight stack to your left, grab the handle of a low-pulley cable with your left hand and bring it to your shoulder. Stagger

Woodchopper: With your left side toward the weight stack, grab the rope pulley of a high-pulley cable with both hands. Keeping your arms straight, bend your knees and rotate your hips as you pull the rope down and across your body until your hands are just outside your right knee, then reverse the motion. Finish your reps before switching sides and repeating the movement.

Get in the Zone

The "zone"—a mental state that boosts an athlete's performance—is no longer a mystery. In a brain-imaging study, Syracuse University researchers found that when hypnotized athletes relived a prior zone-fueled performance, there was greater activity in the part of their brains that controls coordination. At the same time, other mental wiring became less active, allowing for greater focus and execution.

Try it yourself: Quiet your mind while playing a sport, and you'll be more likely to enter the zone. Specifically, don't pay attention to spectators or to your chances of success.

Pump Up the Volume

There's a reason NBA locker rooms contain as many sets of headphones as they do pairs of

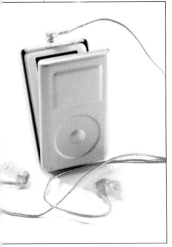

sneakers. Listening to music while warming up will jumpstart your game. Scientists at Israel's Tel Aviv University had 24 volleyball players perform pregame warmups both with music and in silence and found that the tunes were responsible for a temporary 10 percent power boost at game time. Up-tempo music can raise your heart rate and level of blood epinephrine, a hormone that helps fuel exercise.

Choose your tracks and volume wisely, though. The study authors recommend listening to songs with tempos of at least 140 beats per minute (Green Day's "Boulevard of Broken Dreams" weighs in at 167) at about 60 percent of your music player's max volume.

Breathe Freely

Pack some broccoli in your cycling jersey: Nitrate-rich foods such as spinach and strawberries can boost breathing during workouts, reports an *Acta Physiologica* study. Nine men ingested either placebos or nitrate supplements for 4 days. On the fourth day, the volunteers pedaled a stationary bike at varying intensities. The supplement swallowers consumed 5 percent less oxygen, which improved their muscle efficiency by 7 percent.

Nitrate helps produce nitric oxide, a chemical compound that improves blood and oxygen flow to your muscles, the researchers say. Nosh pregame on salads with strawberries and grapes.

Stretch It Out

Stay strong and limber by stretching at the right time. Static stretches—the stretch-and-hold technique you're familiar with—can reduce strength and power when done before your workout, according to a report in *Strength and Conditioning Journal*. Stretching causes muscle fibers to relax, thus inhibiting the amount of force you're able to produce. Know what to stretch when, for great results. Hold each stretch for 30 seconds.

WHEN TO STRETCH	WHAT TO STRETCH	WHY
When you wake up	Stretch your hip flexors, quadriceps, and neck muscles.	These muscles are often tight because of the way most men sleep, with their legs bent and shoulders rounded.
Before your workout	Steer clear of static stretches for 1 to 2 hours before you train.	Try calisthenics instead.
After you train	Stretch all the muscles used in your workout, and stay consistent.	Gains in flexibility accrue over time.
In the evening	Stretch your hamstrings, lower back, and glutes.	Long hours at your desk tighten these areas.

Eat Jelly Bellys to Take Off Your Jelly Belly

Workout candy? Please. But the University of California at Davis laid doubt to rest: Specially formulated Sport Beans boost exercise performance as much as carb-loaded sports drinks and gels. Researchers compared 16 cyclists who got either water or a sports drink, a gel, or the jelly beans during a long race. The beans stood up to the other supplements, all of which shaved 32 to 38 seconds more off race times than the water.

"Carbohydrates optimize performance by conserving muscles' fuel, and the source doesn't seem to matter," explains study coauthor Gretchen Casazza, PhD. Try 50 calories from any high-carb supplement every 20 minutes during intense exercise. Find Sport Beans ($11.50 for 12 packs) at jellybelly.com.

Bounce Back

Holding a stretch is so 1980. Instead, bounce. Brigham Young University researchers found that ballistic stretching increased basketball players' vertical jump by about $1^1/_2$ inches. That means bouncing at the end of your range of motion, one bounce per second for 30 seconds. For 8 minutes, the players performed lunges, reaches, and heel lifts. Static stretches showed no vertical benefit.

Stay Smooth

A shocking revelation: Dual-suspension mountain bikes are as fast as their hard-tail counterparts, say Swiss researchers, who dispelled the long-held belief that single-suspension bikes are faster. After sending 13 riders on a mile-long climb, the researchers found that suspension type had no effect on pedaling efficiency. Although the additional suspension does absorb some of the extra pedaling energy, the researchers speculate that that energy somehow goes back into turning the tires.

Go Faster with Goo

Sucking on protein gel will boost your pedaling performance, according to research out of James Madison University. When compared with cyclists who used carbohydrate-only energy gels, cyclists who consumed gels that contained both protein and carbohydrates were able to ride 13 percent farther. One possible explanation is that the protein increases the number of carbohydrates that pass from your intestines to your bloodstream, and from there to your energy-hungry muscles.

To slurp the same gel used in the study, check out gusports.com. The study authors recommend pounding a pack of goo for every 15 minutes you pedal.

Start Fast to Finish Faster

Pedaling fast for the first 10 seconds of a bike race will improve your power output at the end of the race, reports the journal *Medicine & Science in Sports & Exercise*. Going hard early jumpstarts your breathing pattern. Researchers had eight cyclists perform three 4,000-meter trials. Over the first 2,000 meters, the cyclists either increased their power output, decreased it, or kept it steady. They then pedaled hard to the finish.

Study author Florentina Hettinga, PhD, a professor of movement sciences at Amsterdam's Vrije University, says the fast starters performed best at the end. Cyclists should follow their fast getaway with a gradual increase in speed until

the midpoint—then sprint. This pacing preserves anaerobic energy for the finish, she says. Speaking of pacing, a study in the journal *Sports Medicine* found that knowing your route helps. The brain uses the knowledge to calibrate power output and metabolic rate.

Pull for Speed

Hitting the hills? Pull your bike's pedals for a faster ride, according to a study out of London's Brunel University. The researchers observed trained racing cyclists as the riders demonstrated three different pedaling strategies: pedaling in an even circular motion, pulling on the upstroke (the shoes need to be clipped onto the pedals), and pushing during the downstroke. Their finding: Pulling was the most efficient pedal stroke.

The technique may give you an edge during sprinting and climbing because it forces your hamstrings and hip flexors to work together during each upstroke, which results in a more powerful downstroke and greater speed, says study author Thomas Korff, PhD. For long, flat rides, he suggests pedaling however you're most comfortable; it'll save you energy.

Be a Visionary

You already spin and pump—now beef up your eyeballs. A new athletic program at the Vision Care Institute in Jacksonville, Florida, is helping Olympic hopefuls in softball, volleyball, archery, and soccer fine-tune their visual skills. The AchieveVision Program increases athletes' reaction times with exercises that sharpen hand-eye and foot-eye coordination.

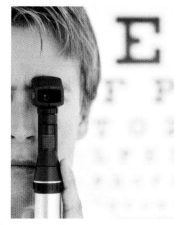

Try it: String a piece of flexible plastic tubing through red, blue, green, and white Wiffle balls; secure the ends to create a hoop. Have a friend throw it to you while calling out a color; as the hoop spins, try to catch the right ball.

Train with TiVo

Not that you need a reason to watch more ESPN, but seeing A-Rod hit a homer will make you a better hitter. The reason: Through imitation, we're able to learn tasks—such as swinging a bat—much better than was previously thought, says Yigal Agam, a neuroscience expert at Brandeis University. He

found that it took only a single viewing of a movement for people to retain and replicate it effectively. The more they viewed it, the more exact their imitation became.

One note of caution: Another study in the *Journal of Sports Sciences* found that you can subconsciously pick up bad habits by watching mediocre athletes. So flip past the K.C. Royals. Got TiVo? Intermittently pausing an action will make it easier to learn, Agam says.

Pop This Pill for Speed

Maybe this is the pill Floyd Landis should've taken. Quercetin supplements increase an athlete's endurance. Pepperdine University researchers found that elite cyclists taking 600 milligrams of the antioxidant daily for 6 weeks improved their 30-K time trials by almost 5 percent. The best news: The athletes were particularly fast in the last 5 kilometers, when

they should have been the most fatigued. Why? Quercetin appears to reduce inflammation and muscle damage. Try GNC's Quercetin 500 ($12 for sixty 500-milligram tablets).

Mouth Off

Yes, they're annoying. But contrary to popular belief, wearing a mouth guard doesn't hinder breathing and may boost your performance, according to a study in the journal *Medicine & Science in Sports & Exercise*. Researchers tested athletes with no guards against athletes using either custom-made or cheap "boil-and-bite" guards. Custom-made models improved airflow during exercise by creating a smoother oral cavity, making breathing less turbulent. And visual reaction time was not affected.

Flex Your Muscle Memory

Phil Mickelson's preshot waggle and Derek Jeter's tugging on his batting gloves aren't quirks: One of the best ways to master a skill is to use a premove routine. Why? It makes it easier for your brain to implement the desired movement, says Mark Churchland, PhD, a neuroscientist at Stanford University who studied muscle memory. Researchers say the brain has difficulty repeating trained movements precisely, but it gains consistency when actions are preceded by specific cues.

Watch and Learn

Get pumped to kick butt. Scientists from the University of Illinois at Urbana-Champaign surveyed 16 people and found that when they believed strongly that they could push through discomfort while maxing out on a stationary bike, they did. Train your brain to push your body by developing an "If they can do it, I can do it" mentality. How? Rent a flick. Here are five films to stoke your finish-line fire.

WHEN	WHAT	WHY
Training for a 10-K	*Personal Best* (1982)	The Olympic track team gets heated—in more ways than one.
Entering a bike race	*Breaking Away* (1979)	One of the most inspiring films of all time—a classic.
Learning to surf	*Blue Crush* (2002)	Talented surfer almost loses serious focus over random guy.
Joining a soccer team	*Bend It Like Beckham* (2002)	Sticking it to tradition to play "football."
Getting in the ring	*Rocky* (1976)	The Italian Stallion never gets old.

Burn Fat Like Beckham

Here's why you never see chubby soccer players: Soccer is a potent fat-burning workout, according to an Italian study. In a 30-minute pickup game, competitors exercised above 70 percent of their maximum heart rate 91 percent of the time.

"Even during periods when you're not running as hard, your heart rate stays elevated because of the constant changing of direction," say the study authors. Boost soccer's fitness potential even further by playing both sides of the ball. An Irish study found that midfielders—who play both offense and defense—sprinted 60 percent more during games than did strikers and defenders.

Kick your body into shape by playing pickup soccer. You'll burn 400 calories in just 30 minutes of play.

Slack Off

Training hard? Cut back: Reducing workout length before competition gives you an edge, reports a *Medicine & Science in Sports & Exercise* study. Investigators found that athletes who trimmed their workout length by 41 to 60 percent for the 2 weeks before an event while continuing to work out as intensely, and as often, boosted their performance by 2 percent—enough to shave 60 seconds off a 50-minute 10-K.

Tapering for 2 weeks allows you to recover energy after tough training; 1 week won't reduce fatigue, and 3 weeks can degrade your fitness, says lead author Laurent Bosquet, PhD. So, if you've built up to a 30-mile training week, cut that by 12 to 18 miles, and sub in power naps or massages.

Trade Your Sneaks for Cleats

Soccer burns more fat than jogging does, reports a University of Copenhagen study. Investigators compared 14 soccer players with a group of joggers, measuring their heart rate, muscle mass, and body fat. After 12 weeks of equal exercise time, soccer players had lost twice as much fat (8 pounds versus 4 pounds,

on average) and gained an average of 4 pounds of muscle (runners gained zero). The players lost more flab in part because they spent 20 percent more time at a higher heart rate and built fat-blasting muscle mass with sprints, jumps, and turns, says lead researcher Peter Krustrup, a PhD candidate. Find indoor soccer, volleyball, or basketball leagues at the gym, the YMCA, or active.com.

Play on Clay

If you play tennis for the exercise, do so on a clay court. You'll play longer and run more compared with hard-court games, according to a Canadian study. Balls travel slower on clay, allowing for longer volleys. Go to ustasearch. com to find the nearest clay court.

Throw a Speed Ball

Want a rocket arm? Try overhead medicine-ball throws. Researchers at the University of Delaware found that 8 weeks of medicine-ball training can add 2 miles an hour to your fastball. Here's how: Stand 2 feet in front of a wall while holding a 6-pound medicine ball overhead with both hands. Bend your arms back behind you, then toss the ball against the wall (as if you were throwing a soccer ball into

play). When the ball rebounds, catch it and go into your next rep without pausing. Do three sets of 10.

Training
Tips

Will sex in the evening hurt my athletic performance the next day?

Let the pregame show begin! A Swiss study found no difference in performance between elite athletes who got busy 10 hours before a battery of tests and those who abstained. But much of sports performance is mental, and other studies suggest that if you believe a romp will ruin your game, it will.

My shoulder always hurts after I swim. Any advice?

Easy: Stretch your chest and lats every morning, after you swim, and at night, says Mark Verstegen, MS, CSCS, founder and president of Athletes' Performance, in Tempe, Arizona. Your chest and back muscles are responsible for rotating your arms toward your body's midline, so these muscles tighten with repetitive freestyle and butterfly strokes (or too many bench presses and lat pulldowns in the weight room). Use this new stretch to loosen up your chest and lats, and go to MensHealth.com, keyword Foam, for more stretches and a complete shoulder-strengthening workout.

DYNAMIC CHEST STRETCH

Stand with your feet staggered about 2 feet apart and your arms extended in front of you at shoulder height, palms in. Move your arms out to the sides and behind you while rotating externally so your palms face up. Hold for 2 seconds, then return to the starting position. Do 10 repetitions.

Why am I always hungry after I swim?

Blame your body temperature. University of Florida researchers found that people exercising in cold pool water were 44 percent hungrier afterward than those working out in warm water. The authors think this is due to your body's attempt to reheat itself, triggering you to chow down for extra energy. Try taking a brisk 15-minute walk after swimming to increase your body temperature and combat your postswim cravings.

I want to start cycling. How do I buy the most bike for my buck?

Approach buying a bike as you would a suit: Make sure it's perfectly tailored to your body.

"How you're positioned on the bike is the most important facet of the purchase," says Matt

Heitmann, cofounder of Cadence Cycling Centers, in Philadelphia. A good bike shop will have an expert bike fitter to measure your legs, torso, and arms to determine exactly what you need.

After the fit, the next most important factor is weight. Because the price will rise as the bike's weight falls, keep it between 19 and 23 pounds, plenty light for most novices. Now, with the size and weight in mind, pick out a bike with as many of the quality points listed here as possible. Everything shown can be purchased at cadencecycling.com.

Ⓐ Firm saddle: Match your seat to your body type. "A bigger guy won't want a narrow saddle," says Ken Whelpdale, director of logistics for USA Cycling. Shown: Selle Italia

Ⓑ Aluminum handlebars and stem: Their relative weight is negligible, so save cash with aluminum, says Matt Heitmann, cofounder of Cadence Cycling Centers in Philadelphia. Shown: ITM Visia

Ⓒ Aluminum/carbon frame: Choose a combination aluminum/carbon-fiber frame for vibration dampening and affordable strength. Shown: BMC SL01

Ⓓ Lightweight wheels: Wheels are pricey, so use whatever comes with a bike that fits the bill in other areas. When it's time to upgrade, buy deep-dish carbon rims for speed. Shown: Mavic Elite

Ⓔ Carbon forks: They connect the wheels to the frame, so carbon fiber is critical for vibration dampening. Shown: Easton EC70 fork

Pain-free fit: Pressure is equally divided among your feet, hands, and seat on a bike that fits. If your neck or shoulders hurt, your ride is the wrong size.

I regularly bicycle 20 miles nonstop with no respiratory problems, but when I try to jog a quarter of a mile, my lungs start to hurt. What gives?

It's a good bet that you're compelled to run faster than you should because you're accustomed to your bike's cruising speed. When you ride, the bike supports all of your body weight. When you run, you have to carry a lot more poundage—that's one reason you're sucking wind sooner.

To keep your pace in check, track your heart rate on a comfortable bike ride. (You can talk, but only in one-sentence spurts.) Then try maintaining the same heart rate on your next run, even if it means going a little slower than you'd like.

Is there anything I can do to have a faster first step in sports?

To run fast, you have to train fast. This drill, combined with running sprints three times a week, will train your central nervous system to respond to quick movements.

How to do it: Imagine a large X on the floor and stand in the middle of it with your feet pointing at a 45-degree angle toward the top left of the X. Keep your shoulders facing forward as you rotate your hips and feet back and forth toward each end of the X. To counterbalance the movement, shift your arms to the right when your hips rotate left, and vice versa. Rotate back and forth for 6 seconds at the start of each sprint.

What's the best way to improve my putting game?

Buy a strobe light, then turn it on in a dark room and start putting into a cup. The visual noise created by the strobe will train you to keep your head down and your eyes focused on the top of the ball. (If you don't, you'll be more likely to top or miss-hit the ball.)

In normal light, it'll be easier to concentrate because your eyes will have grown accustomed to the flashing light. The ball will also appear to move more slowly under the strobe light, allowing you to determine the spin you're putting on the ball—cut, slice, end over end—and correct your stroke accordingly.

How long should you ice an injury? My doctor always says "20 minutes on, 20 minutes off," but my trainer suggests less time. Who's right?

Trainer wins. Actually, until last year, no one had really studied the best way to ice injured muscles. But research published in the *British Journal of Sports Medicine* suggests that 10 minutes of on-off icing (try to keep it up for an hour) is more effective than the universally prescribed 20 minutes because it keeps the temperature of the muscle lower longer.

When in doubt, though, see a doctor—especially if you're in a lot of pain, the swelling hasn't gone down after 24 hours, or you're unable to put pressure on the muscle.

Image Credits

Cover Photograph
© Scott McDermott

Interior Photographs
Courtesy of Advanced Fitness Group: page 83

© Almay: page 280

© Matt York/AP Images: page 313 (baseball player)

© Ed Zurga/AP Images: page 330 (right)

Courtesy of Peter Arnell: page 50

© Banana Stock: pages 57 (bottom), 61 (bottom), 108, 239 (left), 271 (right)

© Beth Bischoff: pages 64, 66, 67, 68 (exercises), 69, 73, 74, 75, 76, 79 (prone cobra, knot reliever), 80, 81, 82, 120, 121, 123, 127, 128 (exercises), 129, 130, 131, 132, 139, 148, 185, 190, 191, 192, 193, 196, 197, 198, 199, 202, 203, 204, 205, 208, 209, 210, 211, 213, 214, 215, 216, 218, 221, 222, 223 (left), 224, 225, 228, 229, 230, 231 (left), 232, 234 (right), 235 (bottom right), 236 (bottom right), 237, 272, 294 (right), 295, 296

© Brand X Pictures: pages 57 (top), 235 (top right)

© E.J. Camp: page 314

© Corbis: page 52 (bottom)

© Randy Faris/Corbis: page 332

© Patrik Giardino/Corbis: page 90

© Bob Jacobson/Corbis: page 240 (top)

© Jupiter Images/Corbis: page 183 (top)

© Mika/Zefa/Corbis: page 65

© Craig Cutler: pages 16, 18, 25, 27

© Davies & Starr: page 262

© Digital Vision: pages 53 (bottom), 59 (top)

© Eyewire: page 126

© Andrew French: page 113 (right)

© Getty Images: page 179 (top & right)

© Blend Images/Getty Images: pages 61 (top), 260

© Bongarts/Getty Images: page 259

© Cultura/Getty Images: page 281

© Emmanuel Faure/Digital Vision/Getty Images: pages 330 (left)

© Digital Vision/Getty Images: pages 34 (right), 270, 323 (right)

© Image Source/Getty Images: page xii

© PhotoAlto Agency/Getty Images: page 331

© Photodisc/Getty Images: pages 116, 179

© Rubberball/Getty Images: page 282

© Stockbyte/Getty Images: pages 28, 277 (left)

© Fredrick Bass/fStop/Getty: page 273

© Hayley Baxter/Gallo/Getty Images: page 242

© Chris Cole/Iconica/Getty Images: page 245 (left)

© Nicolas Russell/The Image Bank/Getty Images: page 158 (left)

© Markus Amon/Photographer's Choice/Getty Images: page 150

© PE Reed/Photonica/Getty Images: page 38

© Jan Stromme/Photonica/Getty Images: page 36

© China Tourism Press/Riser/Getty Images: page 34 (center)

© Dominic DiSaia/Stone/Getty Images: page 308 (basketball player)

© Loungepark/Stone/Getty Images: page 152

© Carl Lyttle/Stone/Getty Images: page 48

© Whit Preston/Stone/Getty Images: page 244

© Mark Hanauer: pages vii (top), 2, 4, 6, 8, 10, 15, 70, 77, 79 (dumbbell incline fly), 122, 284, 287, 289, 290, 298

© Jeff Harris: page 128 (pasta)

© Colin Hayes: pages 245 (right), 246, 311, 312

© Christian Hogue: page 119

© Todd Huffman: pages 56

© Imagebank: page 114 (right)

© Monte Isom: pages 143, 144, 145, 146

© Pearl Izumi: pages 58, 112, 263, 271 (left), 274, 324 (left), 329 (left), 336 (left)

© Devon Jarvis: pages 261, 327

© Anna Emilia Lundgren/Johner Images: page 34 (left)

© Blend Images/Jupiter Images: page 234 (left)

© Ed Landrock: page 277 (right)

© Joel Lardner: page 258

© Jason Lee: page 315

© Henry Leutwyler: page 110

© Adam Levey: pages vii, 31, 32

© Jennifer Levy: page 275 (right)

Courtesy of Life Fitness: page 86 (bottom)

© Matt Mahurin: pages 161, 162, 171

© Michael Mazzeo: page 168

© Scott McDermott: pages v, vi (middle), 188, 189, 194, 200, 206, 207, 212, 219, 226

© Kagan McLeod: pages 45, 55, 91, 107, 158 (right), 159, 177, 217, 223 (pain killer exercises), 231 (jump shrug), 233, 239 (right), 241 (bottom left), 247, 268, 269, 275 (exercises), 308 (exercises), 309, 313 (exercises), 316 (stroke), 317, 321, 325

© Ryan McKnee/NCAA Photos: page 292

© Kyle Carter/Reuters/Newscom: page 303 (football players)

Courtesy of Octane Fitness: page 85 (left)

© Sophie Pangrazzi: page 310

© Scott Peterson: page 238

© Plamen Petkov: pages 41, 42, 46, 278

© Pixland/Jupiter Images: page 184

© Chris Philpot: page 97

© Photodisc: pages 52 (top), 60 (left & right), 109 (bottom), 111 (right), 236 (top right), 241

© Melissa Punch: pages 124, 335

© Stockbyte/Punchstock: page 44

© Rodale Images: pages vi (top), 180 (right), 302, 303 (football plays), 305, 326 (right), 328

© John Hamel/Rodale Images: pages 316 (swimmer), 323 (left), 324 (right)

© Heather Jones/Rodale Images: pages 84, 85 (right), 86 (top), 164, 165, 166, 167, 185 (right), 320

© Mitch Mandel/Rodale Images: pages 181, 185 (bottom), 186, 326 (left)

© Margaret Skrovanek/Rodale Images: page 337

© Kurt Wilson/Rodale Images: pages 59 (bottom), 114 (left)

© Rubberball: pages 181 (left), 182

© Embry Rucker: pages 136, 137, 138, 141

Courtesy of Carole Segel/SciFi Channel: page 89

© Carlos Serrao: pages 92, 95, 96, 98, 300, 304, 306

© Piotr Sikora: page 156

© Empics/Sportschrome: page 111 (left)

© Stockbyte: pages vi (bottom), vii, 53 (top), 62, 88, 118, 178, 180 (left), 235 (bottom left), 322, 329 (right), 334, 336 (right)

© Art Streiber: pages 100, 102, 105

© Tim Tadder: page 236 (bottom left)

© Alex Tehrani: pages 293, 294 (bottom left)

© Joe Toreno: pages 248, 249, 250, 255, 256

© Tim Turner: pages 12, 68 (cookies), 78, 133

© Mark Ulriksen: pages 285, 286, 288, 291

© Blend Images Photography/Veer: page 109 (top)

© Somos Photography/Veer: page 266

Courtesy of Versa Climber: page 113 (left)

Courtesy of Warner Brothers: page 101

© Mark Weiss: page 265

© Workbook Stock: page 333

© Jim Wright: page 318

© David Zickl: page 115

Index

Boldface page references indicate photographs and illustrations.
Underscored references indicate boxed text.

Plank, 80, **80**, 167
   with diagonal arm lift, 208, **208**, 210
   on Swiss ball, 179
   with weight transfer, 232, **232**
Plantar fasciitis, 264, 273
Plate size, effect on eating, 30
Platform stepdown, 169
Plyometrics, 257, 261, 274–275, **275**, 298
Positive attitude, benefits of, 267
Posture
   checklist before lifting, 304–305
   cycling, 320
   exercises for
      prone cobra, 78–79, **79**
      squat, 157
Potassium, 40, 43
Potatoes, baked, 47
Potato-sack squat, **123**, 123–124, 124
Power clean, 12
Power skip, **45**, 45
Power training program, 138–142
Prisoner squat, **91**, 91
Proanthocyanins, 44
Progressive overload, 139
Promises, as motivation booster, 49
Prone cobra, 78–79, **79**
Prostatitis, exercise for relief of, 110
Protein
   daily intake, 155, 157–158
   intake before and after workouts, 178, 185
   role of muscle mass in metabolism, 153, 154
   shakes, 178, 179
Prowler, 149
Psychologist, weight-loss, 53
Pull exercises, 140, 169, 174–175
Pullup, 200, **200**, 203
   incline, 165, 169
   interrupted, 233, **233**
   with leg raise, 269, **269**
   mixed-grip, 230, **230**
   neutral-grip, 215, **215**
   one-arm horizontal, 231, **231**

Punch and pull, **325**, 325
Push exercises, 140, 169, 174–175
Push jerk, 229, **229**
Push press, 194, **194**, 197
Pushup
   benefits of, 65, 65
   crab-walk, 233, **233**
   decline spider-man, 130, **130**
   dumbbell pushup row, 68, **68**
   dumbbell underhand, 68, **68**
   explosive crossover, 68, **68**
   incline, **55**, 55, 165, 169
   medicine ball archbishop, 65–66, **66**
   plus, **239**, 239
   spider-man, **107**, 107, **107**, 107
   stop-and-go, **158**, 158, **158**, 158
   Swiss-ball, **235**, 235
   Swiss-ball pushup plus, 67
   triple-stop, 66, **66**
   wide-grip, 81
Pushup plus, **239**, 239
   Swiss-ball, 67
Pushup test, 87
Putting, improving, 336

Q

Quercetin, 330
Quinn, Brady (football player), **300**, 301–309, **303**, **304**, **306**
Quinoa, 133

R

Rack walk-up/walk-down, 134
Railing step-over, step-under, 169
Reaction time, improving, 329
Rehabilitation, machine-based training in, 172
Repetitions, number of, 9–10
Resistance training. *See* Weight lifting